Case Studies in

Foreign Language Placement:

Practices and Possibilities

Case Studies in Foreign Language Placement:

Practices and Possibilities

edited by
THOM HUDSON
MARTYN CLARK

NATIONAL FOREIGN LANGUAGE RESOURCE CENTER
University of Hawai'i at Mānoa

2008 Thom Hudson. Some rights reserved.
See: http://creativecommons.org/licenses/by-nc-nd/2.5/

Manufactured in the United States of America

The contents of this publication were developed under a grant from the U.S. Department of Education (CFDA 84.229, P229A060002). However, the contents do not necessarily represent the policy of the Department of Education, and one should not assume endorsement by the Federal Government.

ISBN(10): 0-9800459-0-8
ISBN (13): 978-0-9800459-0-1

 The paper used in this publication meets the minimum requirements of the American National Standard for Information Sciences–Permanence of Paper for Printed Library Materials.   ANSI Z39.48–1984

book design by Deborah Masterson

distributed by
National Foreign Language Resource Center
1859 East-West Road #106
Honolulu, HI 96822-2322
nflrc.hawaii.edu

About the
National Foreign Language Resource Center

THE NATIONAL FOREIGN LANGUAGE RESOURCE CENTER, located in the College of Languages, Linguistics, & Literature at the University of Hawai'i at Mānoa, has conducted research, developed materials, and trained language professionals since 1990 under a series of grants from the U.S. Department of Education (Language Resource Centers Program).
A national advisory board sets the general direction of the resource center. With the goal of improving foreign language instruction in the United States, the center publishes research reports and teaching materials that focus primarily on the languages of Asia and the Pacific. The center also sponsors summer intensive teacher training institutes and other professional development opportunities. For additional information about center programs, contact us.

Richard Schmidt, Director
National Foreign Language Resource Center
University of Hawai'i at Mānoa
1859 East-West Road #106
Honolulu, HI 96822-2322

email: nflrc@hawaii.edu
website: nflrc.hawaii.edu

NFLRC Advisory Board

Robert Bickner
University of Wisconsin–Madison

Mary Hammond
East-West Center

Frederick Jackson
independent language education consultant

Madeline Spring
Arizona State University

Elvira Swender
American Council on the Teaching of Foreign Languages

Contents

1. Designing Sorting Hats: Foreign Language Placement Processes
   Thom Hudson & Martyn Clark 1

2. Filipino (Tagalog) Language Placement Testing in Selected Programs in the United States
   Leo Paz & Linda Juliano 7

3. Towards a Heritage-Learner-Sensitive Filipino Placement Test at UCLA
   Nenita Pambid Domingo 17

4. Placement Test and Course Objectives: The Case of the Filipino Program at the University of Hawai'i at Mānoa
   Sheila Zamar & Lilibeth Robotham 29

5. Current State and Issues of the Japanese Placement Test at the University of Iowa
   Yukiko A. Hatasa 39

6. Current Placement Test and Future Developments: The Japanese Program, Yale University
   Yoshiko Maruyama 53

7. A Case Study: Japanese Placement Process and Issues
   Eiko Torii-Williams 63

8. A Case Study From a Community College
   Emi Ochiai Ahn 71

9. Placement for Mixed Populations in a Relatively Small Program
   Mieko Ono 81

10 Placement Within a Changing Curriculum: Russian Heritage Speakers at Montclair State University
    Jessica Brandt 89

11 Placement Examination for a Heterogeneous Group of Russian Heritage Learners
    Irina Dolgova 99

12 Yet Another Test? Placement Issues in the Chinese Language Program at the University of Colorado, Boulder
    Madeline K. Spring 105

13 Using a Web-Delivered Questionnaire to Improve Placement in Chinese
    Rongzhen Li 111

14 Developing a Chinese Placement Instrument in Response to the Diversity in a Student Population at the University Level
    Song Jiang 119

15 Placement Assessment Issues for the Southeast Asian Studies Summer Institute
    Robert J. Bickner 133

16 Placement Issues in Study Abroad Programs: The Case of the Intensive Advanced Swahili Group Project Abroad
    Masangu Matondo 145

17 Placement Testing For a Large Spanish Program With Separate Tracks for Heritage- and Second-Language Learners
    Derek Roff 159

18 Asterix in Testland: Can a Large Department Resist Tests as a Part of Its Placement System and Get Away With It?
    Francoise Sorgen-Goldschmidt 167

19 The Challenge of Placing Hindi Heritage Students
    Rakesh Ranjan 177

20 A Case Study of Thai Language Program Placement Testing: Incorporating News Articles Into the Thai Placement Process
    Chintana Y. Takahashi 187

21 Challenges in Placing Korean Heritage Learners: Validity, Heterogeneity, and the Foreign Language Requirement
    Seungja Kim Choi 197

Designing Sorting Hats: Foreign Language Placement Processes

Thom Hudson
Martyn Clark
University of Hawai'i at Mānoa

Early in *Harry Potter and the Sorcerer's Stone* (Rowling, 1997), Harry arrives at Hogwarts School and attends the Sorting Ceremony before the start-of-term banquet. This is the ceremony in the Great Hall by which the first-year students of wizardry are assigned to one of four houses, Gryffindor, Hufflepuff, Ravenclaw, and Slytherin. Professor McGonagall places a pointed wizard's hat atop a four-legged stool in front of the students. As Professor McGonagall calls their names, they step forward and don the hat. The hat, sometimes quickly, sometimes after awhile, shouts out to the whole hall the name of one of the houses: "HUFFLEPUFF!", "RAVENCLAW!", "GRYFFINDOR!", or "SLYTHERIN!" This declaration places the students into the houses in which they will live for their time at Hogwarts learning to be wizards. As they were selected, they sit at the tables associated with their houses. Harry, of course, is placed into Gryffindor, and the rest is history, as they say.

Most people who are involved with language placement wish they had devices like sorting hats. They would make life so much easier for everyone concerned. We would not need to write tests or interview students for placement purposes. A sorting hat does not make errors resulting from haste or exhaustion. Every student would be in the right class, whether they were rank beginners or heritage learners. Unfortunately, the sorting hat is J. K. Rowling's creation, and it does not exist for language programs. Those of us involved in language programs have to come up with our own procedures and processes. This book is about the procedures and processes that have been used by a group of tertiary-level language teachers and administrators who attended a workshop at the University of Hawai'i at Mānoa in the summer of 2005. A number of different languages were represented, most of them less commonly taught.

When we began to put the workshop together, being researchers, we decided to research the current state of foreign language placement testing. To our surprise and chagrin, we discovered that there is very little literature on the language placement process. Lots of people use placement in their programs, but few people research it as a process or attempt to carefully articulate its bases. Much research uses placement tests, looking at statistical or content

---

Hudson, T., & Clark, M. (2008). Designing sorting hats: Foreign language placement processes. In T. Hudson & M. Clark (Eds.), *Case studies in foreign language placement: Practices and possibilities* (pp. 1–6). Honolulu: University of Hawai'i, National Foreign Language Resource Center.

characteristics, but almost no research has examined the process itself. What became clear throughout the workshop was that placement happens and that to a large extent, all placement is local. We initially wanted to write a book that we would describe as "best practices." However, we found that best practices really cannot be defined in general without considering the particular context of a language program. Particular placement practices, satisfactory or unsatisfactory, reflect a history of pedagogical motivations and evolving personnel. So, in this volume, we present case studies from across the US that discuss the nature of the programs in terms of course placement.

Several of the case studies describe societal and historical developments in how particular foreign languages migrated to the U.S. institutions in which they are taught today. These discussions are fruitful in the way that they provide insights into how different languages are perceived in the academic community as more or less privileged. Also, many of the case studies describe the context of their language programs at length. This reflects how placement issues are part of the overall curriculum in which decisions are made. Sometimes, no placement tests are in place in the programs described in the case studies. Thus, the suggested placement procedures are often exploratory in nature. Often, a "test," as typically envisioned, may not be the most appropriate means for placement in a particular context. Additionally, in most foreign language programs, the person in charge of the placement process is not someone trained in testing and measurement. This adds to the somewhat non-systematic way that placement has been addressed.

A number of types of learners often need to go through the placement process: those who have just been promoted, those who have come from institutions with articulated programs of transfer, those who come from institutions with very different course requirements and curricula, and those who have taken prerequisite course levels but have been out of school for some time since. The issues of articulation of placement are not only those of placing high school students in tertiary-level courses; they are also issues across tertiary-level intuitions, such as community college students being placed into state universities. All of these conditions affect the necessary complexity of the structure of the placement process.

A primary determinant in how a language program addresses placement concerns relates to the extent to which a heritage-language population seeks to enroll in courses. For language programs identified with traditional foreign languages such as French and German, identifying initial course levels is generally unproblematic. These programs are often involved in the placement of true beginners. Those students who have never studied the language before are placed into the lowest proficiency level in the program. In many tertiary contexts, placement is essentially self-placement, particularly if the language is being taken as part of a university foreign language requirement. Some issues may arise with students who studied the language in high school, but most programs have some formula for determining how many years of high school language equate with how many semesters or quarters of university language training.

Additionally, within U.S. university placement processes are issues of how to place students whose native languages are cognates of the target language but not English. For example, undergraduate foreign language programs fulfilling a language requirement may need to determine how to place a student whose native language is Japanese into a Chinese foreign language course. Such students may have less difficulty with learning new orthographic characters than students who natively speak English but not have advanced proficiency with tone.

However, in many contexts, true beginners are rare because the programs may have students who have resided in foreign countries for some time before beginning formal study, matriculating students who have studied the target language in high school, or students from a heritage-language background. Broadly speaking, a heritage language is one that is not viewed as "foreign" to the learners, either because of prior exposure at home or through cultural heritage and identity. As such, the term is used in descriptions of very different learner contexts. Often an issue in the placement of heritage-language students or students who have spent time in a foreign country is whether the target language uses orthography different from that of the learners' first language. So, for example, some students may know some Korean by virtue of having someone in the family, such as a parent or grandparent, who speaks Korean periodically at home. Such students may have some listening or speaking ability but most likely have little reading or writing proficiency. This will certainly affect placement into courses that integrate all of the language skills.

Logistic and pragmatic considerations also affect course placement. Placement into courses is sometimes affected by the size of the language program. In low-enrollment language programs, the courses are sometimes modified to reflect the student population rather than the students being selected to fit a particular curriculum. In these cases, placement may be determined in a relative manner to control class size. In such situations, the content for any particular course may change from semester to semester depending upon the particular constellation of students. The logistics are also affected by such institutional conditions as the amount of time within which students are allowed to change from one course to another at the beginning of the academic term.

Throughout the case studies presented here, logistic issues abound. Some institutions require that all registration take place prior to the beginning of classes. This has implications for entering freshman in how they access university-required testing or other placement processes. In other cases, the placement takes place during an orientation period before the semester begins, and students must be placed within a limited time frame of, for example, 50 minutes.

Placement issues are also affected by the role that is played by the language courses within the larger institution. For example, in some contexts, a language is taken as part of a university requirement, meaning that students may stop studying the language as soon as the requirement is fulfilled. In other situations, students may not be taking the language as a part of the university requirements. In such cases, the students may go beyond the three- or four-semester requirement.

All of these issues affect placement into foreign language programs throughout North America. The case studies reported here are examples of a wide variety of foreign language contexts in which course placement must take place. In some cases, the placement system can be very simple. In others, many variables enter into the design of the placement system. In some cases, the language placement responsibility is addressed by administrators who have expertise in the statistical and psychometric issues of assessment. In other cases, the language placement responsibility falls to the most recently hired assistant professor in the department.

Organization and use of this book

This text is intended to provide information to readers about many of the real-world contexts in which language placement takes place. Each chapter represents an existing situation and suggests changes in the process where such changes are deemed to be needed. We assume that readers of this book will be interested, at least initially, in contexts similar to those with which they are involved, either in terms of the particular language taught or in terms of the program profile. Thus, we provide a brief description of the chapters below.

Although by definition, all placement is program-specific, the chapters in this volume are arranged roughly into groups that share or illustrate common concerns. The first three case studies help to survey a range of situations in which placement decisions are made for a growing heritage language, Filipino. In Chapter 2, Leo Paz & Linda Juliano provide a complete overview of Filipino language teaching in the US. Discussed are the history of the Filipino language in the US and its incorporation into modern language programs, materials, and curriculum development, issues in teacher training and certification, articulation, and issues with the placement of traditional and heritage learners. In addition, the chapter highlights the specific placement procedures at four U.S. universities. Chapters 3 and 4 examine placement practices in two specific Filipino programs. In Chapter 3, Nenita Domingo discusses the usefulness of language background questionnaires in a program that, though composed predominantly of heritage learners, is not currently a heritage program. After a detailed discussion of the current placement process, a need is outlined for a new placement test that is heritage-learner sensitive. In Chapter 4, Sheila Zamar & Lilibeth Robotham provide a detailed examination of the placement test content and process for a decade-old Filipino test. Their case study includes a look at the relationship between the content of the test and the course objectives in the program and a consideration of how well the current system meets the needs of the students and the administration. These two chapters can serve as models for other programs interested in critical self-appraisal of current placement practices. The three chapters together provide insight into practices that have emerged as this heritage language has increased in its number of learners and formal instruction available.

Chapters 5 through 9 look at placement in one language, Japanese, across a range of institutions, providing insight into how unique institutional factors influence placement procedures within a single language. Chapter 5 reports an investigation into placement in a university-based Japanese language program with primarily traditional students. In this program, placement test creation coincided with a curriculum renewal project in the mid 1990s. The chapter includes a discussion of the factors that influenced the placement procedure and illustrates how thoughtful curriculum renewal can provide the basis for future placement test refinement. Chapter 6 looks at placement in another Japanese language program in the context of a new foreign language requirement. In this chapter, Yoshiko Masuyama details the student population and placement procedures. A unique feature of the current system is an emphasis on instructor consensus for placement. Ideas for revising the current test are also discussed. Writing samples and interviews figure prominently into the placement process of the small Japanese program described in Chapter 7. This case study by Eiko Torii-Williams also deals with articulation issues of students who have studied the language in high school and university students who are returning from study abroad. Chapter 8 is a discussion of placement in a relatively large community college Japanese program. The unique situation of community colleges makes articulation issues challenging, as such colleges traditionally serve a number of populations and student types. This case study by Emi Ahn describes such challenges and provides reflection on the potential future placement procedures that are needed in such a situation. In a similar vein, Chapter 9 looks at arguments in support of a standardized placement test in a small Japanese program that currently uses informal interviews rather than explicit tests. As with all of the chapters in this group, contextual factors play a large role in determining the approach to placement taken.

The next two chapters look at two different Russian language programs and examine how increasing numbers of heritage learners changed the dynamics of the programs, which had primarily been composed of traditional learners. In Chapter 10, Jessica Brandt shows how careful investigation of a current placement test can help to identify problematic content for a changing population of learners. This case study also helps to examine two relatively common misperceptions—that placement tests are necessarily invalid simply because they are old and that tests that have been shown to be reliable do not need to be revised. Irina Dolgova's case study in Chapter 11 also deals with the issue of heritage language learners. Here, she contrasts the types of errors made by traditional and heritage learners as the basis for proposing a new placement exam specifically geared towards placing heritage students. Though both of these programs are still in the process of revising their placement tests, these case studies provide insights into the tough process behind such revisions in response to changing student populations.

Placement procedures in three Chinese language programs are presented in Chapters 15 through 17. A common thread that runs through these case studies is the need for placement procedures that are practical given the time constraints under which placement decisions must be made. In Chapter 12, Madeline Spring discusses placement procedures that, while generally effective, rely on the availability of a small group of key faculty members. In the search for a test that would be less reliant on particular individuals, institutional constraints on test adoption are discussed. Chapter 13 is a discussion of plans for a web-based placement test for a university Chinese program. Such a test is needed as students are required to take the placement test the day before classes start, creating a need for a quick turnaround of test scores. In this chapter, Rongzhen Li discusses the format of such a test and the reasons for each proposed test section. In Chapter 14, Song Jiang looks at the placement of a wide range of learner types using a hybrid process consisting of interviews and final exams from various course levels. Students from eight distinct types of backgrounds all need to be placed in an efficient manner. The ramifications of the current system are discussed, including its great reliance on teacher intuition and the importance of careful thinking about placement decisions.

Chapter 15 and 16 are discussions of issues of placement in two very special contexts. In Chapter 15, Robert Bickner illustrates the process of language placement in a summer institute that must place students from all over the country into multiple levels of multiple languages for short-term, intensive courses. The chapter highlights contextual challenges brought about by the transitory nature of the institute, which changes its host institution every couple of years. The chapter also details the placement procedures in the nine less commonly taught languages offered in the institute, nicely illustrating how different languages tend to attract different populations of learners. Masangu Matondo's case study in Chapter 16 presents yet another challenge—the placement of advanced students into a study abroad program. Unlike local misplacements, which can be corrected in-house, study abroad presents a unique challenge because the screening procedures take place on a different continent than the actual language program. As in Chapter 15, the placement process is made more difficult because the participants are drawn from a variety of language programs, each having their own curricula and pedagogical priorities. The connections are discussed between program goals and placement as well as the adverse effects of not having systematic placement procedures in place.

Chapters 17 and 18 address placement in two language programs that teach more commonly taught languages, Spanish and French. They indicate how different concerns can be depending upon whether heritage speakers are an issue. In Chapter 17, Derek Roff looks at placement in a very large language program with separate tracks for heritage- and second-language learners. The two tracks result in two placement tests being used, one commercial and one locally developed. This chapter discusses the various issues associated with each one from the students' and instructors' perspectives. In contrast to Chapter 17, Francoise Sorgen-Goldschmidt's description of placement in a French language program in Chapter 18 highlights the placement options available when dealing with predominantly traditional language learners. The program uses self-placement, as opposed to more rigid language testing. Again, the importance of clear goals and objectives in providing the basis for smooth articulation are not

The preceding chapters having looked at the breadth of placement possibilities, the final three case studies examine how the distinction between heritage and traditional language learners can affect placement in university-based language programs. In Chapter 19, Rakesh Ranjan continues to explore issues with placing heterogeneous populations, this time in the context of a university-based Hindi language program. As this case study shows, heritage learners, though often treated as a homogeneous group distinct from traditional language learners, are anything but homogeneous, and even the definition of what constitutes a heritage learner is dependent on many linguistic and cultural factors. The final two case studies deal with the placement of heterogeneous populations in small language programs. In Chapter 20, Chintana Takahashi describes the placement procedures used in a Thai program designed to produce literate users of the language. As such, emphasis is placed on reading and writing. The small size of the program facilitates personalized meetings with the students to determine appropriate placement. In Chapter 21, Seungja Kim Choi discusses the impact of a new language requirement on a small Korean program. One particular challenge for the program is the placement of heritage learners with heterogeneous language abilities, often manifested as a gap between written and oral skills. This becomes especially important in the placement of advanced learners because the advanced course is not divided into heritage and non-heritage tracks.

Summary

Most foreign language programs have some process for placing students into appropriate course levels. However, little research has been carried out on the process or best practices. The case studies in this volume are included to provide a broad picture of the process used in a number of different places. The strength of this book, we think, is that it opens up these different foreign language contexts and the placement decisions that are made. We hope that this will help start a serious examination of foreign language placement and some of the issues that need to be addressed. That said, we also know that the chapters in this volume do not represent a random sample of all foreign language placement contexts. The cases included highlight the situations of many less commonly taught languages rather than those of traditional modern languages. However, we believe that they are windows into the ways in which language placement is carried out in many programs around the US today.

Reference

Rowling, J.K. (1997). *Harry Potter and the sorcerer's stone.* New York: Scholastic Press.

Filipino (Tagalog) Language Placement Testing in Selected Programs in the United States

Leo Paz
City College of San Francisco
Linda Juliano
University of Pennsylvania

We hope to trace the beginnings and development of language testing placement in Filipino educational institutions in the United States. A number of publications and articles on Filipino are about teaching methods and materials, but very few are on placement testing. Furthermore, only aptitude tests are given to foreign service or military personnel going into Philippine language studies. Literature on placement tests for the K-12 levels in Filipino may not exist either. We will give a general background about Philippine languages in the US and describe the beginnings of placement testing in this less commonly taught language. We will also analyze the existing approaches in Filipino and describe the specific challenges and needs of various sectors using the language. The latter part of this chapter will point out possible future directions and strategies for placement testing in Filipino.

Context

Filipino language

Filipino is the national language in the Philippines, based on Tagalog. It is the native tongue of the people in Central Luzon. It was declared the national language in 1937. It was renamed "Pilipino" in 1959. The new Constitution of 1987 officially renamed the language "Filipino." The law provided for enriching the Filipino-based national language with borrowings from other Philippine and foreign languages. Filipino/Filipino and Cebuano/Visayan have the greatest number of speakers among over a hundred languages spoken in the archipelago.

Filipino is taught in many parts of the US at both college and K-12 levels. According to Teresita Ramos of the University of Hawai'i, Filipino is taught in 28 colleges and 22 high schools. Across California, 94 classes in Filipino are taught in 21 schools. According to the San Diego-based association of educators, FILAMEDA, in 2003, among the statewide total of 2,500 students that attended Filipino classes, 1700 were from San Diego.

Paz, L., & Juliano, E. (2008). Filipino (Tagalog) language placement testing in selected programs in the United States. In T. Hudson & M. Clark (Eds.), *Case studies in foreign language placement: Practices and possibilities* (pp. 7–16). Honolulu, HI: University of Hawai'i, National Foreign Language Resource Center.

Filipino language in the United States

Philippine languages were informally taught in the US when an influx of migrant workers came to Hawaiʻi and the mainland US in the early twentieth century. This movement was driven by a need for cheap labor in U.S. agriculture and the ready availability of workers from the new Philippine colony. Workers informally taught their children their native languages, Ilokano, Filipino, Cebuano, and others. Those wives who were able to join their husbands may have taught Philippine languages to children in their transient homes and shelters. Scholars from various universities and disciplines went to the Philippines for governmental and educational administration, field study, and research. Among these were scholars who investigated the languages, folklore, and literature of the new colony. These scholars published many works on the Philippines. Grammars and dictionaries on Philippine languages also were published. Many Filipinos came to U.S. schools to study in various specialties and disciplines. Among these were the "Pensionados" and "Fountain Pen Boys." Many of these students went back home and worked in the colonial administration and in the public education system established by the American rulers. However, many Filipino workers remained in the US and worked in service jobs in cities, fish canneries in Alaska, and in the planting and harvesting of produce throughout the West Coast.

The Second World War became a "watershed," as described by Ron Takaki, and many Filipinos inducted into the armed forces were also sworn in as U.S. citizens. After serving overseas, they often came back with war brides from the Philippines, bought homes, and raised families. The new generation grew up wanting to learn about their American and Filipino heritage.

New immigrants, many of whom were professionals such as doctors, nurses, engineers, and teachers, came to the US after 1965, encouraged by new immigration laws aimed toward the unification of families. This growing number of Filipino-Americans (Fil-Ams) composes the second largest Asian population in the US next to the Chinese, and Filipino is the sixth most commonly spoken language in the country. Second- and third-generation Fil-Am students have clamored for and are getting more opportunities to study their heritage language in our schools.

Key issues in Filipino language teaching in the US

Filipino language teaching in the US faces the following challenges:

- introduction of more Filipino language classes in schools and colleges and recruitment of students to enroll in these classes
- development of curriculum, textbooks, and teaching materials
- articulation of classes from the K-12 to college/university levels
- recruitment, training, and credentialing of qualified teachers for all levels and compliance with the No Child Left Behind legislation in K-12
- development of curriculum for heritage language students
- placement of traditional and heritage language students.

Introduction of more Filipino language classes in schools and colleges and recruitment of students to enroll in these classes

Although a number of institutions offer Filipino language classes, their enrollments are only a small percentage of the large Fil-Am population, estimated at 2.1 million from the 2000 Census (U.S. Census Bureau, 2004). Most of these schools are concentrated in California, where half a million Filipinos reside, primarily in the counties surrounding Los Angeles, San Diego, and San

Francisco. A few universities in the Midwest and on the East Coast offer Filipino language classes. Classes for K-12 are only available in the San Diego and San Francisco areas. These opportunities are not available for the majority of the student population outside of California.

Administrators of federal and state sources of funding and education administrators who approve the opening of classes must be aware of the need for Filipino language classes and the presence of a large Fil-Am population that fuels this need. They also need to be cognizant of the cultural and politico-economic contributions of this group. New classes cannot be opened without funding.

At the college/university levels, students have often been the catalyst for the opening of classes. Fil-Am student organizations have mobilized and started signature campaigns asking that administrations create Filipino sections. Classes at the University of Pennsylvania, Diablo Valley College, and City College of San Francisco started this way. At Stanford University, the Language Center will offer a class if at least five students request one. Teresita Ramos started teaching language classes without pay at the University of Hawai'i to expand the Filipino program. University of California (UC), Davis students have sacrificed by going to Filipino classes taught by a visiting instructor from a nearby community college on an inconvenient class schedule. At Drexel University in Philadelphia, Pennsylvania, the instructor taught the first level of the language to 20 students, but because of funding constraints, the program did not continue to the next level. Community group action has also been responsible for expansion of classes. The School Board approved the addition of Grade 6 bilingual classes in Filipino and English at Bessie Carmichael/Filipino Education Center in San Francisco at the request of community and parent groups. At the University of Pennsylvania, the Filipino program started as a volunteer project with a community-based approach and continued for five summers with children and youth from ages 7 to 18 and a few adults who wanted to learn the language.

Development of curriculum, textbooks, and teaching materials

Before any classes can be opened, curricula for these language classes must be prepared and approved. Textbooks and teaching materials need to be prepared or at least acquired from various sources within or outside the state. These must also pass the standards and requirements of the educational systems where they will be used.

The pioneer and moving spirit behind the preparation and publication of textbooks has been the University of Hawai'i's Department of Indo-Pacific Languages. Ruth Mabanglo and Teresita Ramos have prepared many textbooks and other materials that have been published by the University of Hawai'i Press and the National Foreign Language Resource Center. Recently, DVDs and CD-ROMs with accompanying manuals and texts have also been produced. Other early materials are the UC texts written by Professors Bowen, Schachter, and Otanes and those of John Wolfe of Cornell University. Many teachers have developed materials on their own to augment the limited resources available. Books have been imported from the Philippines, particularly for use in K-12. In the 1970s to 80s, bilingual education programs in California prepared and disseminated Filipino language materials used in K-12 classrooms. In 2004, a Bay Area group of educators under the leadership of Leny Strobel of Sonoma State University started a funded project for preparing teaching materials in Philippine history, culture, and language, also for K-12.

Articulation of classes from K-12 to college/university levels

The ideal situation is to have curricula well-seamed from K-12 levels to 13-14 at community colleges and to the higher university levels. This will require coordination and communication among these three sectors. Reciprocity agreements also need to be established between states. Articulation between high schools and colleges on Philippine language matters is almost non-existent. The rule specifying two terms of high school studies being equivalent to one term at the college level is sometimes observed. However, articulation about the level and content of studies is almost nil. Some schools have tried 2+2+2 systems granting credits across high school, community college, and university systems. This has been done in commonly taught languages but may also be tried in the less commonly taught ones. Articulation exists between community colleges and universities, whether public or private. In California, for example, coordination is maintained through a group called IMPAC. This group of administrators, teachers, and counselors regularly reviews articulation agreements, course content, and skill requirements from one system to the other and strives for clearer transfer exit and transfer and exit requirements. These articulations are for educators and students on the web under software called ASSIST. Articulation guidelines like these should also enhance the placement process for language students.

Heritage language students and development of appropriate curriculum

The focus on heritage languages in the US was heightened because of the first nationwide conference on heritage languages in Long Beach, California in October 1999. This was reinforced by the first National Conference on Preservation of Less Commonly Taught Languages in San Diego in January 2005. In 1999, Irma Pena Gosalvez of UC Berkeley surveyed nine instructors of Filipino from various institutions in the US who were asked to assess their heritage students' proficiency in listening, speaking, reading, writing, and culture. She also administered a needs-assessment survey of twenty heritage students of Filipino at UC Berkeley. Highlights of the study were published in the Berkeley Language Center Newsletter.

Gosalves (1999, p. 15) defined the "heritage Filipino learner" as one who comes from a home in which Filipino is spoken and Filipino culture is lived to any degree. This is close to Guadalupe Valdés' definition of a heritage learner, "a language student who is raised in a home where a non-English language is spoken...speaks or at least understands the language, and is to some degree bilingual in that language and in English."

The faculty survey confirmed the results from the student questionnaires. Heritage students comprised 95% of the class; 95% were of Filipino parentage, and Filipino was their primary language; and 5% were of mixed parentage. Half were born in the US, and the other half, Philippine-born. Of the latter, 70% moved to the US at 6 to 13 years of age, and 30% migrated before age 6. Students whose parents spoke only Filipino and no other Philippine language had higher listening comprehension enhanced by hearing Filipino at home and viewing Filipino movies and television. They had more familiarity with the language's sound, intonation, and rhythm. They understood approximately 25 to 75% of conversations at home. Filipino instruction is necessary to improve the students' listening and speaking skills. Heritage students tended to pronounce words more correctly than non-heritage students. They were also able to apply words in the proper contexts more readily than the non-heritage students. Their errors appeared to be ingrained and more difficult to correct. Because they think in English, they may fail to use the appropriate honorific particles and respectful pronouns when speaking to parents, elders, and persons of higher status. Gosalves suggests that "maintenance and acquisition of formal, respectful speech should, therefore, be a primary objective in first-year heritage Filipino instruction."

Heritage students showed no marked advantage in reading and writing skills over their non-heritage peers because they had limited opportunities for using these at home. Heritage students will benefit from strategies transferring their superior skills in listening and speaking to reading and writing. In the area of culture, heritage students, because of their life experiences, possess an advantage in tasks requiring knowledge of day-to-day cultural practices.

Students scored poorly when tested on their knowledge of Philippine history, geography, literature, and the arts, which Gosalves termed "high culture." She recommended the following for a first-year Filipino curriculum:

- Teach functional vocabulary.
- Structure interactions with native speakers of Filipino in a school context to promote interest in pursuing similar interactions elsewhere;.
- Structure class work requiring participation in varied activities to develop sociolinguistic competencies.
- Introduce various text types.
- Teach grammatical strategies for tackling a Filipino text.
- Incorporate reading and writing activities that take into account the student's home language background and interest.
- Teach reading and writing on varied topics on Philippine/Filipino culture beyond the daily cultural practices in the home.
- Structure classroom activities that contribute to a positive attitude about the language, culture, and oneself.
- Undertake ethnographic projects in the language in the Filipino community.
- Encourage the use of Filipino in context in various situations and with a variety of interlocutors.

Gosalves (1999, p. 15) concluded that "rather than simply look at our students as 'slow learners' and 'fast learners,' or as 'good speakers' and 'poor readers,' practitioners would be well-served to acknowledge the wealth of cultural and linguistic knowledge that heritage students bring to the classroom to the benefit of all." This survey served as a catalyst for more projects on heritage language students in the UC system.

To address these heritage issues, a Filipino heritage language course was introduced at UC San Diego in 2001. In 2004, a project, funded and sponsored by the UC Consortium for Language Learning and Teaching, was started by four UC campuses to develop and establish a first-year Filipino curriculum that addresses the needs of the heritage learners who make up 95% of the classes in these institutions.

Placement of traditional and heritage-language students

Although the Filipino language is taught in many universities, community colleges, and secondary schools, only a few use formal placement tests. The University of Hawai'i, UC Los Angeles (UCLA), Cornell University, University of San Francisco, and University of Pennsylvania have placement tests. Most of the other schools that offer courses in Filipino use formal or informal interviews, survey questionnaires, or final/exit tests as bases for placements. Below are brief descriptions of the Filipino language programs and placement tests at Cornell University, the University of San Francisco, University of Hawai'i, UCLA, and University of Pennsylvania.

Cornell's foreign language requirement and placement test

At Cornell, the Filipino language is taught at various levels—beginning, intermediate, and advanced. Beginning courses involve thorough grounding in basic speaking and listening skills with an introduction to reading. The intermediate and advanced levels develop all four language skills—speaking, listening, reading, and writing. Directed studies may also be arranged to address particular student needs. The catalog notes that

> The faculty considers competence in a foreign language essential for an educated person. Studying language other than one's own helps students understand the problems of language, our fundamental intellectual tool, and enables students to understand another culture. The sooner a student acquires competence, the sooner it will be useful. Hence, work toward the foreign language requirement should be undertaken in the first two years.

Foreign languages and literature are taught in the College of Arts and Sciences in Asian Studies, and Filipino is one of them. According to the catalog, a placement test is *not* needed for:

- Entering students who have studied the language for less than two years in high school. You may enroll directly in the elementary level. (exception: bilinguals, native speakers, or those who have spoken the language at home).
- Students with no background in the language at all. You may enroll directly in the elementary level.

A placement test *is* needed for:

- Students who have had two or more years of high school study in the language.
- Students who are bilingual or native speakers or who have spoken the language at home.
- Students who have been awarded credit for language work at another college or university and wish to continue with the language at Cornell.
- Students with an SAT II score or AP exam score. The instructors will still want to test you to judge which level will best suit you.

Being placed into a 200-level course does not earn credit toward the degree. Credit is earned only for high school work equivalent in level to language courses numbered 200 and above.

University of San Francisco Filipino placement test

The University of San Francisco (USF) requires three semesters of study of a language for the BA degree. It requires two semesters of study of one language to get the BS degree. A student who requests a waiver of the language requirement is required to take a placement test. The cutoff scores specified by the University are 52-63 for the BS and 64-80 for the BA. USF adapted the Brigham Young University (BYU) Placement Test for Filipino in the mid 1990s. The BYU test for Filipino is a paper-and-pencil test for reading, writing, and listening. Note that USF introduced a minor in Philippine Studies in 2003. A year later, it offered Filipino language classes with credits applicable to the Philippine Studies minor. Students can now opt to take language classes earning credits towards the minor and choose not to take the placement tests that exempt them from the language requirement.

University of Pennsylvania Filipino program and placement test

The University of Pennsylvania established the Penn Language Center (PLC) in 1989 to expand, intensify, and enrich Penn's language curriculum. It has a long and distinguished record in the teaching of foreign languages and plays a leading role in many foreign language research fields. Language learning is highly integrated into both the curriculum and the research effort of the academic community. The most significant feature of the PLC has been its structural flexibility that has made it possible to respond to changes in demand for instruction in a variety of languages. The PLC has been able to serve growing language instruction needs that could not be covered within the regular programs of established departments. As of spring 2005, 35 less commonly taught languages were being taught through the PLC. Filipino is one of these.

The PLC coordinates foreign language competency testing services for students who seek exemption from the foreign language requirement at the School of Arts and Sciences or other schools that have similar policies. It also provides testing services for students from other universities who need to demonstrate competency in a language offered at Penn. The foreign language competency test consists of four components that measure one's ability to communicate, read, and write in a foreign language. The duration of the test varies depending on the language and can be approximately 1.5-2 hours. The foreign language competency test assesses the student's command of a foreign language and determines how well s/he uses the language in specific communication tasks. A test includes an oral interview between the test candidate and the tester, a reading comprehension assignment, and a writing sample.

The Filipino language program started in 1997, in response to a petition served by more than 100 students. Since then, four levels of the Filipino language have been taught, with an average of 10 students per class. Approximately 90% of the students are of Filipino heritage, and 10% are non-Filipino who take these courses for personal, business, or graduate purposes. As of spring 2005, 128 students had completed four levels of the language, and 20 students had passed proficiency tests to fulfill Penn's foreign language requirement. At least 10 students were from nearby universities such as Bryn Mawr College and Swarthmore University and enrolled in and completed the fourth-level Filipino course, and five external students underwent proficiency tests.

Beginning Filipino 1 is designed for beginning learners. The themes include everyday greetings; describing objects, people, and things; introducing members of the family; and expressing likes and dislikes. The lessons are organized through the use of listening, writing, and vocabulary-building exercises. A cultural workshop is included, which is cooking Filipino food with the students in Tag 2.

Beginning Filipino 2 is also designed for beginners—particularly those who have taken Beginning Filipino 1 or those who have some basic knowledge of the Filipino language. To determine students' eligibility, a placement test is required. The themes include making requests and giving commands, telling time, describing ownership and possession, talking about tenses, and expressing ability and obligation. The lessons are organized through the use of listening, writing, and vocabulary-building exercises. A trip to a cultural site followed by a dinner at a Filipino restaurant is included in the schedule.

The Intermediate Filipino 1 lessons are designed for those who have already completed Beginning Filipino 1 and 2. A placement test is required for those who would like to attend this course to determine their eligibility. The lessons include cultural activities and situations using forms and skills previously learned. A special project is assigned to this class, which is adding information to the Filipino website. A cultural workshop is included, which is cooking Filipino food with the students in Intermediate Tag 1.

Intermediate Filipino 2 is a continuation of the lessons from Intermediate Filipino 1. A trip to a cultural site chosen by the students is part of the schedule. A dinner at a Filipino restaurant follows.

A placement test exists for Filipino, but it has not been used for a number of years. Each fall term, an invitation is sent to all freshman and current students to attend a welcome and orientation on the Filipino language program. At least 40 people, mostly heritage students and members of the Penn Philippine Association, attend this orientation. Non-heritage students who intend to enroll in Filipino are given 10-minute oral interviews to appraise their knowledge of the language and scored from 0 to 10 points. Because of the limited enrollment of about ten each semester, all students are placed in the Beginning I class. Should a student be "misplaced," s/he is given a two-hour written and oral test based on the final examination for the next level. The Filipino language teacher plans to update the placement test based on the input from the 2005 NFLRC workshop on designing effective foreign language placement tests at the University of Hawai'i (UH) for possible reintroduction in the future.

University of Hawai'i placement test and objectives

The largest Filipino language program in the US is at UH. It offers eight language courses from beginning to advanced levels. It averages over 200 students in several classes each academic year.

UH conducts a Filipino language placement test to properly place students into five different levels. It is now being revived, and two UH faculty members will review the placement test and make recommendations to modify and improve the current version. The review is to assess the validity and practicability of the current system to serve both the students and the program and to identify certain administrative areas that may need modification.

The placement test contains the following sections: grammar, which is focused on knowledge of verb forms, markers, and ligatures; writing, which asks examinees to write about themselves; reading, which contains a short story followed by a 30-item comprehension and vocabulary test; listening, which includes a five-minute viewing about a Filipino celebration; and speaking, which is a 10- to 15-minute interview to check proficiency in performing speaking tasks.

Commercial placement tests for Filipino

Brigham Young University in Utah is one of the nation's leaders in foreign languages placement test development. They have a computer-based system called "Webcape," which is used by numerous institutions. It has tests for a number of less commonly taught languages that may be purchased in limited or large numbers. One of these is the previously mentioned placement test for Filipino, which is now used by USF.

An early test published in 1986 used to assess speaking and listening skills for K–12 placement is the Basic Inventory of Natural Languages developed by CHECpoint Systems, Inc. The Inventory is mainly a measure of oral language. It elicits oral language using large photo posters depicting multiple cultural scenes. It uses two scoring options: counts of the number of target language words per sentence and the calculation of scores for linguistic complexity based on a point system. The points may be optionally calculated on a computer. Each grade level's scores are then classified into Non-Pilipino Speaking, Limited-Pilipino Speaking, Fluent Pilipino Speaking, and Proficient Pilipino Speaking. This is a relatively old inventory and may not be in wide use.

UCLA sensitive placement test in Filipino

According to a UCLA Filipino faculty member, Nenita Pambid-Domingo, the current Filipino placement test is used to determine a student's speaking, listening, reading, and writing proficiency and fluency as well as command of grammar and vocabulary. The completion of this exam allows a student to either enroll in one of the Filipino classes offered or waive the one-year foreign language requirement. Most students taking this placement test will be allowed to enroll in the Filipino courses to fulfill their foreign language requirement. Ninety percent of the students are of Filipino heritage.

The Filipino language placement test at UCLA is handled using a thorough and systematic written schedule. The test is given at the beginning of the fall quarter, and the date, time, and location are noted in the schedule of classes. Students are provided with a table on the placement calculation, specifying the minimum score for each level. That the students should "not email or call the office for results" is also emphasized in writing.

Possible future directions and strategies for placement testing in Filipino

Formalized placement tests in the Filipino language are not readily available in the US. Only a few of the 28 universities and colleges reviewed use a formalized placement test. A number of effective Filipino language placement instruments may need to be designed.

Some programs, especially the ones with one or two sections per term and with two levels, find the undertaking too difficult or technical and often expensive. Often, the programs have very small faculties, often adjunct/part-time. Thus, they may continue their practices where a formal or unstructured interview is coupled with a written test developed within the organization. Sometimes, these tests are simply final or exit exams used for the targeted level. These programs may also purchase commercial tests. In these cases, cost may be a factor. Other programs lean towards copying and adapting placement tests from schools like UH or UCLA. This may work, but it may not work in schools whose student bodies and circumstances are quite different from the source of the test.

San Diego State University's Language Acquisition Resource Center recently embarked on a project to create a placement test in Filipino and provided some funding for the effort. A test has been created with the help of four Filipino teacher volunteers. It tests multiple levels and is composed of writing, reading, listening, and speaking subtests. It is due for pilot testing, and cutoffs for the various levels will be established later. The tested items are attuned to American Council for the Teaching of Foreign Languages (ACTFL) levels. In the near future, this test may be a valuable resource for both high schools and colleges with placement testing needs.

The 2005 NFLRC workshop offered great impetus for the development of these tests. The workshop offered a balance between theoretical issues such as assessment, placement assessment, and psychometric analysis through computer applications. In support of the short-term goal that language professionals expand their knowledge of foreign language placement assessment issues, our team will produce placement tests and procedures, considering issues of validity, reliability, and practicality. The team will also consider alternatives in assessing placement tests. The information from the workshop session on developing and improving test items (determining whether items are ambiguous) will be very important in refining the test further. The team will also read and analyze actual Filipino placement tests acquired from other Filipino language professionals.

Once formalized and approved, this placement test will be introduced to the team members' university/college administrators and to colleges and universities near the University of Pennsylvania including Drexel University, Bryn Mawr College, Swarthmore College, Temple University, and Philadelphia Community College. The test may also be shared with universities and colleges near the City College of San Francisco such as Skyline College, Diablo Valley College, San Francisco State University, California State University at Hayward, and Stanford University. This placement test will also serve as a recruitment tool for these targeted schools with the purpose of opening up more Filipino language courses in these areas.

References

Gosalves, I.P. (1999). Toward developing a curriculum for heritage students of Tagalog. *Berkeley Language Center Newsletter. 14*(2), 15–16.

U.S. Census Bureau. (2004). *2000 census of population and housing unit counts.* Washington, D.C.: U.S. Dept. Of Commerce and Statistics Administration.

Towards a Heritage-Learner-Sensitive Filipino Placement Test at UCLA

Nenita Pambid Domingo
University of California at Los Angeles

I will look at the present approach to placing students in the Filipino language courses of the Asian Languages and Cultures Department of the University of California, Los Angeles (UCLA) to recommend revising it or constructing a new test that is sensitive to heritage learners. I give a brief history of the Filipino/Tagalog language program of UCLA, the institution of the placement exam, and the need to change the current exam to reflect the current curricular goals and changing needs of the students taking the courses, particularly heritage learners, who comprise 90% of enrollees.

Context of the program

Tagalog was the first of the Southeast Asian languages to be taught at UCLA. It was first introduced in the 1960s. The first teachers were Fe Otanes and Agustina Cunanan (Ramos 2005). In the 1970s, when Paul Schacter was writing his Tagalog grammar textbooks, Tagalog was taught in the Linguistics Department.

In the 1990s, Tagalog was taught as part of a student-initiated campaign of the Asian Pacific Languages and Cultures Committee, a coalition of Indian, Filipino, Thai, and Vietnamese students, according to Barbara Gaerlan, who was a member of the coalition. The students were sponsored by the Asian American Studies Center and were mentored in lobbying techniques. After two or three years, the University agreed to fund one section of Elementary Tagalog, with the condition that the students find a teacher and a department that would agree to host it. The students found Tania Azores, who was working in Asian American Studies as a demographer, to teach the language, but the East Asian Languages and Cultures Department (EALC) at that time was not in a position to add any new languages to their offerings of Chinese, Japanese, and Korean.

Domingo, N. P. (2008). Towards a heritage-learner-sensitive Filipino placement test at UCLA. In T. Hudson & M. Clark (Eds.), *Case studies in foreign language placement: Practices and possibilities* (pp. 17–27). Honolulu, HI: University of Hawai'i, National Foreign Language Resource Center.

Tagalog was taught through UCLA Extension in 1990 and became established on the main campus in the winter of 1993[1] in the Linguistics Department. Russell Schuh, the chair of the Linguistics Department, was sympathetic to less commonly taught languages. He specialized in African languages, and the Linguistics Department still hosts several African languages that are taught to small numbers of graduate students. Linguistics was also hosting Quechua, and they agreed to host the first Tagalog class. Dr. Azores shared an office with the Quechua teacher in the Linguistics Department (Gaerlan, personal communication, 2005).

In 1995, Tagalog was moved to the Department of Applied Linguistics along with the Hindi, Thai, and Vietnamese languages to become the South and Southeast Asian Languages and Cultures division (Azores, personal communication, 2005). Russell Campbell in Applied Linguistics was instrumental in this move. He convinced his department to "adopt" all the orphan South and Southeast Asian languages (Hindi, Tagalog, Vietnamese, and Thai) in Applied Linguistics. In 1998, the languages were moved to EALC when Robert Buswell became the chair, and Shoichi Iwasaki agreed to be the director of the South and Southeast Asian Languages and Cultures Program.

In 1999, Indonesian was added to the Program under the sponsorship of the Department of East Asian Languages and Cultures, later renamed the "Asian Languages and Cultures Department" in 2004. In 2002, the Tagalog course was renamed "Filipino/Tagalog." In 2005, there was a move to change the name to "Filipino" from "SEASIAN 70 A," "B," "C," and so forth. Filipino/Tagalog was selected to make the courses more visible to interested students and to add advanced courses in Filipino.

At present, UCLA teaches the following courses under the Asian Languages and Cultures Department: SEASIAN 70 A, B, and C, Beginning Filipino; SEASIAN 71 A, B, and C, Intermediate Filipino; SEASIAN 172 A, Advanced Filipino Reading and Writing; SEASIAN 175, Advanced Filipino, Filipino Short Story, and Directed Individual Study; SEASIAN 199; and SEASIAN 197. This year, the Asian Languages and Cultures Department instituted the Southeast Asian Studies Major and Minor in any of the Southeast Asian Languages. Students can declare a major or a minor in the Filipino language, which would require them to take all the preparatory language courses and Filipino upper-division courses.

Description of the process

Course descriptions

The three-quarter sequence of SEASIAN 70 A, B, and C, Introductory Filipino 1, 2, and 3, is designed for the beginning student with little or no knowledge of Filipino. The fall quarter focuses on the sounds and rhythm of the language, vocabulary building, actor-focus verbs *um*, *mag*, and *ma*, object-focus verb *in*, and basic sentence patterns. At the end of the course, students are to be able to talk about themselves, their families, and situations for which vocabulary has been learned. The winter quarter places a stronger emphasis on building vocabulary, mastering Filipino sentence patterns, and developing the students' reading skills. Students are introduced to the object- and goal-focus verbs *i-*, *in*, and *an* and the pseudo-verbs *gusto* and *ayaw*. At the end this course, students are expected to be able to write and talk about their likes and dislikes, follow simple procedures, give directions, and function in social situations for which vocabulary has been learned. The spring quarter introduces more grammatical structures, modals, the

---

[1] I interviewed via e-mail Barbara Gaerlan, assistant director of the Center for Southeast Asian Studies at UCLA; Gyanam Mahajan, a Hindi professor; and Tania Azores. They gave different dates for when the languages came together to become the South and Southeast Asian Languages and Cultures division.

abilitative actor-focus verbs *magpa-* and *makapag-*, object-focus verb *ma-*, and existentials *may*, *mayroon*, and *wala* and integrates the material covered in fall and winter. By the end of one year of studying the language, the students will be able to narrate and use the infinitive, past, present, and future aspects of the most commonly used actor- and object-focus verbs in their writing and to communicate and function in the social situations covered in the class. Each quarter is a five-unit course.

The three quarter sequence SEASIAN 71 A, B, and C, Intermediate Filipino 4, 5, and 6, is a course in second-year Filipino. It is intended to improve the communicative competence of students by teaching social rules along with linguistic rules of Filipino. Students learn the intricacies of the focus system and affixation in the language. Through the year, students are introduced to more advanced vocabulary and grammatical structures in reading, writing, listening, and expanded conversations. Class activities integrate and reinforce the material learned. Each quarter is a five-unit course.

The Introductory Filipino course sequence meets the one-year foreign language requirement. The Intermediate Filipino course can fulfill a general elective or major foreign language requirement. Both courses are tied in with the culture.

SEASIAN 172 A, Advanced Filipino (Reading and Writing), is a four-unit course intended to bring intermediate-level students to the advanced level through selected readings on Filipino language and culture, songs, and excerpts from a drama. The students hone their writing and critical thinking through writing and reading assignments. The prerequisite for this course is completion of SEASIAN 71 C, being a native or near-native speaker, advanced placement, or the consent of the instructor. This course was offered in the winter quarter of 2005.

SEASIAN 175, Advanced Filipino (Filipino Short Story), is a four-unit course that surveys the Filipino short story in Filipino/Tagalog from its beginnings to contemporary times. Students analyze stories using Western and Filipino literary approaches. They may also write their own short stories for their final papers. The prerequisite for this course is the same as that for SEASIAN 172. This course was offered in the spring quarter of 2005.

Registration procedure

Students must obtain permission from the instructor to enroll. Permission is given after a student has taken a placement exam and been placed at the appropriate level by the instructor.

Filipino placement exam

The first placement exam was authored by Tania Azores Gunter. According to her, the first test was simpler and shorter than the placement test used in 2000, but it had both oral and written components. When asked about the time limit and the method of conducting the oral test, she said

> Everyone turned in their test at the end of the allotted time, finished or not finished. I didn't count how many were incomplete. I just graded them. As for oral interviews, they were primarily for those who wanted to be, or whose test scores indicated that they should be, on the 2nd year level. I engaged them in conversation to determine how proficient they were.

According to Gyanam Mahajan, the Hindi professor at UCLA,

> ...everyone saw a need for a placement test and we all did a placement test since the first year we became a group SSEAL [South and Southeast Asian Languages] under LRP [Language

Resource Program] [1994]—but we each did our own thing. We have continued to have our own placement test though most of us adopted some form of a universal background info/biographical data sheet including self assessment of level—this was devised by Asif Agha in 1995 when he was coordinator for SSEAL under Applied Linguistics. Each language then modified it for their use and devised their own portions for each language and determined "placement" for different levels. Each language also determined courses to be offered every quarter and what sequence to follow (thus Thai and Hindi have different choices and sequences even though both have to teach script). I have also used general vs. specific or restricted placement based on their biographical data and their intent (i.e., whether they want admission into a particular level or waiver for a particular level...). (Mahajan, personal communication, 2005).

At present, the Filipino placement exam takes two hours and is used to determine a student's communicativeness, proficiency, and fluency in speaking, listening, reading, and writing and his/her accuracy in grammar and vocabulary. Depending on the test results, completion of the exam will allow a student to enroll in one of the Filipino classes offered or waive the one-year foreign language requirement

Students

Most students take the placement test to be able to enroll in the Filipino courses to fulfill the foreign language requirement of the University. Ninety percent of the students are of Filipino heritage, that is, both parents are Filipino by blood or culture and may not necessarily speak or know Filipino/Tagalog. They may speak any of the 160 Filipino languages. A few hyphenated Filipinos (*mestizos*) also enroll in the class. One or two graduate students at the masters and doctoral levels usually enroll for academic purposes, and two or three students usually take the course for fun or to "retrieve" their heritage because of being "white-washed." Another common reason for a student to enroll in the class is a current or future liaison with a Filipino. Students from the navy or contemplating a nursing career may later realize that proficiency in the Filipino language is advantageous in their careers. Most students complete the first-year beginning Filipino classes. Not many continue on to the intermediate level. Only those who require two years of a foreign language like the English, international studies, Asian studies, Southeast Asian studies, and Asian American studies majors take the intermediate courses. In the advanced Filipino courses, for 2004-2005, 13 students enrolled in SEASIAN 172 A, Advanced Filipino Reading and Writing, and 16 enrolled in SEASIAN 175, Filipino Short Story. The numbers are remarkable because this was the first time that these advanced courses were offered and because these courses had more enrollees than the intermediate classes in the past three academic years. Mostly Southeast Asian studies, comparative literature, world arts culture, and history majors and Filipino language minors who are Filipinos and native speakers from the sciences take the upper-division courses.

The students have varying needs. Generally, heritage learners have good listening comprehension but cannot speak, read, or write. Their language abilities differ in these four skills. Most of them place into the intermediate level.

Distinguishing features of the program

The Filipino placement exam is given at the beginning of the fall quarter. The date, time, and location are noted in the schedule of classes. Students can pre-register in one of the following ways: attending the first day of class, signing up outside the instructor's office, or sending an e-mail to the instructor. The preferred way of pre-registering has been sending an e-mail to the instructor and attending the first day of class. As early as the last week of instruction of the previous quarter, I have received e-mail inquiries about where, when, how, and what the placement test would be and enrolling in the courses.

As noted earlier, Dr. Azores authored the first placement exam. She taught beginning and intermediate Tagalog for nine years. I interviewed Dr. Azores via e-mail about the components of the placement test. According to her, the test had vocabulary, grammar, reading comprehension, and essay assessments. It had an oral component as well. Unfortunately, no systematic records were kept of all those years, and the items, reliability, and validity of the test were not systematically analyzed. When asked about the reliability of the placement test in putting students in classes appropriate to their level, she said, "It worked out very well." She did not, however, elaborate on how the cut-off scores were determined. Because no copy of the placement test developed by Dr. Azores was available, I made my own test that I thought would indicate the levels of students intending to enroll in the Filipino courses.

At present, UCLA has two Filipino language instructors. Because I am the more senior, I am charged with the task of creating and administering the placement exam. Much of the protocol for the administration of the exam was in place when I took over. The exam that I used in the past was interactive and communicative. It was a paper-and-pencil test that was functional-situational. It included an oral interview, during which I noted down the student's pronunciation, the content, whether the student could answer questions given a situation about self, family, and friends and whether the answers were memorized or the student could put words together to communicate, the accuracy of the language, and the choice of vocabulary. It had a writing component, too, using authentic materials from free Filipino newspapers available at Asian seafood markets, suggested topics, or topics of the student's choice to best demonstrate his/her language ability.

What was the goal of the placement test? From my own limited point of view, it was simply a means of classifying or categorizing the students into Beginning A, B, C, Intermediate A, B, C, and Advanced. More recently, I have seen the importance of the placement test as a pedagogical tool. Students complain about classmates who already know the language who are enrolled in the beginning level. Usually only 5 or 6 students in a class of 25 or 10 in a class of 30 are truly second- or foreign-language learners. Teaching effectively in a class where students had varying needs was very challenging. At present, UCLA does not have a separate class for heritage learners.

In the past three years of administering the placement test, I was too engrossed in correcting papers and calculating the scores of the examinees to make full use of the information gathered using a biographical form (Appendix A) that comes with the test. This is used to gather information that may indicate whether students are heritage learners (HLs).

Previously, I was unaware of the impact of a mixed class on both foreign language learners (FLs) and HLs. Some students are ethnically Filipino, but FLs because a Filipino language other than Filipino or Tagalog was spoken at home and because they do not hear Filipino or Tagalog at all. How can instruction better serve both foreign language learners and heritage learners in one class so that HLs are not bored and FLs do not feel uncomfortable and intimidated? The answer is to determine with some reliability what the HLs actually know because separating HLs and FLs is not feasible at the present.

Usually around 80 to 100 students take the placement test. Even before the spring quarter ends, I usually receive e-mails from students inquiring how to enroll in the class or when and where to take the placement test. I tell them to come to the first day of class or on the day of the scheduled placement test. First, I have a sign-up sheet. The system is "first come, first served" because the beginning classes fill up quickly. Each student is given a biographical information form to fill out. In the previous years, I would simply ask the test takers after they filled out the form who among them knew any Tagalog or Filipino. Ninety-five percent would say that they did not know any. I took their word for it and gave them their Permission to Enroll number for Beginning Filipino. I had neither the time nor the resources to probe and interview them individually even for five minutes.

When around 60 of the test takers have placed in Beginning Filipino, I administer the written test to the remaining students who want to waive the one-year foreign language requirement and who really want to spend less time studying a foreign language and devote more time to their major courses. If I am lucky, I will have one or two students from the past year who have completed second-year Filipino as volunteers to help me proctor the exam, collect papers, and do clerical work. The test is supposed to take two hours only, but some students take all the time they can get to answer and review their answers.

The test takers are arranged in alternate rows. Every other row moves one seat over. This information is found on the second page of the biographical information form. See Appendix B for additional information on the page.

Qualified volunteers help the instructor with the oral interview following a list of items like greetings, family, vacation, description, simple negotiation, and so forth with rubrics for scoring. After the test, the volunteers leave, and the instructor is left with 60 or so papers to correct over the weekend. The papers are corrected, and the scores for the written, listening, speaking, and reading comprehension tests are tallied; students are assigned their placement accordingly. The results of the placement test are posted at several locations. The students then get their PTE numbers from the instructor for the classes they wish to enroll in.

Before students take the placement test, they are informed that it is *only* for UCLA students. However, beginning fall 2005, because of the opening of a joint distance-learning class for Beginning Filipino between UCLA and University of California, Irvine (UCI), the same placement test is be administered at UCI.

Only two courses need immediate placement in the fall quarter: SEASIAN 70 A, Beginning Filipino, and SEASIAN 71 A, Intermediate Filipino. Only two Filipino courses are offered regularly each quarter, one beginning and one intermediate.

The different sections of the test are scored differently. I base the points on the grammar and content covered in the test compared to what a student who passed Beginning Filipino 1, 2, and so forth can do with the language. No rigorous content analysis was involved in the creation of the placement test, only a general idea of what the test is trying to measure, like knowledge of grammar, verb conjugation, fluency, reading comprehension, and listening comprehension, which is not directly measured but inferred through the oral interview and communicativeness. For the writing part, I used an ad from the local newspaper with a picture for them to write about. The writing is scored based on its content, organization and coherence, spelling, grammar, fluency, vocabulary, and the register of the language. The score of 100 points for 70 B placement was based on the final exam of 70 A, the grammar and vocabulary that successful students of 70 A would have acquired, and the situations that they would be able to handle.

In June 2004, I was trained to use the Oral Proficiency Interview (OPI). This influenced the rating and the oral exam of the placement test. Thus, the oral component of the test, which is worth 80 points, was structured and rated along the lines of the OPI. Because grading the test was a considerable burden, I made it a Scantron. I still check the written test, and a part-time instructor helps me grade the test after conferring on the rubrics.

The test has a total of 180 points. See Appendix C for a breakdown.

Practical ideas for placement and future development: Lessons learned in UCLA's Filipino placement approach

In the placement test just outlined, the grammar and vocabulary are at the beginning level. What separates the beginning, intermediate, and advanced levels are the writing, speaking, and listening scores. The test does not take into account the common mistakes made by students in Beginning Filipino 70 A, like those involving the use of markers, NG doers and ANG doers, syntax and word order, cases, and focus. It was constructed without regard for the curricular goals and the syllabi of the courses for which the students are testing, but only considers pronouns, cases, and vocabulary words. Section C, testing vocabulary, seems like an IQ test, although one cannot arrive at the correct answer without knowing the meanings of the words.

The test has no regard for heritage learners' different capacities. It has no systematic and reliable testing of listening skills. The test format is not clear. The instructions for Section D of the grammar test simply read, "Choose the correct answer." After 10 items of verb forms/conjugation, the following items deal with different grammar points in the Filipino language: use of the noun markers *ang* and *ng*, proper name markers *si* and *kay*, genitive marker for a direct object, and time marker *sa* and distinguishing between a *sa* pronoun and a *ng* pronoun.

How to improve the placement test

One common problem encountered in accurately determining a student's level is the student's motivation in taking the placement test. Some students are not honest in answering the test questions so that they will be placed in the beginning level to get an easy "A" or simply because they have very low assessments of their own language abilities. Having each student sign an intellectual integrity clause will hopefully discourage students from intentionally scoring low or pretending not to have any language ability. Such a clause would say that says the student is taking the placement test using the best of his/her knowledge to enable the program to place him/her in the appropriate class to maximize learning for everyone and to move them to a higher level of proficiency.

I would ideally have the luxury of a test development phase, piloting, and evaluation, that is, running a test on the validity and reliability of the placement test after each administration of it, analyzing the results, and removing items that are not indicative of the students' language ability. Updating the test items to reflect the changing needs of the student population would be good. UCLA has the technical resources to run validity and reliability tests and analyze tests and items through the Office of Instructional Development but not enough faculty resources. To adapt a popular saying, "It takes a village to write a test."

New test items should be constructed keeping in mind the curricular goals for the different courses being offered at UCLA and HLs' varying language abilities. Authentic audio-video clips could be used for the listening component. This would require a venue for the test that is equipped with computers or at the least a good tape player and amplifier or a monitor and a VCR.

I have also determined something to avoid: as Martyn K. Clark (p.c.) said, "No testing without thinking."

Conclusion

I gave a brief history of the Filipino program and the approach to the Filipino placement test at the Asian Languages and Cultures Department of UCLA. Although the program started in the 1960s, data on the tests administered over the years has not been systematically collected, much less analyzed for the reliability and validity of the tests. The data available for the past three years of testing remains to be processed and analyzed in terms of test items, trends of test takers, and statistical analysis of the last version of the test that uses a Scantron. Here, I analyzed only the items and the content of the last test version available.

Given appropriate content and testing instruments, one should be aware of available statistical tools that can help in creating an effective and reliable placement test. Articulation of the curricula would inform the creation of a placement test that would match teaching goals. One should also take note of practicality and applicability in creating a particular placement test suitable to one's unique situation, including the availability of resources. In UCLA's case, rewriting the placement test to sift out HLs and determine with some accuracy their level of proficiency in reading, writing, speaking, and listening is a very important issue. Knowing the different proficiencies of the students affects the quality of instruction and the quality of learning that takes place inside the classroom. The test should be constantly updated to match curricula and the students' needs and to maintain the quality of the test.

Appendix A: Biographical form for UCLA Filipino placement

Birthplace (city and country) _____

If foreign born, what year did you come to the US? How old were you then? _____

Mother's birthplace _____ Native language _____

Father's birthplace _____ Native language _____

Reasons for wanting to take Filipino:

to fulfill the one year foreign language requirement

to fulfill a GE/Humanities requirement

to do research

_____ other (please explain, e.g., to reclaim my heritage, to be able to understand and talk to my grandparents, etc.)

Have you ever taken Filipino/Tagalog lessons before? If yes, when, where and for how long?

How much exposure do you currently have with Filipino/Tagalog speakers?

No contact					Everyday
0	1	2	3	4	5

Is this contact at home, at work, at school or elsewhere? Please indicate:

In your opinion, what is your present level of proficiency in Filipino/Tagalog?

	NONE				VERY GOOD	
Listening	0	1	2	3	4	5
Speaking	0	1	2	3	4	5
Reading	0	1	2	3	4	5
Writing	0	1	2	3	4	5

What other languages do you speak?

_____

_____

Appendix B: Additional information

Placement calculation depends upon your written, oral and listening exam.

The exam has a total of 180 points   minimum score
- to be placed in 70 B   100 points
- to be placed in 70 C   130 points
- to be placed in 71 A   140 points
- to be placed in 71 B   160 points
- to be placed in 71 C   170 points

Test results will be posted by student I.D. No. on the bulletin board outside Hershey 1115 (Instructor's Office) on Friday next week. It will remain posted for two (2) weeks. After that, the notice will be taken down. You can inquire at Royce 290, Asian Languages and Cultures Department for test results. Test results are also posted outside Royce 290.

Do not email or call the office for the results.

Once the exam has started, you must maintain absolute silence. Any question must be directed to the proctor or the teacher, not to the person near you.

When you are finished with the written test, see the teacher or proctor for the oral component of the test. (60 points).

Any questions?

Appendix C: Description of test and breakdown of points per section

Reading comprehension

(Two paragraphs followed by five questions worth two points each. Students write in their responses in complete sentences.) 10 points

Grammar

Choose the correct pronoun. (*ang* pronouns in the nominative case) 10 points

Choose the correct answer. (*ng* and *sa* pronouns in the genitive and dative cases. Nos. 1-10.) 10 points

Interrogatives. (Nos. 11-20.) 10 points

Choose the word that does not belong. (Vocabulary and knowledge of culture. Pronouns, verb forms, adjectives, interrogatives, knowledge of affixation, and stress.) 20 points

Choose the correct answer. 15 points

Verbs *i, in, um,* and *mag* (Nos. 1-10)

    11: Use of the noun markers *ng* and *ang*

    12: Proper name markers *si* and *kay*

    13: Genitive marker used in direct objects

    14: Time marker, *sa*

    15: *Sa* or *ng* doer

Writing

A topic about everyday life (e.g., autobiography, one day in the life of... etc.) 10 points

Description 25 points

Speaking and listening. 80 points

Placement Test and Course Objectives: The Case of the Filipino Program at the University of Hawai'i at Mānoa

NFLRC

Sheila Zamar
Lilibeth Robotham
University of Hawai'i at Mānoa

The University of Hawai'i at Mānoa (UH) Filipino Program is in the early stages of revising its language placement test. The placement tool currently in place has been used by the program for over 10 years but admittedly, does not fully address the placement decision challenges faced by our program every semester. The present study is a move towards developing a more appropriate placement instrument that will help make placement decisions clearer and more efficient. The general objective of this study is to review the Filipino program placement test to identify its strengths and weaknesses and make recommendations on specific areas for modification and improvement. We will review two aspects of the examination: content and process.

The aim of the review of the content is to find out how the existing placement test relates to the objectives of the first four levels of Filipino language courses offered at UH and identify how constructs or test items included in the placement match or do not match specific program course objectives.

The aim of the review of the placement process is to assess how the current system serves students and the program as a whole and identify administrative areas that need modification.

Before discussing the placement process, we will present a brief description of the background of the Filipino and Philippine Literature Program (FPLP) at UH, including its unique and distinguishing features and a profile of its student population.

Program description

FPLP is the third-largest component of the Department of Hawaiian and Pacific Languages and Literature in the College of Linguistics, Languages and Literature of UH. The department also includes the Hawaiian Language Program (the largest component) and other less commonly taught Asian and Indo-Pacific languages including Samoan, Arabic, Thai, and Ilocano.

Zamar, S., & Roboham, L. (2008). Placement test and course objectives: The case of the Filipino program at the University of Hawai'i at Manoa. In T. Hudson & M. Clark (Eds.), *Case studies in foreign language placement: Practices and possibilities* (pp. 29–38). Honolulu, HI: University of Hawai'i, National Foreign Language Resource Center.

FPLP is the largest program of its kind in the United States. It offers eight language courses, from Beginning (101) to Advanced (402) Filipino and a similar number of culture and literature courses. In the spring semester of 2005, over 200 students were enrolled in one or more program classes. This number has been typical of the program enrollment since the early 1990s, when the university instituted a language requirement. The program currently has two tenured professors, one full-time instructor, and two part-time lecturers.

One of the unique attributes of FPLP is its emphasis on reading and writing literacy. It is one of the few language programs in the nation that publishes a bi-annual magazine. This magazine, called *Katipunan*, is produced and edited by the advanced-level students and features essays, poems, and other written compositions from students enrolled in all levels of the program. The magazine is circulated to other colleges and universities that offer Filipino and serves as resource material for use in classroom teaching.

Katipunan is also the name of the co-curricular laboratory component of the curriculum that aims to promote Philippine culture and language skills outside of the classroom. Near the beginning of each semester, all the students of the language and literature classes participate in a program picnic that highlights Filipino games and food and allows all students to get to know the program faculty and their peers in a social setting. A song festival in the fall semester and a drama festival in the spring semester allow the students, beginning and intermediate in particular, to learn traditional and contemporary cultural values through songs and short skits, respectively. *Katipunan* also facilitates and sponsors literary events and community outreach activities that further expose students to other aspects of Philippine language and culture. The school year ends with a banquet in the spring semester that acknowledges the accomplishments of the program and its graduates and provides an opportunity for fun and fellowship among students.

FPLP is distinguished as teaching one of the first less commonly taught languages in the United States to have an advanced study abroad program. The Advanced Filipino Abroad Program (AFAP) focuses on intensive language and culture training for seven weeks in the Philippines in the summer. Since its inception in 1992, it has attracted intermediate language learners from all over the United States. The program provides an all-expense-paid immersion study opportunity to qualified and accepted students under a very generous grant from the Fulbright-Hays Scholarship Foundation. Upon completion of the program, University of Hawai'i students can petition the university to substitute AFAP for Filipino 301 and 302, thus enabling them to enroll directly in Filipino 401.

Another Filipino program milestone within the last three years is the establishment of a Bachelor of Arts degree in Filipino and Philippine Literature, followed by the establishment of a minor in Filipino about a year later. In the past, the program gave certificates in Filipino to students who finished 402 or the advanced level; however, the minor provides official university recognition to students over and above that provided by the department. As of the end of the spring semester in 2005, the program had graduated five students with majors and seven students with minors in Filipino. At present, six students are in the BA program, and a considerable number are working on minors in Filipino.

Student profile and placement program background

Although Filipino language classes had previously been offered by lecturers and Filipino graduate students in linguistics at the university, the development of the program began with the hiring of Teresita Ramos as the first full-time tenure-track instructor of Filipino in 1970. She developed a curriculum, proposed and implemented new courses, and taught most of them herself. Enrollment in the program was small and mainly consisted of graduate students who had personal interests in the Philippines or were planning to conduct their thesis or dissertation research in the country. Most of these students were not of Filipino ancestry. This demographic changed significantly in the early 1990s, when the university instituted a language requirement for all undergraduate students. This led to a large increase in younger heritage language learners of Filipino parentage. By 2000, over 90% of students in the program were heritage learners. For our case study, we define a heritage learner as one who can trace a connection or roots to the target culture without necessarily having been exposed to the language or having any speaking skills in the language.

The rapid increase in student demand for Filipino classes necessitated the expansion of the program by providing more classes and hiring new faculty. Many of this new wave of learners are second- and third-generation Filipino-Americans who want to learn the language of their parents and grandparents. Some have limited comprehension and speaking abilities, while others have somewhat greater language skills. To address the need to correctly place learners with some speaking ability, the program faculty developed a proficiency examination based on existing tests. This exam served as the tool for placing students in level-appropriate classes. Since then, this test has been used by the program to try to match incoming heritage-language students with the appropriate course level.

In the last four years, more than 100 students have been placed in the 100-, 200-, and 300-level classes. Most of the placement test takers were heritage-language students who were in university programs that have the two-year language requirement. Many were born in the Philippines and came to the United States as very young children with their families. While some have retained some language competence and would like to improve, many non-speakers want to learn the language to be able to function in social situations with relatives who may speak little English and to understand cultural nuances within their families. Based on the student responses to surveys administered in every class at the beginning of every semester, understanding culture, knowing the family gossip, and fulfilling the language requirement are the primary reasons that students take Filipino classes.

Placement test and program course objectives

In this section, we discuss the various parts of the placement test. Following that is a discussion of the course objectives of the first four levels, comprising eight semesters or four years of Filipino language courses at UH.

Content of the placement test

The content of the Filipino language placement test has undergone few changes since its introduction in 1991. A number of items were added, like listening and translation sections, and some items replaced, for example, the content of the reading section, at various points in the last 10 years. The original version of the test included only sections on grammar, writing, and speaking. The current version of the placement test contains five components: grammar, writing, reading, listening, and speaking. Here, we describe each component and try to identify the problem areas that need to be addressed.

Grammar

This section is a comprehensive test focused on knowledge of verb forms, markers, and ligatures. It is divided into two subsections: a 25-item fill-in-the-blank constructed-response test of verb "conjugation" and a 5-item sentence-completion test where examinees need to supply missing markers and ligatures. The items in this section are arranged in ascending degree of complexity of the forms. We found two problems in the grammar section of the test. In the fill-in-the-blank portion, several items have ambiguous prompts, where more than one answer is correct. In the sentence-completion portion, some single items target multiple grammatical points. This is confusing because it does not clearly define the grammatical area being tested.

Writing

This section asks examinees to write about themselves. Test takers are given verbal instructions to use complex sentences and a wide range of vocabulary to demonstrate the extent of their knowledge of the language and ability to use it in writing. The maximum score for this section is 20 points, based on the following criteria: content (5), grammar (5), complexity of structure (5), and mechanics & organization (5). The important considerations for rating the essays are the examinees' ability to narrate and describe using detail. We see three areas that can be improved in the writing portion of the test. First, the instructions need to be more explicit about what is expected from the examinees. Second, the current topic is too limited in scope to elicit a sufficient language sample to determine an examinee's proficiency level. Last, the criteria for rating the writing samples are not well-defined.

Reading

This section contains a short story followed by a 25-item comprehension and vocabulary test on synonyms of words selected from the passage. The reading passage is lengthy and too complex for anybody below the 202 level. This limits our ability to assess students with lower reading proficiency. Another problem in this section is that nearly half of the items do not test reading ability; instead, they test vocabulary knowledge.

Listening

This section includes a five-minute video about a Filipino celebration followed by a 20-item written comprehension and vocabulary test. The listening test is limited to a single cultural topic that uses specialized vocabulary ideal for high-intermediate- to advanced-level students. This does not give any information about the proficiency of lower-level students.

Speaking

This section is a 10- to 15-minute interview aimed at checking the examinees' proficiency in performing specific tasks. The rating was originally based on a 10-item checklist of content areas and tasks covered in the interview. In 2003, the American Council for the Teaching of Foreign Languages (ACTFL) Interagency Language Rating-Oral Proficiency Interview (ILR-OPI) was adopted by the program as its official placement speaking test. The ACTFL rating scale is used for evaluating speaking proficiency. The ratings are then converted into raw scores, from 0 to 25, that are added to the overall placement test score. The OPI allows us to elicit good speaking samples. However, we still need clear-cut guidelines on how the ACTFL rating scale relates to the overall placement test results. The current proficiency rating conversion into raw scores is arbitrary and may not be completely reliable.

Translation

This section is not part of the regularly offered placement test. Rather, it is an additional test administered to examinees who request re-placement to 301 (fifth-semester Filipino—currently the highest placement level) after having been placed in 202 (Intermediate Filipino II/fourth-semester Filipino).

We have described the different components of the placement test, and we now examine how the placement test items relate to specific course objectives of the Filipino program.

Course objectives

In this section, we discuss the specific course objectives and general content areas (themes and functions) for each of the four levels of Filipino language classes offered at UH. Following the description of each level are general observations on how the placement test does or does not reflect their objectives. We assume that the placement test is a tool for making decisions on the suitability of a particular course for an examinee's language learning needs. Therefore, it should elicit language samples that will give teachers and program administrators information not only about proficiency but also level suitability.

Filipino 101 (Beginning Filipino I). The course objectives for this level are as follows.

> *Listening*: understand short, simple dialogs and short descriptive passages.
>
> *Reading*: read maps, road signs, schedules, and simple texts relating to self, work, and family.
>
> *Speaking*: talk about self, family, and work; ask and answer basic questions; simply describe concrete referents, for example, food, places, and common household and classroom objects; and talk about likes and dislikes.
>
> *Writing*: take notes/dictation, fill out forms requiring biographical information, and write a short, simple essay about self and family.

The speaking and writing sections of the placement test match some of the specific objectives of the 101 curriculum. However, the grammar, reading, and listening sections have no relevance to the 101 objectives.

Filipino 102 (Beginning Filipino II). The course objectives for this level are als follows.

> *Listening*: understand paragraph-length texts pertaining to personal and social situations and follow simple instructions and directions.
>
> *Reading*: understand the main ideas from authentic materials pertaining to personal and social contexts and guess the meaning of new vocabulary based on its context.
>
> *Speaking*: narrate past, future, and ongoing activities; make requests; give commands; give and follow simple directions; make comparisons; and describe ailments.
>
> *Writing*: write simple friendly letters, letters of invitation, and a journal of daily activities and experiences.

Sixty-five percent of the grammar section targets some of the specific grammatical areas covered in the 102 curriculum. The writing and speaking sections may elicit language samples that can reveal learner competence in limited areas of this curriculum. The reading and listening sections contain texts and test items that are beyond the scope of this level.

Filipino 201 (Intermediate Filipino I). The course objectives for this level are as follows.

> *Listening*: listen for main ideas and some details from movies, news broadcasts, radio announcements, and talk shows.
>
> *Reading*: understand simple texts such as weather reports, flyers, advertisements, recipes, and short stories.

Speaking: give a detailed narration and description of personal and social activities; retell a story; express compliments, complaints, or reactions based on an event or an object; and appropriately use common idiomatic expressions.

Writing: write short essays on limited topics such as the weather, leisure activities, and sports; write detailed friendly letters; and write summaries of folktales.

Twelve percent of the grammar-section items target two specific grammatical points in the 201 curriculum, on top of the 65% of the test items that target grammar points from 102. Without additional verbal instructions, the writing segment cannot elicit writing samples that show 200-level language competence. About 10% of the items in the reading section address some of the 201 course objectives. The speaking section addresses a limited range of topic areas in this curriculum. The listening test may be too advanced for this level.

Filipino 202 (Intermediate Filipino II). The course objectives for this level are as follows.

Listening: listen for main ideas and some details from movies, talk shows, TV dramas, interviews, and documentaries on a limited range of social issues.

Reading: understand detailed texts such as news and feature stories and simple literary texts and essays on Philippine customs, traditions, values, and beliefs.

Speaking: give detailed narrations and descriptions of personal and social activities, retell a story, express opinions for or against issues, give compliments, accept or refuse an invitation using culturally appropriate language, and make short presentations on topics revolving around Philippine culture.

Writing: write essays on topic areas such as Philippine festivals, customs and traditions, family values, and courtship; and write simple, short narratives.

Roughly 10% of the grammar section items target a specific grammatical point in the 202 curriculum, in addition to the 72% of the test items that are within the scope of 102–201. In the writing section, additional verbal instructions are necessary to elicit language samples that will demonstrate 202-level abilities. The topic of the reading passage is within the scope of the curriculum, but a considerable amount of the vocabulary and linguistic structures are beyond it. Furthermore, almost 50% of the items test knowledge of vocabulary and do not directly address the goal of the reading test.

Filipino 301–302 (Third-level Filipino I & II). These courses cover conversation, reading, and writing focused on the Philippine history and cultural heritage. Semester I focuses on topics like nationalism and historical figures and events. Semester II includes ethnic dramas, religious practices, and folk theater.

The speaking, listening, and reading components of the test seem to address some 300-level course objectives. The grammar and writing sections do not test 300-level competencies.

Filipino 401–402 (Fourth-level Filipino I & II). These courses cover advanced reading and composition focused on academic writing and contemporary literature covering a variety of social and cultural issues. Some Semester I topics revolve around issues on language, education, and popular culture. Examples of Semester II topics are migration, globalization, and challenges confronting indigenous cultures.

The speaking component can elicit language samples that address 400-level competencies. No other sections target any of the course objectives of this curriculum.

Placement process

Students who are interested in taking the placement test in Filipino can call the program for test dates, which are usually two weeks before the beginning of the fall and spring semesters. They may also set up appointments to take the test during the regular semester. The test is administered in the program office.

Prior to the written test, the test administrator conducts a background interview to determine the examinee's exposure to the language and culture and his/her reasons for taking the placement test. The interview is conducted in Filipino or English, depending on the examinee's language ability.

Before proceeding to the written sections of the test, the test administrator explains the different components of the test: grammar, writing, reading, and listening, and clarifies the instructions on how to complete the test. The test taker is given 90 minutes to complete these sections. Upon completion of the written sections, the test taker makes an appointment for the oral proficiency interview.

The interview (ILR-OPI) is in Filipino and takes 20 minutes. Examinees are given ratings between 0+ and 2+ based on the ACTFL ILR-OPI rating scale, which are converted into raw scores and added to the written test points to get the overall placement scores.

The placement of students into the different class levels is based on their aggregate scores from the five sections of the placement test. Table 1 shows the cut-off scores for each level.

Table 1. Cut-off scores for each class level (maximum points=125)

overall raw score	placement
120–125	Filipino 301
100–119	Filipino 202
80–99	Filipino 201
60–79	Filipino 102
59 and below	Filipino 101

When students are placed in any level above 101, they can petition for free back credits upon completion of the course level they are placed in if they receive grades of C or higher.

To address possible misplacement of students, the instructor is advised to observe the students' performance and make recommendations on the appropriate classes for the students within the first two weeks of the semester. In the ten years of administering placement tests, only been a small number of questions have been raised about misplacement.

Problem areas

Information about the placement test schedules is disseminated at the New Student Orientation held during the summer for fall semester registration and during the Transfer Student Orientation in the fall for spring semester enrollees. While placement test dates are designated as two weeks before the fall and spring semesters, no one comes in to take the tests during this period. As a consequence, the placement tests may be taken at any time during the regular semester that is convenient for both the student and the test administrator. While this is not ideal, this practice actually helps the Filipino program boost enrollment, especially in the intermediate and advanced levels.

Because few examinees take the placement test at any given point, it is usually administered in an office shared by four faculty members. This is not a venue very conducive to test taking because of student and instructor traffic in the office, leaving the examinee with very little quiet and privacy to concentrate on the test. For the listening segment, the test taker has to move to a senior faculty member's office that has the video equipment needed. Of course, this is only possible if the professor is in her office and the room is available.

On the scheduled date of testing, the examinee is given a verbal description of the different areas of the test and the expectations for each section. The explanation may vary depending upon the test administrator. The lack of a written test description with specific and well-defined instructions is one problem that can be easily remedied in the placement process.

The two components of the placement test, the written test and the OPI, are always administered by different people. The written part of the test is scored manually, usually by the person who gave the test. Spelling is not given much weight as long as mistakes do not change the context or meaning of the structures. However, grammatical errors in all sections of the written test are marked, and points are deducted. The writing section has no set criteria for grading, and only one person rates this section. This is another area that needs to be addressed in the near future.

The oral test uses the ACTFL ILR-OPI rating scale for scoring, but only one person rates it. The interview itself is not documented, so it cannot be reviewed. Videotaping or simply recording the interview would address this problem.

Students are placed in the course levels that match their total scores on the test. Their levels are determined by arbitrary cut-off scores set by the program coordinator. These scores do not necessarily relate to the percentage of the test that matches the different course curricula. They also do not correspond to the specific items that were answered correctly.

The program has collected and kept all test papers pertaining to all placement tests that were taken since 2001, but no data has been compiled from these tests in either a handwritten or digital format. As a result, we have no records on student profiles, item analysis, or basic statistical analysis that could provide information on scoring and placement or test reliability. This may be a reason that no changes, major or otherwise, have been made to the test since it was first administered over 10 years ago. Of course, time, money, and personnel are also factors contributing to the lack of revision.

Recommendations

Having reviewed the UH Filipino program placement system, we now move on to some concrete, actionable ideas for modifying the existing test content and placement process to make the system a better tool for the placement needs of the program. In this section, we offer some recommendations for modifying the placement system, identifying particular areas that need to be prioritized in the revision process.

Recommendations regarding the placement test content

Before embarking on a major project to develop test items, it would be wise to look at the existing items and do a thorough item analysis based on existing data to find out if any of these items actually work for the purpose of placing students, that is, test these items for validity and reliability. The results of such an undertaking would be very helpful in weeding out bad test items and retaining good ones. In addition, this process would allow us to get rid of outdated items and help identify areas that no longer match our curricular goals, thus leading to important changes.

The archiving of data accumulated on examinees and their scores would also be very useful in a number of ways. It could give the program very robust data on a number of salient points regarding placement and misplacement, learner profiles, and changes in the program student population over time. A review of these test papers would also give us valuable insights into the degree of effectiveness of the cut-off scores in correctly placing students and provide us with much-needed information on how accurate and consistent the ratings are for the rated data, that is, the speaking and writing sample scores.

We find the constructs currently being tested to be appropriate, and we would like to retain these components (grammar, reading, writing, listening, and speaking). However, as mentioned above, certain areas need major modifications. We outline here some specific recommendations for each section of the test.

For the grammar section, we recommend revising ambiguous items and removing items that are confusing due to unclear presentation. These items need not even be considered in the recommended item analysis prior to being revised. Creating an item bank is highly recommended. This would allow for easier periodic updating of the grammar section or even the formulation of multiple versions of the test.

For the writing section, we recommend having multiple writing prompts or topics. Each of these topics can be associated with certain writing requirements reflecting the targeted language samples being elicited from beginning- through advanced-level examinees. The instructions should clearly state the goal of the test, the expected output from the examinees, and the general criteria that will be used for rating the output.

For the reading section, having multiple short reading passages rather than one long text would be more useful for eliciting information on the language abilities of test takers from the beginning to advanced level. The passages and their associated test items can be arranged in ascending degree of difficulty, targeting competencies in the different levels. As in the other parts of the placement test, the items need to be reviewed and piloted to ensure their appropriateness.

For the listening section also, we recommend multiple topics targeting multiple proficiency levels. Having several topics geared towards examinees of varying proficiencies allows the program to collect more information on the listening abilities of a wider range of test takers. Other issues that need to be considered are those of cultural knowledge and the inclusion of specialized vocabulary. We find doing so to be very limiting and therefore, not a very efficient way of testing students' listening comprehension.

For the speaking section, we find the ACTFL ILR-OPI to be effective in matching proficiency ratings with program course objectives. However, we need to look at the data on the placement of students and track the students' progress to see whether it is indeed a good placement instrument for our program. Test takers need to be made aware of the goals of the interview and the general criteria for rating. We highly recommend that interviews be tape recorded, not only for archiving purposes, but more importantly, for reference in case questions of misplacement arise.

A useful addition to the test, to be added as a pre-test section, would be a one-page student profile sheet where students are asked to provide information relating to their linguistic background and other data that may be useful in making judgments about their placement. These data can be very useful for future program decisions on the placement system as well.

Recommendations regarding the placement process

We have identified a number of issues concerning the placement test process. In this section, we discuss three main areas that need to be addressed to improve the process. These are the issues of administration, scoring, and archiving.

Administration issues

Students are provided with much information about placement tests at the university: the course catalogue, new and transfer student orientations, and the university website all have information about the different language placement tests and testing schedules throughout the year. In our own program, we can add a general placement test descriptor and the testing schedules in a separate brochure and on our program website. Announcements on bulletin boards all over campus before the testing dates would also be helpful for better dissemination of information.

With the availability of more placement testing information, it would be easier to set specific dates for testing not only before the regular semesters but during the semesters as well. If dates are set, reservations of appropriate venues for the examination could be made in advance. Rooms with the correct video and sound equipment, low noise levels, and comfortable surroundings would be more conducive to test taking.

Scoring

Several aspects of scoring the test can be modified and improved. Clear and well-defined scoring guidelines for each skill area are needed, especially for the writing section. A writing rubric is essential to evaluate specific points or goals from the writing samples. Currently, only one faculty member is in charge of scoring the writing test. Having another instructor review and score the writing sample would be helpful in the final assessment of this section. However, the writing composition raters would have no formal training in scoring that kind of test. To give consistent, fair, and accurate ratings, the testing administrators and other instructors in the program should go through a rater training.

The current scoring system relates the total points scored by the students to a set of arbitrary cut-off scores to determine the placement level. We recommend revising the scoring system to reflect the students' performance on each of the skill areas instead of considering only the overall test score. In addition, a method needs to be developed to combine the skill area scores to better identify the appropriate placement levels.

Archiving

Because the placement tests taken in the last three years have been kept in the program office, our recommendation is that the information from these tests be formed into a database that can be used to analyze student profiles, test-item variables, and placement scores. This analysis will hopefully provide valuable information that will aid in evaluating the overall utility and reliability of the current placement test. An archive of test results and examinee profiles will be a rich resource for the program in forming decisions regarding placement and curricular changes in the future.

Conclusion

We have thought through some of the major issues in our program's placement system. A critical review of its content and process is a big step towards identifying areas of priority in the Filipino program's efforts to revise the current system leading to the establishment of an improved one.

Current State and Issues of the Japanese Placement Test at the University of Iowa

Yukiko A. Hatasa
University of Iowa

In languages like Japanese, a well-established commercial placement test is not readily available, and language practitioners are often faced with difficult placement decisions. Those of us at the University of Iowa (UI) are no exception, and we have struggled to come up with a placement test that serves the purpose of our Japanese program.

The purpose of this case study is to illustrate and review the process of developing a mechanism for placing students in our program so that future development can be conceived and planned. More specifically, I review the following topics that are relevant to the development of the placement test. First, the regional characteristics of the university and its undergraduate and graduate programs that have relevance to Japanese language programs are illustrated. Second, the Japanese language curriculum and its development process are described. The placement test was created in accordance with the curriculum development from 1994 through 1998, and therefore, the chronological development of the language curriculum is closely related to the test development. Third, our placement procedure is explained. This includes the test construction and pre-testing process, test format, design and items, administration procedure, and the treatment of misplaced students. Fourth, the features that are characteristic of the UI Japanese program and its placement test are discussed. Based on these reviews, in the final section of this paper, I discuss plans and ideas for future development to improve the placement system as a whole.

Context of the program

University and its regional characteristics

The University of Iowa is one of two major research institutions in the state of Iowa, with a special emphasis on liberal arts, law, and medical science. It has approximately 27,000 students. The majority of the undergraduate students are from Iowa, though a number of students are from Illinois or Nebraska due to the relatively low out-of-state tuition among the states with Big 10 universities. The graduate students come from all over the world, constituting a highly heterogeneous population.

Hatasa, Y. (2008). Current state and issues of the Japanese placement test at the University of Iowa. In T. Hudson & M. Clark (Eds.), *Case studies in foreign language placement: Practices and possibilities* (pp. 39–52). Honolulu, HI: University of Hawaiʻi, National Foreign Language Resource Center.

Degree and certificate programs requiring Japanese language training

The Japanese Program in the Department of Asian Languages and Literature offers the only Japanese degree program in Iowa. It offers a BA in Japanese language and literature. Undergraduate majors are required to complete three years of Japanese, totaling 32 credit hours. Furthermore, they have to take a minimum of five upper-level Japanese literature and linguistics courses (15 credit hours). The program also offers an MA in Asian Civilizations, which is subdivided into teaching Japanese as a foreign language and Japanese literature. Graduate students in the MA program are assumed to have near-native or native proficiency and are not required to take language courses. Non-native candidates with insufficient Japanese language proficiency are usually required to take one or more upper-level language courses as a prerequisite.

The program offers all levels of modern and two classical Japanese language courses. In addition, it offers a variety of linguistics courses such as Japanese linguistics, sociolinguistics, discourse analysis, Japanese pedagogy, and other applied linguistics courses. Furthermore, a full range of courses are offered on modern and classical literature, cultural studies, art, painting, society, history, sociology, and religions.

The Japanese program also has a close relation with one degree program and one certificate program. First, the Department of Curriculum and Instruction offers a K-12 teacher certification. Students who wish to be certified in Japanese need to complete the fourth-year Japanese courses or to show an equivalent proficiency. They are also required to take such courses as Japanese Linguistics and Japanese as a Foreign Language: Practical Application. Second, the International Program offers a major in international studies, in which Japan can be selected as one area of concentration. This is a relatively new major program established a few years ago, and it requires rather rigorous language studies. Students majoring in international studies are required to complete three years of Japanese language courses, just like students majoring in Asian languages and literatures. In addition, they are required to take 6 hours of foundation courses and 12 hours of courses in Asian studies such as history, political science, literature, sociology, and work on a senior thesis. Furthermore, they are strongly advised to participate in a study abroad program, and they receive a stipend to do so.

Japanese language program

Although UI has offered Japanese language courses since 1967, no attempt to develop a placement test was made until the mid 1990s. The placement test was constructed as a part of a curriculum development project that started in 1994. Information obtained through various surveys and an evaluation to develop the new curriculum and the structure of the curriculum shaped the placement test. For this reason, this section provides an overview of the curriculum development process and then a description of the curriculum of the Japanese language program.

An overview of the curriculum development
Student characteristics and needs. As a first step in developing a new curriculum, a series of needs and readiness analyses, demographic questionnaires, and formative/summative evaluations of all courses were used from 1994 through 1996 to obtain information about student characteristics and the quality of the existing courses.

The results showed the following demographic characteristics: First, among the 100 students enrolled in the Japanese courses, the majority of them were Caucasian-American. Less than 10% of the student population came from other ethnic backgrounds. Most non-Caucasian students were Chinese or Korean. Heritage students or transfer students were extremely rare, and the number of students who studied Japanese in high school was relatively small (about 15 or less) because of the small number of high schools offering Japanese language courses. Approximately 30 to 40 students majored in Japanese language or literature or Japanese studies. [1]

In terms of students' needs, over 80% of the students were interested in modern Japanese culture, especially pop culture such as anime and film. They did not need to use Japanese in their daily lives. However, they had a strong interest in becoming proficient in oral communication, and many hoped to become friends with Japanese natives and/or visit Japan. Only a few students had a strong academic or career-oriented goal in studying Japanese.

In addition, most students spent a few hours every day studying Japanese outside of the class, but they had virtually no opportunities to practice Japanese outside of class except for activities organized by the Japanese Students' Association and a weekly brown-bag lunch session organized by the instructor.

The formative and summative evaluations of the courses tended to indicate a low level of student satisfaction, which was reflected in a high attrition rate in the first- and second-year Japanese courses. The following are the major reasons:

- The instructional approaches were very grammar oriented and did not help students to engage in conversational interaction even at the intermediate or advanced levels.
- Students in the third- and fourth-year courses disliked the teaching materials because they were written exclusively in Japanese with very little explanation.
- The first- and second-year Japanese courses met six hours a week, causing scheduling problems. Credit hours in these courses were high, and this increased anxiety for some students.
- Non-intensive first semester courses, which covered the content of the first year in two semesters, did not work. Non-intensive courses were designed so that the first-semester course began in the spring semester, and the second half was offered in the fall semester. The fall course was supposed to attract students with some background in Japanese. However, many students preferred to take the first semester of Japanese during the fall semester. As a result, students who studied Japanese in high school and those who were studying it for the first time were placed in the same class. Experienced students tended to find the course boring and lose motivation, whereas those without any background felt that they were put in comparably disadvantageous positions.
- Many students developed unbalanced skills at the third-year level because of the strong emphasis on reading and writing and the lack of emphasis on oral-aural skills. This was problematic in fourth-year courses, in which continuing students and those who had returned from the study abroad program and were generally proficient in speaking were usually placed together.

Institutional goals and practical issues

To balance students' needs and the objectives of the Japanese section in the department, the mission statements of the school and the descriptions of relevant majors and certification

---

[1] The Japanese studies major was available until 2001, but it was replaced with the International Studies major. The former required only two years of Japanese instead of the three years required in the latter program.

programs were examined. Contrary to students' expectations, the department expected students to become literate enough to read newspaper articles, short narratives, and descriptions in Japanese so that they would be prepared to handle some authentic texts at the graduate level. Oral communication was not considered as important as reading. Furthermore, the number of credit hours given to language courses was large in relation to other foreign language majors and prevented Japanese majors from taking a variety of content courses.

In addition, practical issues such as the availability of teaching staff and materials were examined. The instructional staff included one full-time instructor and one visiting instructor, but most of the staff was made up of graduate teaching assistants at the master's level, who had very little or no teaching experience. The textbooks adopted were either outdated or written for students studying Japanese in Japan, and all were based on the audio-lingual approach. Consequently, authentic materials were very rare, except for in the advanced courses, and audiovisual or multimedia materials were not readily available, except for one video series.

Based on the above information, the graduate and undergraduate majors and course offerings in the Japanese language were changed in 1996 and 1997. The effectiveness of the new curriculum was measured using students' course surveys and evaluations and enrollment growth and attrition rates from fall 1997 through fall 1998. The change in curriculum resulted in steady enrollment growth. The enrollment in fall 1994 was 98, but approximately 180 students enrolled in Japanese language courses in fall 2005.

Description of the Japanese language program
Currently, the Japanese program offers five levels of Japanese language courses and one review course at the elementary level. First Year Japanese: First Semester meets every day and accepts only those students who have never studied Japanese. Students with some background in Japanese but who are not as advanced as students in second-year Japanese are placed in Elementary Review, which meets three times a week. Both of these courses are offered in the fall semester, and students who complete either one of the courses are allowed to take First Year Japanese: Second Semester. The second-year Japanese courses also meet every day of the week, and completing them is necessary to satisfy the foreign language requirements. At the third-year level, courses are divided into conversation and reading/writing. This configuration provides students an option of taking both courses at the same time and completing the third year, which is required for the two majors, in one year, or taking one course a year and completing the requirements in two years. Another advantage of this configuration is to minimize skill differences at the fourth-year level, which is, as noted above, required for the teacher certification. All of the courses are offered every year, except for the fifth year, which is offered depending on enrollment needs. (See Appendix A for a description of the courses.)

In terms of syllabus design, the four skills are emphasized at all levels, though the emphasis gradually shifts from speaking and listening to reading and writing. The instructional approach is communicative, but accuracy is also emphasized. The syllabi of the beginning- and intermediate-level courses are synthetic, that is, theme-function combined with grammatical. The third, fourth and fifth year use task-based syllabi. One full-time lecturer, two professors, and seven or eight graduate teaching assistants teach most of the courses as a team.

No students taking any of the language courses in the department are permitted to choose a pass/non-pass option. To be promoted from the first semester to the second semester of the same level, a student must have a grade of C or higher. To take a course in the next level, a student is required to obtain a grade of B− or higher. For example, a student in the first-year, first-semester course must receive at least a C to take the first-year, second-semester course. A student in the first-year, second-semester course must receive a B– or higher to take the second-year, first-semester course. Without these grades, students are not given permission to enroll.

In addition to the language instruction at UI, some students choose to study elsewhere. A few students participate in a summer intensive program outside of UI and several students participate in a one-year study abroad program.

Description of the process

Development of the placement test

The Japanese placement test was developed during the 1996–1998 academic years by the Japanese coordinator and the Evaluation and Examination Services at UI.

The target population of examinees was determined to be students who had some knowledge of Japanese and had not gone through a sequence of Japanese courses at UI. This includes heritage students, students who have studied Japanese in high school, students who have lived in Japan, and students who have taken Japanese courses at UI but have attended summer intensive courses or have returned from study abroad programs.

The skill areas to be tested were reading, listening, and grammar; vocabulary and character knowledge would be tested as a part of reading test. A multiple-choice format was selected, though it was not congruent with the activities in the Japanese classrooms. These skill areas and test format were chosen for the following reasons. First, the test is administered by the staff at the Evaluation and Examination Services who do not understand Japanese. Second, the maximum time allowed for the test administration was 65 minutes, so having many subsections such as a vocabulary or character section, with sufficient numbers of items, was not feasible. Third, the tests must be scored on the same day they are taken during summer orientation sessions. Fourth, most of the testing was done during the summer, and no Japanese language staff were available then, so production tests and oral skills could not be assessed. Finally, the Japanese instructional staff was mostly made up of teaching assistants, some of whom have never taught Japanese previously. Therefore, a high degree of reliability would be difficult to achieve if a test format that required subjective scoring was used.

During the development process, three of the most popular elementary and intermediate Japanese textbooks in the US, one manuscript for elementary and intermediate textbooks, and several popular advanced-level textbooks were analyzed for vocabulary, Chinese characters, grammar, themes, language functions, discourse patterns, and so forth to find common features for each level. Based on the analysis, linguistic items, themes, functions, and so forth were selected to create item specifications. This was necessary because students taking the exam would come from a variety of backgrounds. Basing the test items solely on the textbooks adopted at UI might negatively affect those who used different textbooks elsewhere, while giving an advantage to those who used the same textbook. We were also concerned with the stability of the test. That is, if the test were based on a particular textbook, the test would not be useful if we changed the textbook, and in turn, changing the textbook would be difficult. Furthermore, using multiple textbooks as sources in the database enabled us to keep track of the decision-making process in developing the test items. All of the instructors and teaching assistants were asked to contribute a few test items for each subsection of the test to maximize the variety of personal styles. The coordinator reviewed the degree of item congruency with the item specifications and did pilot testing. The data were machine processed by Evaluation and Examination Services, and all the statistical results were returned to the coordinator, who analyzed and revised the items.

The items were chosen so that some items indicated the mastery of the first-year material, some of the second-year material, and so on. This ensured that the interval between the mean scores of two adjacent levels was large enough and that the overlap in test scores between two adjacent levels was relatively small. In general, avoiding overlaps between levels is difficult, but it was possible in our case for two reasons. First, we did not make a fine distinction based on semesters. Instead, we distinguished the differences by adjacent years. In addition, the difference in proficiency between any two levels could be easily distinguished in our program because of the use of permission codes that ensured only those students with a grade of B− or above could take a course at the higher level.

Four pilot tests were administered to students in Japanese language courses to create an item bank. The pre-tests were analyzed using the following statistical calculations and the entire group of test-takers: a distribution analysis with a histogram, item analyses (item difficulty and discrimination indices of key and distracter items), the mean, median, standard deviation, standard error of measurement, score range, mean difficulty of the test, mean discrimination of the test, and reliability estimate (KR-20). Furthermore, the same set of calculations was conducted for the students in each level. Because the number of students was the largest in the first year and progressively decreased as the levels became higher, the distribution of the entire group of the students was skewed. This made it difficult to analyze the test difficulty and effectiveness of items in discriminating different levels. On the other hand, analyzing each level showed the score distribution of the levels, any overlaps between two adjacent levels, and the effectiveness of items constructed as an indicator of mastery for each level. In addition, the analysis of each level allowed us to compare students' scores on the placement test, their performance in classroom achievement tests and on oral interview tests, and their grades.

Description of the placement test

The final version of the placement test has been used since 1998. The test uses a paper-and-pencil format because many high schools in Iowa did not have computers with Japanese fonts for students' use when the test was developed. It is a multiple-choice discrete-point test consisting of three subsections: reading, listening, and grammar. Each subsection consists of 25 items, for a total of 75 items. The maximum time allowed for a placement test during the orientation session is 65 minutes, so the number of items was chosen through pre-testing to ensure that most students finish the test in time while achieving a reasonably high reliability (see Table 2).

Table 2. Specifications of placement test

subtest	format	number of items	time allocated	scoring
reading	multiple choice	25	20 minutes	exact
listening	multiple choice	25	15 minutes	exact
grammar	multiple choice	25	30 minutes	exact

The texts in the reading section range from simple statements to a short paragraph consisting of several lines. The simple statements are written in Japanese syllabic characters and a limited number of basic Chinese characters. As the complexity of the texts increases, the number of Chinese characters increases. The texts at the advanced levels are written in the same way as authentic Japanese texts. Each text is accompanied by one or two multiple-choice questions, written in English. The directions, simplest text, and first question are shown in Figure 1 as an example for this section.

> Section 1: Reading
>
> *Suggested time–20 minutes*
> Directions: The questions in this part consist of short passages in Japanese, followed by one or two questions in English about the passage and four suggested answers. Choose the one choice which best answers the question, based on the content of the passage. Study the following example:
>
> その本は　じしょです。　きょうかしょは　あれですよ。
>
> Where is the dictionary?
>
> a. Away from the speaker and the listener
> b. Away from the speaker and close to the listener
> c. Close to the speaker and away from the listener
> d. Close to both the speaker and the listener

Figure 1. Directions and sample item for reading section of placement test.

Texts in the listening sections range from a very short dialogue to a dialogue consisting of multiple interactions. Each text is accompanied by one or two multiple-choice questions, written in English. (See Figure 2.)

> Section 2: Listening
>
> *Suggested time–15 minutes*
> Directions: You will hear a short statement or dialogue in Japanese. You will hear it only once, so listen carefully. Each item in this part consists of one or two questions in English about the conversation and four suggested answers for each question. Choose the one choice which best answers the question, based on the content of the passage. Study the following example:
>
> You hear:　A: なんねんせいですか。
> 　　　　　　B: よねんせいです。
>
> You see:　What is the man's academic standing?
> 　　　　　　a. Freshman
> 　　　　　　b. Sophomore
> 　　　　　　c. Junior
> 　　　　　　d. Senior

Figure 2. Directions and sample item for listening section of placement test.

The final section, grammar, consists of 25 multiple-choice items as shown in Figure 3. In this section, all of the Chinese characters have superscripts in syllabic characters, so that lacking knowledge of Chinese characters does not affect performance on the test. At the same time, this format does not negatively affect examinees who are more comfortable reading Chinese characters.

> Section 3: Grammar
>
> *Suggested time—25 minutes*
> *Directions*: The questions in this part consist of short passages or sentences with a blank in Japanese, followed by four suggested choices. Choose the one choice which best fits the blank. Study the following example:
>
> きのうは 海(うみ) 行(い)きました。
>
> a. へ
> b. で
> c. が
> d. を

Figure 3. Directions and sample item for grammar section of placement test.

Description of the placement test score report form

A student who has taken the placement test receives the score report form shown in Appendix B. The form shows a recommendation of the examinee's placement in one of the following courses offered in the fall semester: First Year Japanese, Elementary Japanese Review, Second Year Japanese, Third Year Japanese (Conversation or Reading and Writing), and Fourth Year. Fifth Year is not included because it is not offered every year and because the number of students who could be placed at this level is expected to be very small. The form does not suggest that a student take the conversation course or the reading course at the third-year level. It merely suggests that they take either or both of the courses.

The cut scores were determined based on the results of the pilot testing. For each level, the students' grades and test scores were compared, and the median test score of the students with a B− was used as the cut score.

Placement procedure

The placement test for incoming and transfer students is normally conducted during summer orientation sessions. They take the test in the morning of the orientation, and they receive a score report form in which placement recommendations are made at the end of the day. The report form provides suggestions for placements, and the advisors in the academic advising center enroll students in the recommended courses and/or put them on waitlists for the courses. Occasionally, a transfer student comes in a day an orientation session is not scheduled and cannot schedule the placement test. In this case, the academic advising center makes a tentative decision based on the student's transcripts, and s/he is required to take the placement test at the beginning of the semester to finalize the enrollment. If s/he does not take the test, the instructor in charge of the course may drop him/her if the instructor determines that his/her proficiency is insufficient. The rest of the students (i.e., those with some knowledge of Japanese or students who have taken a Japanese course elsewhere) take the exam at least a week before instruction resumes in the fall semester. They also receive the report form and bring the form to the instructor in charge of the assigned course or the coordinator of the Japanese program to complete the registration.

If a student disagrees with the placement recommendation in the report form, s/he is asked to see the coordinator or the head instructor of the desired course, and that person makes an informal assessment through interviews. In a borderline case, the student is usually asked to go to both the recommended course and the course of his/her choice and make a decision with the instructors during the first two weeks of instruction.

Distinguishing features of the program

Compared to the West Coast and Hawai'i, few schools offer Japanese language courses or a degree in the Japanese language in the Midwest. This is especially the case in the area surrounding UI. For example, major institutions such as the University of Nebraska, the University of Missouri, and Iowa State University do not offer more than two years of Japanese. With the improvement of the Japanese program, more students in these states have transferred to UI recently. This may have caused a change in demographic characteristics. The recent addition of an international studies major may also affect the demographic characteristics of students taking Japanese because the number of students choosing this major is rapidly increasing. At this point, it has had a minimal effect on students needs, but it may change in the future because the international studies major includes such disciplines as business and law that are not included in our major.

Another issue, which is not unique to UI, is the articulation between the high school and college levels. Students who have studied Japanese in high school for two to four years are usually placed in Elementary Review, and this is often discouraging to not only to the students in question but also to high school teachers. So far, we have provided some information through placement reports as to what an examinee's score means in our program, but we have not provided detailed feedback regarding the strengths and weaknesses of the examinee's language skills.

The extremely small size of heritage populations in Iowa and nearby states makes it difficult for UI to accommodate their needs. We receive at most one heritage student a year. Because our placement test is intended for non-heritage students whose development of the four skills is radically different from that of heritage students, the test consistently misplaces heritage students. However, the number of heritage students is so low that offering a course that meets their needs is impossible. For this reason, the Japanese program at UI cannot make adequate placement decisions or provide adequate education for these students.

With regard to test development, one unique characteristic of our program is that the success in one course determines the permission to enroll in a course at a higher level. This practice enables us to maintain a relatively strict achievement standard. The fact that most placement decisions are made within a day during the summer and the lack of Japanese-speaking graders during this period limits the types of placement tests that can be administered.

Practical ideas for placement and future development

Although the current test version works well, it has only one form. Due to a lack of time and personnel, no item bank has been made for systematically developing a parallel form. Having only one form is not desirable in terms of test security, so we need to bank items.

We also need to regularly test our students. Giving the test to current students every year is difficult because of the staff and administrative limitations of the program. However, the students' characteristics may have changed over time, and our head instructors have changed recently, so it is essential to examine whether these changes have had any effects on the students' performance on the placement test, and if so, recalibrating and/or modifying the placement report form is also essential. In an attempt to do so, we administered the placement test to our students at the end of the 2004-5 academic year. The findings show that the test discriminated well across the different levels, but the scores were distributed more widely than in 1998 in both the positive and negative directions. More specifically, the scores of the students in the first- and second-year courses had somewhat lower means, while those of the students in the third- and fourth-year courses had higher means. This shift in distribution may be due to a number of reasons. For example, as the number of students taking Japanese courses increases, students' characteristics may have become more diverse. As we have constantly worked on improving instruction to fit students' needs and curriculum objectives, instruction may have changed accordingly. In addition, recent changes in the head instructors may have resulted in changes in achievement criteria for some of the courses. Further examination of item difficulty for each level and students' demographic characteristics is necessary to find out the cause of the score distribution.

We would like to provide transfer students an option of computer-delivered tests. Computerized tests could provide results almost instantaneously, so students who are unable to come to UI during the orientation session could still take the test when they visited the UI campus. The current system is such that transfer students may be allowed to enroll in a course tentatively during the summer, but they cannot finalize their enrollments until they arrive on campus and take the test. If they can take the test at the time of their campus visit, they can be enrolled in a course and do not have to be concerned with the possibility of not being placed in the same course in the fall semester.

In addition, we would like the test to provide more informative feedback to test-takers and high school teachers. Within the current format, we can provide more detailed information about the correspondence between test scores and course grades, but this still does not tell high school instructors what UI students in each level can do. To address this, a combination of "can do" statements for each level, grades, and test scores can be placed on the web in addition to the description of the test and sample items. Moreover, sample instructional materials and classroom tasks could be provided on the web so that students and teachers may obtain a better idea about instruction at each level.

Another possibility is to consider an alternative test format or criterion-referenced tests. If we can work with institutions with fairly similar institutional characteristics and students, it may help us to collect more data in a short period of time to construct items. For example, we can ask the students in a nearby institution with a similar curriculum to take our placement test and examine the results. If their results coincide with those of our students, we can use both institutions as a data source and use our current placement test as a reference to examine the concurrent validity.

Finally, an Advanced Placement (AP) test in Japanese is currently under construction and is expected to be operational in fall 2007. Therefore, we need to establish a correspondence between our placement test and the AP scores before using the AP scores for placement purposes. To do so, we need to have incoming students who have taken the AP test take the placement test. The collection of such data will help us to determine the correspondence between our placement test and the AP test.

Conclusion

We have provided an overview of the placement practices and the academic program of the University of Iowa in relation to the Japanese language curriculum. We have described the development of the Japanese language program and the placement test. More specifically, we have discussed factors that have influenced the determination of the organization, format, items, and administration. Analyses show that our test is workable but a work in progress and that much needs to be done to improve its stability, validity, and congruence with the curriculum. The analyses also provided us with practical ideas for developing the test and factors for future test development such as the AP test in Japanese.

Reference

Makino, S. , Hatasa, Y. A., and Hatasa, K. (1998). *Nakama 1: Japanese communication, culture, context.* Boston: Houghton Mifflin Co.

Appendix A: Japanese language curriculum at the University of Iowa

course	semester offered	hours per week (credit hours)	number of students per section	number of sections	class format and structure
\multicolumn{6}{c}{first year or elementary level}					
First Semester (39J:11)	fall	5(5)	15	5	A four-skills approach with a special emphasis on conversation, vocabulary, and learning strategies. The textbook, *Nakama, volume 1* (year), is theme-based and synthesized with linguistic content. The first six chapters are covered.
Elementary/Non-intensive (39J:12)	fall	3(3)	15	1	A review course for students who have taken Japanese in high school or have equivalent knowledge. Covers the same content as the first-year, first-semester course but with fewer contact hours. The emphasis is on review and learning strategies.
Second Semester (39J:13)	spring	5(5)	15	5	A four-skills approach with a special emphasis on conversation, vocabulary, and learning strategies. The next six chapters of the textbook, *Nakama, volume 1*, are covered.
\multicolumn{6}{c}{second year}					
First Semester (39J:101)	fall	5(5)	15	3	The emphasis is on the four skills with an increased emphasis on reading and listening to longer discourses. The textbook is *Nakama, volume 2*. The first five chapters are covered in the first semester, and Chapters 6 through 10 are covered in the second semester.
Second Semester (39J:102)	spring	5(5)	15	3	
\multicolumn{6}{c}{third year}					
Conversation I	fall	3(3)	15	1 or 2	The emphasis is on developing conversation and listening skills and applying basics learned in first- and second-year Japanese in varied types of interaction. *Chuukyuu no Nihongo* is the main textbook, though it is used merely to introduce some conversational samples and topics. Chinese characters are used but not significantly increased. Most of the materials are produced in-house.
Conversation II	spring	3(3)	15	1 or 2	
Reading & Writing I	fall	3(3)	15	1	The emphasis is on reading and the reading and writing of Chinese characters. Some writings are produced, such as descriptive and expository. In-house manuscripts are used.
Reading & Writing II	spring	3(3)	15	1	

		fourth year				
First Semester	fall	3 (3)	10	1	The emphasis is on reading, writing, and discussion skills. In-house manuscripts and programs on the TV Japan Network are used.
Second Semester	spring	3 (3)	10	1	
		fifth year				
First Semester	fall	3 (3)	10	1	The emphasis is on academic conversation, reading, and writing skills. In-house manuscripts and programs on the TV Japan Network are used.
Second Semester	spring	3 (3)	10	1	

Appendix B: Score report form for the Japanese placement test

JAPANESE
Language Placement Examination Results

Name _____ Score _____

Social Security Number _____ Date _____

> Note: If your score is above 10, you have a substantial advantage over students just starting foreign language and are strongly advised to continue with your Japanese studies immediately. If you do not register for a Japanese course now, your current skills will decline rapidly and you will probably need to start at a much lower level.

score   **recommended placement**

29 or below   Your score indicates that unless you have strong Japanese skills that were not measured by this test (such as speaking), you may have difficulty in 39J:12, Elementary Japanese: Review. You should start with 39J:11 First Year Japanese.

30 to 46   Your score corresponds to a grade of C or lower in First Year Japanese: Second Semester (39J:13). You should start with 39J:12. Elementary Japanese: Review. If you plan to take Japanese, it is in your best interest to register for course work as soon as possible, since the advantage you now have will be lost over time.

47 to 53   Your score corresponds to a grade of B- or higher in first-year Japanese. You should therefore enroll in third semester Japanese, 39J:101, Second Year Japanese: First Semester. If you have taken four or more year of high school Japanese or have reason to believe some of your Japanese skills (such as speaking) are better than this placement indicates, you should discuss with an instructor in charge of 39J:101.

> Note: A score of 54 or higher qualifies you for the Foreign Language Incentive Program (FLIP) if you register for the appropriate course and complete it with a grade of B- or higher. STUDENTS ARE ELIGIBLE FOR INCENTIVE CREDIT ONLY DURING THEIR FIRST AND SECOND REGISTRATIONS AT THE UNIVERSITY OF IOWA. Consult your advisor for further details.

54 to 58   Your score corresponds to a grade of B- or higher in second-year Japanese and reflects very good Japanese skills. You should therefore enroll in fifth semester Japanese, 39J:105, Third Year Japanese: Conversation I or 39J:107, Third Year Japanese: Reading and Writing I. If you would like to be considered for exemption from the Foreign Language Requirement based on this score, please contact the Department of Asian Languages and Literature (353 - 2206) at the start of the fall semester to schedule an Oral Proficiency Interview.

59 or higher   Your score corresponds to a grade of B or higher in third-year Japanese. This is an excellent score and indicates that you should enroll in a seventh semester course, 39J:121 Fourth Year Japanese: First Semester.

Current Placement Test and Future Developments: The Japanese Program, Yale University

Yoshiko Maruyama
Yale University, CT

The Japanese program at Yale has two sets of placement tests: one for student placement into the Elementary through Advanced-I classes and the other for placement into the Advanced-II class. Because my concentration is the intermediate-level classes, the focus of this case study will be on the first test.

We have been using the same test format for quite a while; it was already being used when I joined the faculty more than a decade ago, and it had already been used for more than a decade before that time. Although we have revised the content and tried to update it every year, the test is due for a thorough review to determine its effectiveness. I will examine the problems with the current test and discuss the creation of a new one.

Language instruction at Yale

Yale University, in New Haven, Connecticut, is a private and independent institution founded in 1701. It is composed of three major academic components: Yale College, the Graduate School of Arts and Sciences, and 10 professional schools. Approximately 11,250 students attend Yale, and out of them, about 5,250 are undergraduate students. The Department of East Asian Languages and Literatures is a part of both the Graduate School of Arts and Sciences and Yale College, and the Japanese program is one of the three language programs the department offers. The other two are Chinese and Korean. Besides those three language programs, the department offers a language and a literature undergraduate degree in both Chinese and Japanese and a literature PhD in Chinese or Japanese.

Including the three languages offered in the Department of East Asian Languages and Literatures, over 50 languages are taught at Yale. For the instruction of these languages, a common source of support comes from the Center for Language Studies. It provides us support for pedagogical innovation and professional development by offering workshops and seminars. The Center also supports the development of multimedia materials. It has multimedia classrooms that any language program can use.

Maruyama, Y. (2008). Current placement test and future developments: The Japanese program, Yale University. In T. Hudson & M. Clark (Eds.), *Case studies in foreign language placement: Practices and possibilities* (pp. 53–62). Honolulu, HI: University of Hawai'i, National Foreign Language Resource Center.

Traditionally, Yale College students were required to complete two years (four semesters) of any foreign language, and those students who demonstrated the equivalent level of proficiency in placement tests could choose to have the language requirement waived. However, a new foreign language requirement will take effect in the academic year of 2005-2006. For the class of 2009 and subsequent classes, all students will be required to take language courses, regardless of the level of study achieved before arriving at the school. The new requirement varies from one to three semesters depending on the students' achieved levels (refer to Appendix A for more details). This change in the language requirement is predicted to have no substantial effect on the Japanese program as a whole, the enrollment of the students in our program, or our placement tests and their procedures.

Japanese program

Our mission statement reads

> The Japanese Language Course at Yale aims to provide students, who plan to pursue studies in academics or work in professional fields, with a thorough knowledge of Japanese language skills. In short, the students will acquire the necessary competence to enable them to communicate smoothly for the purpose of fulfilling academic or professional career tasks. We will instruct them in not only the four language skills, but also provide them the background knowledge of history, culture and society, which is essential to language use. In order to achieve the goals of this mission, we will always first and foremost consider the students' needs, and we will research and develop appropriate teaching methods and materials accordingly.

Four levels of courses in Japanese language were offered until the academic year 2005-2006, when a fifth-year course, Advanced Japanese III, was introduced. Six instructors in our program teach these courses. Each level has its own goals, and we hope that the students will use the knowledge they gain in each of the classes to build a knowledge base to ultimately attain the level of proficiency stated in the mission statement of the program. The goals of the different levels are listed below:

Elementary Japanese (first year, meets one hour every day, five hours a week)

Grammar: basic
Characters: hiragana, katakana, and 300 kanji
Speaking: everyday life
Reading: simple sentences
Writing: simple sentences
Listening: everyday life

Intermediate Japanese (second year, meets one hour every day, five hours a week)

Grammar: basic and review, complex sentence grammar 1
Characters: 300 kanji
Speaking: topics related to students' immediate surroundings and their special interests
Reading: letters, essays, short stories, and poems
Writing: complex sentences, diaries, letters, and essays
Listening: anime, movies, songs

Advanced Japanese I (third year, meets 1.5 hours a day, three days a week)

> *Grammar*: complex sentence grammar 1 review and complex sentence grammar 2
> *Characters*: 300 kanji
> *Speaking*: pragmatic expressions and discussion of social issues
> *Reading*: novels, newspapers, and short academic reports
> *Writing*: multiple paragraphs, essays, letters, poems, and novels
> *Listening*: news, *anime*, and movies

Advanced Japanese II (fourth year, meets 1.5 hours a day, three days a week)

> *Grammar*: complex sentence grammar 2 review and complex sentence grammar 3
> *Characters*: 300 kanji
> *Speaking*: discussion of social issues and abstract ideas
> *Reading*: newspapers, critiques, and short academic papers
> *Writing*: multiple paragraphs and short academic reports
> *Listening*: movies and lectures

Advanced Japanese III (fifth year, meets 1.5 hours a day, two days a week)

> This new course is aimed at further developing skills for use in academic settings, including public speaking, formal presentations, and expository writing based on research. The materials include lectures, scholarly papers, criticisms, fiction, and films.

Recently, the enrollment in our program has been steadily increasing, and a conspicuous trend is that the number of students in the advanced courses is increasing. See Table 1. The increase in enrollment is partly due to a scholarship that was first awarded in 1996. This scholarship supports students who study East Asian languages (Chinese, Japanese, or Korean) to study abroad. About 30 Japanese students have been awarded the scholarship each year for the last three years. Consequently, an increased number of students have spent a summer and/or a year in Japan and continued to take advanced-level courses after returning to the school.

Table 1. Numbers of students in each level of courses, 2001–2005[1]

	fall 01	spring 02	fall 02	spring 03	fall 03	spring 04	fall 04	spring 05
Elementary	57	44	57	57	44	39	47	52
Intermediate	17	18	31	29	36	31	31	31
Advanced I	6	7	13	12	22	20	20	19
Advanced II	6	7	9	7	9	7	16	11
total	86	76	110	105	111	97	114	113

The program consists of mainly undergraduate students, and a majority of them are highly motivated to learn Japanese. The students' majors vary widely, with many majoring in natural

---

[1] In fall 2001 and spring 2002, intensive (10-hour/week) and semi-intensive (5-hour/week) courses were offered in elementary Japanese. The enrollment numbers above are a combination of the two. (In fall 2001, 31 students enrolled for the intensive course and 26 for the semi-intensive, and in the spring of 2002, 21 enrolled for the intensive and 21 for the semi-intensive.)

sciences in addition to humanities. (See Appendix B for their distributions.) Their interests in studying Japanese differ widely as well, including the Japanese economy, culture, movies, martial arts, and pop culture. Recently, we have found that a large contingency of students start taking Japanese courses because of their strong interest in Japanese *anime* or comic books. Although these various areas of interest were their initial sources of motivation to study Japanese, many students' interests grow into more academic fields, such as Japanese history, literature, sociology, international relations, and political science. As they continue to study Japanese and related subjects, some decide to major in East Asian studies.

Placement test

We assess the incoming students' language proficiency using a written test and an interview to place them into appropriate levels. As mentioned above, we use two separate written tests. One is for students who want to place into the elementary level through Advanced-I, and the other is for students who want to place into Advanced-II and Advanced-III. If students are not sure which test to take, the instructors, who serve as proctors, can advise them after getting some information about their histories of studying Japanese. They can switch from taking one test to the other if they find that the test they started is too easy or difficult at any point in time. Depending on the results, the students are placed into Elementary Japanese through Advanced Japanese II or III. For the elementary to intermediate levels, the students may be placed into a class offered in a fall or spring semester. The placement test is also used for those who want to be exempted from the language requirement. However, only a few students each year, if any, take the test for that purpose. If they prove to be proficient enough to be placed into Advanced I, they are eligible for exemption from the language requirement. Again, this does not apply to the class of 2009 and subsequent classes because the new foreign language requirement is in effect for them.

We have about 30 students who take the placement tests at the beginning of each year. The numbers of students who took the test and were placed into each level in 2004 are shown in Table 2. Very few heritage learners take the test. If students miss taking the test, but hope to enroll in the spring term, they are given the same test at a convenient time before or at the beginning of the spring term. Not all students returning from studying in Japan are included in the table because some were simply placed by instructors without taking the test.

Table 2. Placement, fall 2004: Numbers of students in each level and their previous study of Japanese

placed level	number of students	background of Japanese study	changes from placement decision
Elementary-fall	10	college summer program up to 4 yrs. of high school grad. student from Korea	
Elementary-spring	8	3-6 yrs. of high school heritage learner grad. student from Korea	2 decided to take Intermediate-fall
Intermediate-fall	8	college summer program up to 6 yrs. of high school self-taught lived in Japan as a child	

Intermediate-spring	4	grad. student, studied at college, a Japanese mother	
		6 yrs. of high school	2 decided to take Intermediate-fall
		summer program in Japan after elementary Japanese	1 decided to take Advanced I-fall
		grad. student from Korea	
Advanced I	2	4 yrs. of high school	
		1 yr. at a language school in Japan	
Advanced II	1	unknown	

Each year, the tests are given in the morning of the day before class starts at the beginning of the fall term. Before the test, the students are asked to fill in an information sheet that includes

- name (family, given, and middle)
- student ID number
- year and college
- telephone number
- e-mail address
- purpose of taking the test: placement or exemption from language requirement?

While the students are working on the written test, they are called one by one into a separate room for an oral interview, which takes about 10 minutes. After each student finishes his/her interview, s/he resumes and finishes the written test. The students usually finish the written test in 1.5 to 2 hours, but if necessary, they are allowed to spend up to 3 hours. The tests are graded in the afternoon of the day they are given, and the placement results are given to each examinee via e-mail or phone by the end of the day.

Hereafter, I will limit the discussion to the test for the lower levels—the written test for Elementary through Advanced-I and the oral interview for Elementary through Intermediate—because these are the levels that I am more directly involved in teaching and the testing of for placement.

The written test is made up of three sections: *kanji* (Chinese characters used in Japanese writing), Japanese to English translation, and English to Japanese translation. The *kanji* section tests how well the students read *kanji* and understand the meanings of the characters. In this section, students are asked to write the readings of *kanji* words in *hiragana* and write their meanings in English.

Though we want our classes to be communicative and task-oriented, we believe that grammatical accuracy is essential for the elementary- and intermediate-level students to move on to advanced levels. Taking this into consideration, the translation sections of the written test contain problems involving vocabulary and grammar/sentence structures we want the students to have learned before being placed into certain levels of classes. In the translation sections, students are asked to translate English sentences to Japanese and Japanese sentences to English.

Each of the three sections contains 30 items, which progress in difficulty. The 30 items in each section are divided into three subsections, A, B, and C. Students are instructed that they should try to answer as many questions as possible and that they do not necessarily have to finish all the questions.

Our assumption is that those who complete or do fairly well in subsection A of each section have enough knowledge of *kanji*, vocabulary, and grammar to be placed into the Elementary-spring class. Those who complete subsection B satisfactorily are placed into the Intermediate-fall class, and those who complete B but start having difficulty answering the problems in subsection C are placed into either Intermediate-spring or Advanced-I, depending on which items they had trouble with. Those who completed subsection C satisfactorily are placed into Advanced-I or exempted from the language requirement. The students who want to be placed into Advanced I or to be exempted from language requirement can choose to start from C, skipping the A and B subsections. However, if they find C too difficult, they can go back to do B or A.

As mentioned above, while the students are taking the written tests, they are called one by one for an oral interview in a separate room. Those students who are taking the lower-level test go to a room where two instructors who teach elementary or intermediate classes conduct an interview. (Two instructors who teach Advanced-I and Advanced-II interview those students who are taking the higher-level test.) To gather information about their backgrounds in Japanese study and to assess oral proficiency, one of the instructors asks about their histories of studying Japanese—how long and where they have studied Japanese, the reasons for studying Japanese, what they can do in Japanese, and so forth—and questions pertaining to their immediate personal surroundings in Japanese—their families, trips to New Haven (where the campus is), and so forth. When making the decision on placement, the results of the written test are weighted heavily, and the results of the oral interview are supplementary.

All of the instructors are involved in the decision-making process of student placement. To determine where to place a student, the responses on the written test are evaluated for the number of items answered in each section, level of sentence structure, grammatical accuracy, and knowledge of vocabulary and *kanji*. Typically, one instructor will grade the test of an individual student, and s/he receives consensus about her/his decision of placement from other instructors who teach that level. Because we believe that acquiring accuracy in grammar and sentence structure is critical for students, our emphasis during the first and second years of study is on understanding the fundamental structure of the Japanese language. Therefore, when making a placement decision, we place the most weight on the students' proficiency in these areas. We also check their oral interview results to see if they are congruent with the results of their written tests. If the two have a significant discrepancy, we make the adjustment necessary for the final decision. Again, the most consideration is given to the student's level of grammatical accuracy and sentence structure.

After learning the test results, some students come to the instructors with their desires to be in different levels (usually higher ones). In such a case, the instructor who is in charge of the course a student wishes to be in reviews the student's test and may allow him/her to take the higher-level course on a trial-basis. This action always comes with a recommendation of what the student has not learned and how s/he is to make up for it. For the first week or two, the instructors closely monitor these special cases so that all the students are in the appropriate classes, and necessary further changes are made by the time the shopping period for registration ends.

We have been using this format of written test (translation) for quite a while. Although it has satisfactorily served its purpose, I feel that creating a new test in a new format would be appropriate at this time, for the reasons discussed below.

First, the content of the current written test is based on the content of our various levels of classes in its vocabulary, grammar/sentence structure, and *kanji*. Therefore, although the test results generally show the students' proficiency in the areas covered in our classes, they often do not reflect the students' true language abilities, especially for those who studied in other institutions or have acquired language skills not through formal education but by living in Japan or by being exposed to the language at home. Second, in translation problems, although we can usually judge where a student failed to correctly translate an item, whether the error occurred because of the student's lack of knowledge in grammar or in vocabulary is difficult to determine. Third, because reading is stressed in Advanced-I, we need to create a new test to measure students' reading abilities, which our current test does not do. Last, we give no numerical scores to the test, and the decision is based on the teachers' experience and intuition for placement. The subjectivity of the placement process may reduce its accuracy.

In the light of the problems within the current test, the following points need to be considered in creating a new test. The new test has to be in a format such that the scoring will be easy and will not depend too much on the grader's experience or intuition. The test needs to have discrete items to test *kanji*, vocabulary, and grammar, and those items need to be more comprehensive. The test should allow us to have a clear scoring system and cut scores for placement into different levels.

Future developments

The new written test should include the following sections in the formats stated.

- *kanji (reading)*: multiple choice
- *vocabulary*: multiple choice
- *grammar*: multiple choice
- *reading comprehension*: multiple choice
- *writing*: on a given topic (rubrics needed for grading)

The instructions on the test should be simple so that the students will be able to easily follow them. To ensure the students' comprehension of the format, each section of the test should start with an example problem and response. We have to work toward a valid scoring system; that is, we need to determine what the cut scores are for each section and how much weight each section carries in the decision-making process. We also need to think about how to incorporate the oral interview results in the process.

Since receiving insight into practical ideas and motivation for test improvement at the NFLRC summer workshop in 2005, I have begun writing test specifications and test items. I plan to complete a test draft during the summer so that I can share it with my colleagues to receive their feedback and prepare it to be used as a new placement test, or at least as a pilot test, by the 2005–2006 school year that begins in the fall. I plan to complete the test-making process in two or three years and to continue improving the test, assessing its validity, measuring its reliability, and maintaining its quality so that the test will be an effective and useful assessment tool.

Conclusion

During the workshop, an important point was raised: We need to see placement tests as educational and not as simply a bureaucratic necessity. I strongly agree with this point, and I want to incorporate it into our placement procedure. In this light, we need to improve our communication with students regarding the placement test, explaining fully its purpose and process. Information can be added to our departmental web page where our placement tests are announced. Example test items for students to review in preparation for the test could add to the validity of the test results as indications of their linguistic abilities. The test itself can accomplish the same kind of communication with students. We can explain what we are trying to assess in each section of the test and why we are trying to assess it, for example. I believe that a new, sound placement test with proven validity and reliability will become complete with this student-friendliness in mind.

For many of students, taking the placement test is an introduction to our program. With the new placement test, which will hopefully be in place in the very near future, I hope that the beginning of the school year will be a smooth transition period for the students and for the instructors.

Appendix A: Excerpts from the coming year's Yale College programs of study on the foreign language requirement

The study of languages has long been understood to be one of the distinctive and defining features of a liberal arts education, and in the world of the twenty-first century, knowledge of more than one language will become increasingly important. The benefits of language study include enhanced understanding of how languages work, often resulting in heightened sophistication in the use of one's own language; unmediated access to texts otherwise available only in translation or not at all; and the ability to recognize and cross cultural barriers.

All Yale College students are required to engage in study of a foreign language, regardless of the level of study achieved at the time of matriculation. Students who have not studied a foreign language before arriving at Yale, and those whose prior language study does not qualify them for placement into a second-year course, are required to take three terms of foreign language study to fulfill the distributional requirement. Students who can place into the third term of a language program must successfully complete two terms, and those who can place into a fourth term must successfully complete one term, of further study in that same language. Students who can demonstrate ability beyond the fourth term of language study, either by a score of 4 or 5 on an Advanced Placement test or by a requisite score on a placement test at Yale, must either successfully complete one term of further study in that language, or successfully complete instruction in a different language through the level designated L2. Students must enroll for at least one course credit toward satisfaction of the foreign language requirement by the end of the fourth term of enrollment and the requirement must be completed by the end of the sixth term of enrollment.

Students may complete an approved study abroad program in lieu of intermediate or advanced language study at Yale.

Appendix B: Student majors, 2004–2005

	total number undergrad/graduate		major
	fall	spring	
Elementary	47	52	Anthropology, Art, Comparative Literature, Economics, Electrical Engineering, English/East Asian Studies, History, International & Development Economics, Molecular Biophysics, Music, Neurobiology, Physics, Psychology, Undecided (many)
Intermediate	31	31	Biology, Computer Science, East Asian Studies, Economics, Electronic Engineering, English, Japanese, Linguistics, Music, Philosophy, Undecided (about half of the students)
Advanced I	20	19	Art History, Biology, Economics, French, History, International Relations, Linguistics, Math, Political Science, Psychology, Spanish, Undecided (some)
Advanced II	16	11	Applied Math, Architecture, Art/History, East Asian Studies, Economics, History, Linguistics, Literature, Undecided (some)

A Case Study:
Japanese Placement Process and Issues

Eiko Torii-Williams
Wellesley College, MA

I discuss the placement process that our small Japanese program currently uses and the placement issues that may need to be addressed. Prior to my involvement in the program, the reading sections of the final exams for each year were administered along with a short interview to place students into appropriate courses. Although this process did not present any major problems, the results of the exams clearly did not provide the type of information that was needed for placing students into courses: only partial reading comprehension skills with some language background information was evaluated, resulting in the misplacement of some students. For example, a student who appeared to have fairly good listening and reading comprehension skills based on the exam was placed at the third-year level. She turned out to know only basic grammar patterns and have weak writing skills. She would have been more properly placed at the second-year level. After several incidences such as this, another instructor and I were asked to create more suitable placement exams for each level. Based on prior experiences, it was critical to measure students' knowledge of basic grammar and *kanji* in addition to listening and reading comprehension skills; thus, in constructing the current exams, the core content of the course material was carefully examined and was incorporated into the exams.

I intend to provide an overview of our program's approach to placement testing and issues that are particular to our program.

Context of the program

Program

Our institution is a small liberal arts women's college outside of Boston. The student population is approximately 2400. The Japanese Language Program was established in 1986 and became its own department in 1995. In July 2003, the Chinese and Japanese Departments were consolidated to form the Department of East Asian Languages and Literatures.

Torii-Williams, E. (2008). A case study: Japanese placement process and issues. In T. Hudson & M. Clark (Eds.), *Case studies in foreign language placement: Practices and possibilities* (pp. 63–70). Honolulu, HI: University of Hawai'i, National Foreign Language Resource Center.

The Japanese Language Program offers language courses at all levels, as well as courses in classical and modern literature, gender and popular culture, animation, theater, and film. The faculty consists of two literature specialists who normally teach the fourth-year-level courses, two language specialists, one language instructor, and one teaching assistant. The Japanese language and literature major consists of a minimum of eight units (courses) and normally includes the second semester of the second-year-level language course, the first and the second semester of the third-year-level language courses, and five additional units. At least two must be non-language units, and at least two must come from the 300-level (upper undergraduate level) courses within the department. No Japanese minor is offered.

Students

The first-year student enrollment is approximately 25 to 30. Of these, 20 to 25 students usually continue to the second year. The third- and fourth-year classes normally have 10 students each. About two-thirds of our students are Asian (Korean/Chinese) or Asian-American, the remainder being a diverse mix of non-Asian heritage. Traditionally, very few Japanese-heritage students enrolled into our program, though recently, the numbers have been increasing; thus, a new advanced course addressing this group's unique needs was created in the fall semester of 2005. In the 1980s, most students wished to study the Japanese language to use it in their business careers; thus, a large number of students enrolled in the first- and second-year courses (approximately twice as many as today), and a very small number in the third- and fourth-year courses. As the Japanese economy started to falter, the first-year enrollment figures also decreased, which affected the figures in the second year. However, the number of students in the third- and fourth-year courses remained the same and has recently begun to increase. More students continuing on to the upper levels seems to be a trend. Compared to the 1980s, when most students were economics majors, the students' majors now vary widely. They are more interested in Japanese popular culture, animation, drama, fashion, music, and so forth. Almost every student who continues on to the upper levels goes on a study abroad program to Japan, which is available for a summer, a semester, or a whole year. Most upper-level students have double majors, one of which is Japanese.

Description of the process

Course description

The Japanese Language Program offers four levels of language courses. The first- and second-year-level courses are called "Beginning" and "Intermediate." *Japanese: The spoken language, parts I–III* by Eleanor H. Jorden and Mari Noda (1987) are used as the main textbooks with supplementary reading and writing material for the first two years; the classes meet five days a week (for one hour). Although the textbooks are based on the audio-lingual approach, the teaching methodology is quite communicative, and reading and writing are also emphasized. The main objective of the first two years is the acquisition of the four basic skills in Japanese. The third-year-level course is called "Selected Readings in Advanced Japanese," and it meets three days a week. The students begin to read newspaper/magazine articles and portions of novels/essays with the help of grammar/vocabulary lists. Although the title of the course includes "Readings," development and refinement of oral skills is also emphasized through class discussion, presentations, interview projects with native speakers, and so forth. This course acts as a transitional stage between the textbook or "controlled" Japanese and "authentic" Japanese because the students deal with newspapers, novels, classical literature, and so forth. Depending on the year and the semester, two or three of the following courses are offered at the fourth-year level: Readings in Contemporary Japanese Social Science, Directed Readings in Modern

Japanese Prose, Readings in Classical Japanese Prose, and Contemporary Japanese Narrative. All these classes meet two days a week with one independent tutorial or discussion section. The students are expected to read a variety of texts and conduct individual projects that they present to the class. Writing and/or translation skills are addressed through assignments. Beyond the fourth-year level, a research/individual study course is available for students who wish to undertake independent projects of their interest under the supervision of their advisors. Senior thesis research is also possible with the permission of the director.

Type of information needed for placement

Because one series of textbooks is used and the courses are very structured for the first two years, the placement exam for the second-/third-year level should measure whether a student has knowledge of the core grammar patterns and vocabulary that are covered in our first-/second-year material. We should also measure whether she can read and write all the Japanese characters and some *kanji* (Chinese characters). Emphasis is placed on oral skills in the courses as well; thus, all areas of how well students understand and express themselves need to be tested.

As noted in the previous section, the third-year level is a transitional course to authentic Japanese, and the students read a variety of text types at the fourth-year level. Therefore, the placement exam for the fourth-year level should measure whether a student can grasp the general idea of a given body of text with the assistance of a small vocabulary list. It should also measure whether she can express herself fairly well in both written and oral contexts.

Placement procedures

During the orientation week for incoming students, which is the week before classes begin, a day is designated for the foreign language placement exams. The exams are scheduled from 9:00 to 12:00am and 1:00 to 4:00pm; a student can take an exam anytime during these hours.

The exams for all levels consist of two main parts: oral and written. The oral part of the exam is a 5- to 10-minute interview with two instructors. This interview has two purposes: to examine the student's oral skills and to find out the student's background in language studies. After a couple of warm-up exchanges and questions, for example, "It's a nice day isn't it?," "When did you arrive?," and "How is your dorm?," a list of guided questions with regard to the student's language background is asked. Some examples are "Where did you study Japanese?," "How long?," "How many hours per week?," "What textbook did you use?," "Did you learn the writing systems?," and "How many *kanji* (Chinese) characters do you know?" More specific questions with regard to the basic grammar are asked for placement in the second-/third-year levels, such as the student's familiarity with direct forms, potential forms, causative forms, and so forth. These questions, with the results of the interview, help the examiners to determine which level of written exam (second or third) the student should be taking. Note that all of these questions are asked in Japanese, including the warm-up exchanges and questions, unless the student does not understand the questions. Likewise, the answers are expected to be in Japanese unless the student does not know how to express herself. In some instances, the placement decision need not be made if the student realizes that she cannot understand and/or answer even the simplest question and resigns herself to enrolling in the first-year level.

After the initial interview, the student takes a written exam for the target course. The exams for second- and third-year levels consist of grammar/vocabulary, reading comprehension, and *kanji*. The grammar/vocabulary sections have 14 (second year) or 4 (third year) fill-in-the-blank questions, 10 (second/third year) multiple-choice questions, and 12 (second year) or 21 (third year) cloze questions. In the reading section, a short passage is provided, and the student taking the second-year exam is expected to answer four questions regarding the passage in English and two questions in Japanese, while the student taking the third-year exam is expected to answer three questions in Japanese. In the *kanji* section, the student needs to provide the readings or writings of 16 (second year) or 17 (third year) *kanji* characters that are used in sentences. See examples in the Appendix.

The current format of the exam for the fourth-year level consists of *kanji*, grammar/vocabulary, and reading comprehension. The format of the *kanji* and the reading sections is very much like the placement exam for the second-/third-year levels, except that the content is more difficult. The *kanji* section tests 26 characters, and the reading comprehension section asks five questions in Japanese. The grammar/vocabulary sections have 20 fill-in-the-blank and 2 sentence-completion questions. The student also needs to create five sentences by using certain grammar patterns/vocabulary. When a student finishes the written exam, she meets with the examiners again, where she will be asked how she thinks she did on the exam in English. At this point, or even in the middle of the written exam, some students realize that they will not be able to function in the targeted course and ask to be placed in lower levels. This is also a chance for examiners to ask a few more questions if additional information or clarification is needed. Otherwise, the student is asked to leave her contact number and will be notified of the results on the following day.

While the students are taking the written exams, the two examiners discuss the results of the oral interviews and compare their notes for each examinee. As the students finish their written exams, the examiners grade them. The maximum score of the exams is 50 points, and the cut score is 25. For those students who score at/near the cut score, the examiners examine their notes from the oral interviews and decide on an appropriate placement. Students who score far above or below the cut score are normally placed as the results suggest unless the written exam and the oral interview results have a large discrepancy, in which case the student is normally placed in the lower level.

The first two weeks of the semester is the add-drop period, during which the students may be placed in different levels if misplacement occurs. Therefore, the instructor of each course pays special attention to the students who took the placement exams to determine if the placement is appropriate.

One of the main goals of the Japanese program is to provide students with proficiency in all four skills: listening, speaking, reading, and writing. In particular, some of the upper-level students who major in Japanese wish to study Japanese in more depth at graduate schools; thus, being able to read and translate authentic material is emphasized.

Distinguishing features of the program

Normally, 15 to 20 freshman students take the placement exams at the beginning of each academic year, most of whom wish to be placed in the second-year level. However, only a few students succeed in bypassing the first-year level. Most of those who fail to qualify for the second-year level studied Japanese at their high schools for a year or two and do not mind starting all over again from the beginning after learning that the college Japanese curriculum is much more rigorous and intensive than that of their high schools. However, a problem arises when a student has invested four or five years in studying Japanese and ends up being placed at the beginning level. This is quite discouraging for the student, and in most cases, she will quit studying the language. An articulation problem is apparent between our college curriculum and some of the curricula of high schools because the instructional emphasis of most colleges is on language learning, whereas that of most high schools is on cultural exposure.

Approximately five students return from study abroad programs each semester, and they are normally placed in the third-/fourth-year levels. These students usually display great oral fluency due to their extended exposure to native speakers, though their reading and writing skills are less proficient. Longer exposure to the target language equates with greater oral fluency. Thus, placement for these students can be problematic because they may be as fluent as the fourth-year-level students in terms of oral skills, yet their reading and writing skills are at the level of the third-year students. A different track would ideally be available for these students. However, because the length of the programs vary, so does the proficiency of the participants, so having multiple tracks that perfectly suit the needs of students with vastly different proficiencies unfortunately does not seem realistic in terms of time and resources.

Over the past few years, the number of Japanese-heritage students has begun to increase, and they have often been placed at the fourth-year level. However, both heritage and non-heritage students have been dissatisfied in being placed together because the heritage students who can express themselves like native speakers normally take over the class discussions, which is quite intimidating for the non-heritage learners. In addition, the larger number of the heritage students has made it impossible for instructors to supervise them as individual study students. Therefore, beginning in the fall of 2005, a new fourth-year-level course for heritage students was offered to resolve this issue.

Practical ideas for placement and future development

To help solve the articulation problems mentioned above, the incoming students should be provided with information regarding the placement exams, not only the time and place of the test, but also information about the content and procedure before the exam. In that way, a student can get a general idea of what is expected to be placed at the level that she desires, and knowing the format of the test in advance should reduce any anxiety about taking it.

The current written exam for the fourth-year level should be reexamined because the results of the written exam do not always accurately provide the type of information needed for placing students into the fourth-year-level courses. As mentioned previously, the placement exam for the fourth-year level should measure whether a student can grasp the general idea of a given body of text with the assistance of a small vocabulary list and whether she can express herself fairly well in both written and oral contexts. However, the written exam tests only samples of *kanji*, vocabulary, grammar knowledge, and some reading comprehension skills of the students. Having a larger reading comprehension section and an essay section seems more appropriate for meeting the criteria for placement in the fourth-year level.

Although the exams for the second-/third-year levels do not seem to have any major problems, reexamining them would be good because a variety of issues such as validity and reliability were not considered during their construction. The exams were constructed without asking why fill-in-the-blank questions are used in certain parts of the exam, why the cut score is 25, and so forth.

Conclusion

As Thom Hudson (p.c.), the director of the 2005 NFLRC workshop: Designing Effective Foreign Language Placement Tests, said, "It takes a village to make a placement exam." Because of the urgent need for constructing something better than final exams, a colleague and I created placement exams over a decade ago. Although the content of the exams was carefully considered, many other issues, such as validity and reliability, were not. To help cope with articulation problems, the placement procedures and guidelines should be described in writing and made available to the faculty and students. New issues have arisen, such as an increasing number of heritage learners and students returning from study abroad programs; thus, this time seems good to reexamine the current placement exams as a whole.

Reference

Jorden, E. H., & Noda, N. (1987). *Japanese: The spoken language, parts I–III.* New Haven: Yale University Press.

Appendix: Sample placement exam questions

Fill in the blank

Supply a particle in (   ). Mark with X where ungrammatical. Do not use は.

A: すみません。このへん（　　）ぎんこう（　　）ありますか？
B: ええ、この道（　　）まっすぐ行って左のほうです。
　　ぎんこうは九時（　　）三時（　　）ですよ。

Multiple choice

Choose the appropriate answer.

A: 行きませんでしたね。
B: (a. はい；b. ええ；c. いいえ) 行きましたよ。

Cloze

Supply a predicate (verb, noun or adjective) in its appropriate form.

A: 高かったですか？
B: いいえ、あまり _____。

Reading

やさしいむすこがいました。お父さんが弱かったので、むすこが毎日仕事をしていました。お父さんはおさけがすきでしたが、おかねがないので、家には何もありませんでした。むすこはお父さんにおさけを買いたいといつも思っていました。。。。。。。。。。。。。。。。。。

Answer the following questions in English.

What drinks did they have at home? _____

Answer the following questions in Japanese.

お父さんは仕事をしていましたか？　どうしてですか？

_____

Kanji

Give *hiragana* under the *kanji* and write *kanji* in the space.

妹は今年、八つになりました。

_____、_____で勉強するけど、_____から_____みです。
まいあさ　がっこう　　　　　　らいしゅう　やす

Fill in the blank

（　　）に適当な助詞を入れなさい。ただし「は」は使ってはいけません。

若者は母親を背負って山に登ること（　　）した。何時間（　　）歩いている
途中で若者は背中の母親が何（　　）同じ動作を繰り返している（　　）気がついた。気（　　）つけている（　　）、
母親は道のそばにはえている木のえだ（　　）折っているのだ。

Sentence completion

_____ に適当な日本語を入れなさい。

A: となりのステレオがうるさいねえ。

B: そうねえ。 _____ 言ってきましょうか？

Compose a sentence

次の日本語を使って文を作りなさい。

まるで。。。。。みたい

_____。

A Case Study From a Community College

Emi Ochiai Ahn
Mesa Community College, AZ

Community colleges are in a unique situation. They are often viewed as bridges between high schools and four-year universities. However, they are not limited to those roles. They serve students of a variety of ages, educational and environmental backgrounds, and motivations for education. Because of the variety of abilities resulting from these backgrounds, students must frequently be placed in appropriate language classes. Placing students is one of the most common activities for community college language teachers prior to or at the beginning of a semester. Japanese language teachers are no exception. To accommodate for this need, placement tests should be administered. However, to my knowledge, almost no placement tests are available for community college students of Japanese.

In this case study, I analyze the unique situation of the Japanese program at Mesa Community College, advocate implementation of a placement test for the foundation-track courses, and discuss what needs to be considered in developing a placement test.

Japanese program at Mesa Community College

Program structure

Mesa Community College (MCC), located in a suburb of Phoenix, is the largest community college in the Maricopa County Community College District, which encompasses ten community colleges. MCC has approximately 27,000 students, including full- and part-time, and serves as a feeding school for four-year universities. The majority of our students transfer to the three Arizona state universities (Arizona State University, the University of Arizona, and Northern Arizona University). The school offers apparel merchandising, biotechnology, business and industry, fire science, interior design, mortuary science, network academy, nursing, and other programs. The Office of Research and Planning of MCC reported in fall 2004 approximately 15,000 full-time students with the following demographics (Office of Research and Planning, 2004):

- average number of semester credits taken per student: 8.1
- average age of the students: about 26

Ahn, E. O. (2008) A case study from a community college. In T. Hudson & M. Clark (Eds.), *Case studies in foreign language placement: Practices and possibilities* (pp. 71–80). Honolulu, HI: University of Hawai'i, National Foreign Language Resource Center.

- students younger than 17 and older than 40: 12%
- students between the ages of 17 and 30: 76%
- male students: 53%
- student ethnicities: White, 66%; Hispanic, 15%; Asian/Pacific Islander, 4%; Black, 4%; and American Indian (Native American), 3%
- daytime students: 46%, evening students: 30%, students taking both daytime and evening courses: 24%

The Japanese program at MCC is in the Foreign Language Department, which offers 12 languages including Japanese. The Japanese program began in 1987 and has grown into the fourth-largest program in the department after Spanish, American Sign Language, and French. A temporary full-time Japanese position was first opened in the spring of 1992. The position was institutionalized in 2000 with assistance from a grant from the Japan Foundation. As of fall 2005, the program was run by one residential (full-time) faculty member and four adjunct (part-time) instructors. Only one instructor among them is a non-native speaker of Japanese.

The Foreign Language Department at MCC offers two different tracks: foundation and conversation. The foundation-track courses are five credits a semester (300 minutes of instructions per week), while the conversation-track courses are only three credits (150 minutes per week). The details of the tracks are available at http://www.mc.maricopa.edu/dept/d16/foundation.html and http://www.mc.maricopa.edu/dept/d16/conversation.html.

The foundation track prepares students for courses above the 200-level at any university. The courses, 101, 102, 201, and 202, are university equivalents. This track is also for those desiring a balanced program. The four skills are included (listening, speaking, reading, and writing). This track includes these courses:

101, Elementary Level I
102, Elementary Level II
201, Intermediate Level I
202, Intermediate Level II
265, Advanced Level I
266, Advanced Level II

The conversation track emphasizes the speaking and listening skills. It is for tourists and those desiring minimal conversational abilities only. Some of these courses are related to specific areas of employment, such as Spanish for Health Personnel. This track includes these courses:

115, Beginning Conversation I
116, Beginning Conversation II
225, Intermediate Conversation
226, Intermediate Conversation
235, Advanced Conversation I
236, Advanced Conversation II

The Japanese program at MCC offers Japanese (JPN) 101, 102, 201, 202, 115, 116, 225, 226, 235, and 236. Because any course is susceptible to cancellation depending on enrollment, in the 2004–2005 academic year, only JPN 101, 102, 201, 202, and 115 were actually taught. Only one

Japanese course was offered in 1987, when the program was inaugurated. The program has grown gradually, and in the 2004–2005 academic year (including summer 2005), it offered 19 courses: Ten JPN 101s, four JPN 102s, two JPN 201s, two JPN 202s, and one JPN 115. At the highest point of enrollment in each semester of the 2004–2005 academic year, approximately 200 students were enrolled. Considering that the school is located in a community with a Japanese population of a moderate size and a moderate number of Japanese enterprises, the enrollment in the Japanese program at MCC is large. In the Maricopa County Community College District, only five colleges, including MCC, offer Japanese courses, and among them are only two full-time Japanese teachers supplemented by adjunct faculty members.

Foundation- and conversation-track courses, which are equally important, have different characteristics. The foundation-track courses are transferable toward language requirements in four-year universities throughout Arizona. The conversation-track courses at MCC, none of which have precise equivalents at the three Arizona universities, can be transferred to the universities, but only as electives. Many of the students in the conversation-track courses appear to take them out of pure interest. Some use the courses as a preparation for foundation-track courses, although JPN 101 is designed for true beginners. The administration favors the foundation-track courses in that conversation-track courses require higher enrollments to avoid cancellation. Because a placement test for the foundation-track courses is immediately needed in the Japanese program at MCC because of articulation requirements and administration priorities, the focus of further discussion will be on foundation-track courses.

Students in Japanese foundation-track courses at MCC

The population of students should be thoroughly analyzed before making plans for placement. Thus, students' backgrounds in terms of their history of Japanese study and their motivations for learning Japanese will be discussed. A close analysis of these aspects of the students' backgrounds will guide to us in determining for whom we should create placement tests, what kind of tests are needed, and why.

While any student, including absolute beginners, may take JPN 101, the students in JPN 102, 201, and 202 fall into the following categories:

- promoted students who have passed the prerequisite course at MCC
- promoted students who have passed the prerequisite course at an in-state university
- promoted students who have passed the prerequisite course at in-district community colleges other than MCC
- students who have spent two years or longer in Japan for missionary or military purposes
- promoted students who have taken Japanese classes at high schools in Arizona
- students who have taken Japanese at Saturday schools
- promoted students who have taken Japanese classes at high schools not in Arizona
- heritage students
- others

The majority of students belong to categories 1 through 6. Because the school is located in a community with a large population of members of the Church of Jesus Christ of Latter-day Saints, a significant number of students return from church missions in Japan. Compared with students who fall into other categories, those students have much higher communication skills (listening and speaking), while their writing and reading skills and grammatical and *kanji* knowledge vary considerably from one student to another. Students from the local Saturday school show a variety of levels in their skills. The school offers two different tracks: one for native Japanese students from kindergarten through junior high and one for teenage non-native Japanese speakers. A small number of heritage students attend the tracks according to their levels of comfort with the language. The track for native speakers follows a curriculum based on the standards of the Japanese Ministry of Education, while the curriculum of the non-native track differs from those in schools in Japan. Students are basically allowed to attend the school as long as they want, until they reach the age to graduate from high school. Therefore, not only are they of diverse ages (anywhere in the teens), but they also have spent different numbers of years studying Japanese at the school. Thus, having had differing curricular tracks means that their skills are variable. Accordingly, an evaluation is needed for them to be placed into appropriate language levels at MCC.

Should promoted students also take a placement test?

The students who have passed the prerequisite course at MCC, other Maricopa County community colleges, and Arizona state universities are automatically promoted to the next level course because an orderly transfer system has been established between MCC and these institutions. A student who took courses at other schools, however, needs a signature from an MCC advisor to register for a course above JPN 101 because curricula, seating hours per credit, and credit hours for courses of the same level vary at different schools. Naturally, the students from other schools need placement. At the same time, we have found that not all promoted students have taken the prerequisite courses immediately prior to taking the next level course at MCC. Some students have waited years before moving on. Detecting this group of people is important because some of them may not have retained the skills and knowledge needed to be ready for the next level.

Japanese 101 students

The categories of JPN 101 students are:

- students who have no experience with Japanese language learning
- students who have taken JPN 115 (and JPN 116) at MCC
- students who have taken JPN 115 (and JPN 116) at in-district community colleges other than MCC
- students who have taken Japanese courses at high schools in Arizona
- high school students whose schools do not offer Japanese courses
- homeschoolers
- students who have taken Japanese courses at Saturday schools
- students who have taken Japanese courses at high schools other than in Arizona
- heritage students
- others

Students with other statuses

An increase in students with special statuses has been noticeable. Theses students are high school students whose schools do not offer any Japanese courses or any higher-level Japanese courses and homeschoolers. MCC allows any student who has passed the assessment testing for

English, reading, and math to be admitted. The web page of the Testing and Assessment Services says:

> Assessment testing (ASSET) for English, Reading, and Math is required for all new students and for students who need to meet a prerequisite for a class. New students, or students with no college level credit in these three subject areas, test in a "block" format at scheduled times. (http://www.mc.maricopa.edu/services/testing/index.html)

ASSET is a standardized test and provides each taker a standardized score. The Foreign Language Department has set a cut score for the English and reading tests and has a policy that only students whose English and reading scores are above these cut scores are allowed to ask the instructors of the courses in which they want to register for approval signatures to enter classes.

Student motivation

Students' motivations for learning Japanese should be considered when planning placement procedures. Students' motivations for learning the Japanese language at MCC appear to have changed over the years. Recently, they appear to have decided to learn Japanese because they

- want to fully enjoy Japanese animation, comics, and computer games.
- are fascinated with Japanese martial arts.
- think it may be helpful for their future careers in fields such as computer graphics and business.
- love the Japanese culture.
- want to sustain the language skills that they have acquired in Japan.
- are closely acquainted with Japanese persons (friends, soul mates, spouses, and family).
- want to try something different.
- are required to learn it because of their current job assignments.

During the 1980s and 1990s, a larger proportion of students took Japanese for future career purposes or job requirements, but the number of those students has decreased.

Compared with students in other language courses, Japanese students' level of motivation is high, according to Japanese teachers observations in class, although the retention rate does not necessarily reflect the level of motivation. The drop rate, especially, at the elementary level, is high. The primary reasons for dropping a class are academic overload and job schedule changes. Before the semester begins, most students seem to underestimate the hours they have to spend on the course. However, many students who have dropped do retake the same course after a semester or two. From this fact, we can say that their motivation level for learning Japanese is high.

A placement decision is influenced by the student's level of and basis for motivation, especially when the student's skill falls between two courses. If the student sees Japanese study as a long-term project or the student's motivation involves more personal than career reasons, s/he should be placed in the lower-level course. If a student's concern is graduation, the student may want to be placed to be in a higher-level course to accelerate progress. Students' personalities should be also considered. For students who do well at things when they feel comfortable, placement in a lower-level course is better.

Placement test issues for evening, summer, and online courses

As at many community colleges, the MCC Japanese program offers evening, summer-intensive, and online courses in addition to regular daytime courses. Although college-age students represent a large proportion of the evening course population, evening courses also have many high school students, office workers, and community members. A large number of college-age students in both daytime and evening classes at MCC have full-time jobs. Evening and summer-intensive Japanese courses are identical to regular daytime courses in terms of seating hours, credits earned upon completion, operational curricula, textbooks used, instructors, instruction quality, and other features. The only difference is the length of each session. For the 15-week semester, daytime courses are either five days a week, 60 minutes per day, or three days a week, 100 minutes per day, but evening courses are twice a week, 150 minutes a day. Summer-intensive courses are four hours a day, four times a week for five weeks. Online courses are the same except that they are delivered online. Although online courses have no seating time, we expect students to use 13 to 15 hours a week for 15 weeks. Evening, daytime, and online students are not mutually exclusive categories. Due to schedule changes, one student may, for example, take a JPN 102 daytime course in the semester following an evening JPN 101 and move on to JPN 201 online. The first four courses in the foundation track (JPN 101 though 202) are transferable to four-year universities, whether evening, daytime, or online. Accordingly, the differences between daytime, evening, and online courses need not be considered in planning the content of the placement test and its cutoff scores.

Current testing status

Currently, the MCC Japanese program has no placement test. Students can end up in courses that are too elementary or too difficult for them. In the first case, students may not understand the concept of a "true beginner" because we have had students who had lived several years in Japan with no formal Japanese study in JPN 101 courses, thinking that they are true beginners. The placement process has been conducted using personal interviews either in person or on the phone. The process is not, unfortunately, even remotely systematic. Because a student wishing to take JPN 102 or a higher-level course without taking the prerequisite(s) needs to obtain approval from an advisor to register for the course, the student must visit the advisor prior to the start of the semester or during the first week (drop-add week). The advisor is often a Japanese teacher. All residential (full-time) faculty members at MCC are required to be at the school one week prior to the start of the semester (the week of accountability) for this advising purpose.

The instructor-advisor usually asks the student's history of Japanese study and attempts to determine the student's knowledge by asking for a self-assessment. The questions often asked include:

> Can you read and write all *hiragana* and *katakana* characters (the Japanese syllabic writing systems)?
> How many *kanji* (Chinese) characters do you think you can read and/or write?

The teacher also often shows textbooks to the student and asks him/her to read aloud a passage typical of the proficiency that students should attain at the time of the final test. After that, the teacher asks if the student felt comfortable reading it. Finally, the teacher recommends the student take a particular class. If the teacher feels the student can take either of two, s/he suggests that the student register for one of the courses yet attend both during the first week and consult with the teachers of the classes. Based on the first week's instruction and through discussion with the teachers of the courses, the student decides which course s/he will attend for the semester.

In harmony with the trends of the world, MCC has started to offer online registration to students. Previously, students who registered for classes online had the leeway to register for any course without seeing an advisor. Problems arose because this did not allow teachers to screen students who registered for their courses without the prerequisites or approval. To solve these problems, online registration currently allows students to freely register for courses that do not have any prerequisite courses, but requires students to contact an advisor for approval before registering for higher-level courses.

In light of the background explained above, the current placement process in the MCC Japanese program has room to improve for the following two reasons: Students who should be advised to take a course higher than the first-semester course can, without advisement, register for the first-semester course because they believe that their skills are not strong enough to register for a higher-level course; and the student's self-assessment that the advisor considers to place the student may not be as accurate as we hope it is. Therefore, all students who wish to take upper-level JPN courses, except for students immediately promoted from the previous semester, should take placement tests to be more accurately placed.

Issues to consider for planning a placement test

Initial stages

Because we currently do not have a placement test, we should plan the steps we need to take to develop an appropriate one. First, we need to make explicit the purposes of the placement testing. Should we use the placement test as the only assessment tool to place students or as a screening tool for further investigation? If we decide to use the test as a simple screening tool, what procedure should we follow to make a final decision to place students? Should the test serve the needs of each individual student's learning or the teacher's class management and instruction? We must decide whether we will use the test results for awarding credits or simply for placement purposes. We should also consider what the test is for because some placement tests may serve to protect students, while others are intended to protect institutions.

Next, we should decide if we will consider articulation issues when we develop the test. If we decide to do so, we need to plan an opportunity to discuss the issues with teachers at universities, other community colleges, and high schools. This may result not only in decisions regarding the placement procedures at MCC, but also in alterations and revisions of our operational curriculum. Accordingly, we may need to revise our syllabi. If we decide not to consider the articulation issue at this moment, our faculty members need to discuss what the objectives of the test should be.

Following that, we need to decide the format and content of the test. Which skills of the language should be tested? What delivery method should we use: paper-and-pencil or computer? If we deliver the test via computer, should it be over the web or computer-adaptive? When and where should the test be administered? Should we have one test at different levels or should separate tests be developed for each of the four foundation courses that are regularly offered each semester? Should we use norm-referencing or criteria-referencing approaches? How about alternative methods such as portfolios and self-assessment? Will students receive grades or points for the results of the test? We need to check that the test format and content motivate test-takers to do their best without any academic dishonesty.

Before implementing the test, we need to decide how we can verify its validity. Should we rely on some authority who can give us advice about the validity? Should we experimentally try out the test? If so, who should be the subjects—promoted students at MCC or students outside? What should we compare the results of the tests with—GPA, grades in Japanese classes, or results of other tests?

After determining all steps of the development of the placement test, we need to examine the resources necessary to proceed with each step. We need to check what resources are already available and what resources need to be explored. We need to decide who should develop the test—do we use an expert in placement-test making, or do we need to train someone to make a good test? Will the test-maker have time to make the test? Where should the content come from—other Japanese placement tests or tests used in our school? Do we have the physical facilities to develop the test—computers and software, if necessary? If we decide to check the validity of the test using trial runs, do we have the physical facilities for that? Who will administer the test? Should the proctors go through training? What will the training cost?

Suggestions in planning for Japanese placement tests at MCC

Although we have a long way to go to answer all of the above questions, here are some suggestions and opinions regarding the development of the Japanese placement test at MCC. The general purpose of the placement test should be to screen students. We actually do have another test called "Credit-by-exam," which awards a student a letter grade and credit if s/he earns a D or higher on the test. Therefore, the placement test to be developed will not need to duplicate this exam. Although we should definitely consider articulation issues with other institutions, making a placement test would be substantially delayed if we attempted to involve all other institutions that might be interested. In fact, approximately three years ago, officers of the Arizona Association of Teachers of Japanese started an articulation effort. Although the effort of the officers of the organization deserves everyone's recognition, due to the diverse locations of each institution, differences in textbooks, and availability of time, complete articulation throughout the community was not possible in the short time allowed for the project. From this reality and considering the fact that the number of students transferring from MCC to Arizona State University exceeds those who transfer to other institutions by a large margin, at this point, we should rationally focus on good communication with the program at Arizona State University when we develop our placement test, at least to start with. Nevertheless, we must publicize the existence of the test and a detailed explanation of what content is tested by what delivery method. A sample test can be made available for public use so that other schools can see our expectations.

Requiring the placement test seems necessary for all students who attempt to register for any Japanese course, except for promoted students. The test should catch students who think that they should register for the elementary course but who actually have the skills to take a higher-level course. This action requires the cooperation of the registration office, general advising center, and IT staff. The registration process on the phone, in person, or online should determine whether a student has been recently promoted. If not, s/he should be required to take the placement test before registering.

Because this test has to be taken by a large number of people and considering that increasing numbers of students are registering online, the test should be available on the web. Because this is not a test to award credits, students have no motivation to cheat. Being placed in a higher class than one in which they can succeed is not advantageous to students. Although students can compile portfolios on the web, time limitations suggest that a better format for both students and teachers is selected-response or constructed-response. If students choose to take the test on campus, they should be sent to the Foreign Language Department language lab. Having students take the test at Testing and Assessment Services would be ideal, but the office currently is short on space and staff. Also, Testing and Assessment Services may not be able to offer the necessary Japanese-capable computers. Many of the workers in the office are students and are frequently replaced, so training them to deal with Japanese-capable computers could be cumbersome and inefficient. Unlike the situation in Testing and Assessment Services, the Foreign Language Department language lab has a fixed full-time worker who is proficient in the Japanese input system. Furthermore, all the computers in the lab are already Japanese-capable. When students choose to take the test online, off-campus, we need to make sure that the computers they use for the test are either Japanese-capable or can be made so. For those whose computers can be made Japanese-capable but are currently not, a website must be prepared with instructions on how to enable Japanese.

Proposed placement test structure

The placement test should consist of at least two sections. The first section should be multiple-choice questions to discriminate true beginners from the rest. The section should tell us if the student has ever taken Japanese before, has ever lived in Japan, is a returning or heritage learner, or is a false beginner. On top of this, the section should ask about students' motivations and personalities; this information can be helpful if the results indicate that a student's skills (tested in the second section) fall between two course levels. Those who are assessed as true beginners would be encouraged to stop taking the test. This section would provide teachers with background information on each incoming student.

The second section of the test should focus on students' language skills so that teachers or advisors can place the students into classes at the appropriate levels. To maximize the accuracy of placement, we should test as many skills as possible. At the same time, we want to take advantage of selected-response tests, which have the advantages of easy scoring and a fairly high degree of objectivity. Selected-response questions are known to be relatively difficult to create. We need to

- avoid ambiguity, especially in instructions, and clarify what language function is tested using a given question.
- avoid trick questions because the results from them may reflect something other than the students' language skills.
- avoid giving unnecessary information to students because this may confuse and frustrate them.
- present the test in an orderly way because students take tests with certain expectations.
- avoid giving away the answers.
- use appropriate language.

Because the placement test is an instrument we plan to use for a long time, a long and thoughtful planning period is acceptable.

Selected-response tests are easily created for web delivery. Because we do not expect to have a large budget for making the test, we should use a delivery system we already have. MCC currently owns a school license for WebCT. WebCT is a course management tool that has a function for easily creating a quiz. Because the Foreign Language Department offers online courses in Japanese, Spanish, French, and German via WebCT, most faculty members are fairly familiar with the tool. However, IT specialists will need to add a function for logging into a special system because the students who will take the test may be new to the school and may not have student IDs and passwords, which are usually required to log into any WebCT site.

The second section, which evaluates students' language skills, should contain items that test the skills to identify the correct

- usages of characters and their meanings.
- usages of and meanings of words that represent the themes dealt with in each semester (e.g., the themes dealt with in JPN 102 are weather, hobbies, food, and fashion).
- usage of grammar points.
- interpretation of short written passages.
- interpretation of short audio dialogs.

Before the placement test is used, it should be pilot tested to check its reliability and potential validity. The easiest and the most feasible way to do so is to use students who are currently taking Japanese at MCC. An effective pilot would involve administering the test at the beginning of a semester to each of the students that are already placed in each class and comparing the results of each student's test with his/her performance throughout the semester.

As mentioned above, currently available technological resources may be enough. However, developing the test will require a significant investment of faculty time. Because all residential faculty members at MCC must teach 15 to 16 credit hours per semester, finding the time to develop a test is almost impossible while teaching during the regular semester. The faculty member or members in charge of developing the test definitely need release time to be exclusively spent on developing the test. Fortunately, the faculty members at MCC can apply for several campus-wide and district-wide grant opportunities, which would either award them release time (usually three to six credit hours per semester) or provide a stipend for the time they spend during a summer.

Conclusion

I introduced the Japanese program at a community college in the Phoenix area, and similar needs exist in many community colleges throughout the US. Because of the characteristics of the diverse students, a placement test is needed for the foundation-track courses. The placement test should have two sections: one that queries background information and one that tests language skills. The test will serve students and faculty best if it is delivered online.

References

Office of Research and Planning. (2004). *Student Profile: Fall 2004*. Retrieved May 5, 2008 from http://www.mc.maricopa.edu/about/orp/statistics/studentprofileFall2004.pdf

Placement for Mixed Populations in a Relatively Small Program

Mieko Ono
Miami University of Ohio

I reviewed the placement procedure in the Japanese program at Miami University of Ohio. The purpose is to revise the current methods to fit the program situation and needs, given the relatively small, yet diverse population of placement candidates we encounter

Currently, we do not have any placement tests. Instead, we administer placement interviews. However, practical and pedagogical reasons warrant the use of standardized placement tests. The practical reasons are

- to have a placement assessment tool that does not excessively burden the staff. Placement assessments are often requested during the summer orientation period because of a registration deadline for the fall semester, but our staff is not always available to test students during the summer.
- that because taking a language is a college requirement, quasi-native speakers of Japanese sometimes want to satisfy this language requirement in Japanese. College policy prohibits using one's native language to satisfy the language requirement, but occasionally, we get students in a grey area, that is, students who have near-native fluency because of their language backgrounds. A placement test score could help to convince them that they are far beyond 402.

The pedagogical reasons for the use of a standardized placement test are that

- using placement test scores, anyone in the Japanese program could access the past data and the analysis of the results, which means that we could have an objective and uniform procedure that could be administered by any instructor.
- the cumulative test scores will provide statistical data to predict adjustments that transfer students may have to make or may allow predictions regarding the post-transfer learning curve.
- the test scores and item scores will help instructors determine what types of special learning tools/practices are needed for these students.

Ono, M. (2008). Placement for mixed populations in a relatively small program. In T. Hudson & M. Clark (Eds.), *Case studies in foreign language placement: Practices and possibilities* (pp. 81–87). Honolulu, HI: University of Hawai'i, National Foreign Language Resource Center.

- the majority of candidates for a placement test either took Japanese in high school or are transfer students. We are particularly interested in students' rates of recovering their language skills. Students who have studied a language before can recover their skills once they are in classes, and in-class performances are often not directly related to placement scores when a student has an interval (a summer break, a semester, a year, etc.) before resuming his/her study. Placement test data might provide insights into post-placement performance or recovery curves, thereby enabling better study guidance for those students.

With the above points in mind, we will look at an overview of our program.

Context of the program

The program is small to medium, with a comprehensive coverage of first- to fourth-year levels and literature and linguistics in English. Approximately 50-60 students enroll in the first year, 30-35 in the second year, 10-15 in the third year, and 5 in the fourth year. The textbooks we use at each level are

101-202: *Learn Japanese Vols. I-IV* (Young and Nakajima, 1985) with basic sentence patterns, grammar notes, dialogues, and oral drills with supplemental materials and activities).

301-402: *Integrated Approach to Intermediate Japanese* (McGloin and Miura, 1994) with many supplemental reading materials depending on the student population and instructors).

In 101-301, students are trained in speaking and listening, basic writing and reading skills including the Japanese writing systems with some *kanji* characters (500), fundamental vocabulary, and expressions. Classes are geared toward a communicative approach, but weight is placed on accuracy, too. The language classes are also aimed at the Liberal Education goal of understanding other cultures. In 302, students start reading longer passages from various materials, and in 401-402, they read about and discuss Japanese society, people, and culture through reading materials like newspapers and writing weekly journals, critical essays, and so forth in Japanese. Essay writing is assigned from 101 through 402.

Currently, the program offers a Japanese minor, and an East Asian Major (Japanese and Chinese) is in preparation. Two years of Japanese satisfies the Arts and Science language requirement. Beginning in 2005, the JPN 201-301 sequence satisfies one of Liberal Education's sequential course requirements. Japanese language credits also satisfy some other programs' requirements, that is, East Asian Studies, International Studies (Asian Concentration), International Business (Asian Concentration), and the English Department's foreign language requirement for graduate students.

Students' motivations for taking Japanese have shifted from business career needs to interests in Japanese culture, including pop culture such as anime, games, and music. The majority of placement candidates are those who have studied Japanese in high school and some transfer students from other universities. Occasionally, we have heritage-language learners, self-taught students, returnees from study abroad (one summer, one semester, and one year), and students who have lived in Japan for many years with or without formal language education.

Description of the process

We do not administer a placement test during the orientation period but offer placement interviews during the summer and at the beginning of each semester. Approximately 6 to 12 students need placement interviews per year; most seek them in the fall. This is a relatively small number of students considering the size of the program. Possible reasons for this will be discussed in Section 4, "Distinguishing features of the program." The program has two regular faculty members and one teaching assistant. For placement interviews, I am responsible for the first-year (basic level) and fourth-year (advanced level) language classes, which I usually teach, and the other instructor is responsible for the second- and third-year (intermediate level) classes, which she usually teaches. The largest population of placement candidates is for the first-year classes because the majority of students who have studied Japanese at high schools (1-3 years or so) are placed in either 101 or 102. I decide whether students should enroll in 101 or 102 or should move beyond 102. Possible intermediate students are sent to my colleague. If she determines that a student's language skills are beyond 302, the student is sent to me, and I conduct an interview to determine whether the student should be in 401 or 402. The two instructors make the major decisions, that is, whether a student is basic, intermediate, or advanced; students who are on the borderline of 102/201 and 302/401 are interviewed by the two instructors, and the rest, by the instructor who teaches that level. Because few students are in the 400-level classes, the class content and level can be changed depending on who is currently registered for the classes. The interviewer will consider the student population in the current 401/402.

The placement interviews I give to the first-year candidates consist of two parts. In part I, I collect indirect data: I ask about the number of years of Japanese studied, textbook, instruction method, and so forth in English. (Students are told beforehand that they will be asked about the textbook used, past exams and assignments, projects, and grades.) In part II, I collect direct data: I conduct a reading test using passages from the 101 or 102 textbooks to check whether the student has mastered all *hiragana/katakana* and some *kanji*; I ask for a summary or rough translation of the passages they are given (usually from the dialogue sections of the current textbooks to compare to those of students who are already in classes); I engage each student in a mini conversation using basic questions, for example, I ask his/her name, age, about family members, number of years studying Japanese, hometown, and so forth using sentence patterns we cover in 101/102.

The time spent on each student varies depending on the complexity of the students' backgrounds but is usually 10-20 minutes. In part I, an interviewer can gain a rough idea about where the student will be placed based on past cases of students with similar backgrounds. In part II, a *hiragana* reading passage is the first thing to be tested. If a student can hardly read *hiragana*, or even if s/he can more or less read but cannot figure out the meanings of very basic sentences, s/he will be placed in 101. In this case, the interview takes only a few minutes, and we always have a certain number of these cases. My criterion for the placement interview is whether a student's language ability is equivalent to or higher than the C students in 101 and lower than C students of 102. For the fourth-year class, students are sorted into 401-402 and the level beyond 402 (or under 401). If a student is beyond 402, s/he is advised not to take the course, but the final decision is left up to the student. If we determine that a student is on the borderline, we also leave the final decision up to the student after showing him/her all materials including sample exams and explaining the content and goals of the two classes.

The purpose of the placement test is to maximize the learning experience of the placed students and to ensure a homogeneous instructional environment for students who are already in class. In other words, placed students should be comfortable and learning something new in class, and their fellow students should not be intimidated or deprived of opportunities by placed students with skills that are too advanced. At the placement interview, we make recommendations for students but cannot force the students to accept them. The final decisions are left to them.

Students tend to place themselves in lower classes than their abilities warrant. Placement decisions are finalized by the end of the second week of the semester. If a student is placed in a higher class than s/he feels comfortable in, the instructor and/or the student usually discovers this quickly. If a student is placed in a class that is too easy, s/he may move to a higher level or stay in the original class, if desired. Students who have decided to stay in classes other than those indicated by an instructor's assessment and recommendation can do so after receiving detailed assessment results and guidance to use classroom experience and materials to polish their language skills.

Some challenges within this process are that

- for first-year students, when a student has had some interruption in his/her language study, his/her rate of recovering language skills is difficult to predict before class starts. A quantifiable tendency has yet to be identified;
- for fourth-year students, a student who is far beyond fourth year or a quasi-native speaker can be difficult to dissuade from taking 402. Some numerical figures and data are needed to place out of 402;
- the number of students who have taken Japanese in high school is increasing. The current method of placement heavily relies on the instructors' experiences and skills, but we will eventually reach the limit of our interview capacity in terms of time availability and staffing, especially when the Japanese major (currently in preparation) is offered.

Distinguishing features of the program

The program has a small but mixed population at a college in the Midwest farming area. The students are 75% state residents and 25% from outside the state. We occasionally have some transfer students in the program. The institution is geographically fairly isolated from major cities, and our students cannot easily get good exposure to Japanese people and culture. The students' language skill retention rate is not very good, probably in part because of poor linguistic and cultural stimulation outside of class. The students' academic performance in general is good, but they tend to be conservative in terms of exposing themselves to foreign cultures, languages, and people. Misplacement occurs mainly when students have had some interruptions in their language learning and initially decide to attend a lower level for reviewing purposes, but quickly recover their skills once the class starts.

Practical ideas for placement and future development

Currently, two of us work as gatekeepers for two placement decision points: whether students should be in the 100 level or higher and whether they should be in the 200/300 level or higher. Students who have taken Japanese before often self-place themselves during registration in March, orientation (June to July), or the summer. We usually interview these students at the beginning of the class. The student information sheets on language background are turned in on the first day of class, and the interviews start on the same day. We would like to create a standardized test to check the mastery of basic items for the 100 level, like Japanese *kana* scripts (reading/writing), basic structural knowledge, and expressions (see more details in Appendix) and administer it during orientation. We will provide the placement procedure and sample questions on the web and make them available for incoming students to get some ideas of the expectations of college-level language classes for self-placement purposes. We will still need individual interviews with some students, but less of them: only for problematic cases that we will deal with during consultation week (a week before class starts). This process may reduce the labor of the instructors and shorten the crucial timeline for placement.

We will also record the test scores to analyze in the future to improve our placement process.

Conclusion

The current number of placement candidates is small but certainly increasing, and the program will be expanding when the Japanese major is offered. The test results can be used not only to place students in a timely manner but also for other purposes, for example, determining a transfer student's strengths and weaknesses and studying the correlation between students' test scores and their post-placement study curves to further customize the placement procedure for our program.

References

Miura, A., & McGloin, N. (1994). *An integrated approach to intermediate Japanese.* Tokyo: The Japan Times.

Young, J., & Nakajima-Okano, K. (1985). *Learn Japanese: New college text.* Honolulu: University of Hawaiʻi Press.

Appendix: Test specifications

100 level

Mastery of writing systems
Kana (*katakana/hiragana*), which are covered in 101

500 *kanji*, which are covered by the end of 102

Grammar
Case marker and other particles

Sentence types
- Noun
- Verb
- Adjective
- Adjectival

Tense (non-past/past distinction for single-clause sentences)
Negatives
Question formation
Yes/no

Wh-

Adverbs (time, place, degree, etc.)
Pre-nominals
Noun modifiers

Relative clauses

Conjugations (plain form, *te*-form, volitional, provisional, etc.)
Demonstrative pronouns (Japanese has a very rich vocabulary in this category)
Conjunctives (coordinate, subordinate, contrastive, etc.)
Others
Numbers/counters

"Give" and "receive" expressions

Writing:
Letter writing to pen pals/friends/family members/acquaintances/and so forth

Reading
Reading dialogues on various topics: studying, shopping, asking directions, using public transportation, and so forth

Listening and speaking
Participating in conversations in various settings: studying, shopping, asking directions, using public transportation, and so forth

Vocabulary
Basic words in first-year textbooks plus some general vocabulary

400 level

Mastery of basic grammar in Japanese

Kanji: 1400–2000 (including educational characters)

Ability to use dictionaries (Japanese-English, English-Japanese, *kanji*)

Reading passages (newspaper articles, essays, stories, etc.) from 401/402, using dictionaries

Speaking and listening knowledge: basic conversation in everyday settings

The higher the level, the more emphasis is given to writing/reading abilities in placement. In Japanese, writing and speaking styles are different. This is not so significant in the basic levels, but the higher a class is, the more apparent is this difference in language skills. The goals of the upper-division courses are more about understanding other cultures and communicating in an intellectual context than about daily conversation skills, although students are highly encouraged to participate in class, which is usually conducted in Japanese only.

Placement (place-out) test for students beyond 402

Reading comprehension and essay writing (following ACTFL guidelines)

Placement Within a Changing Curriculum: Russian Heritage Speakers at Montclair State University

NFLRC

Jessica Brandt
Montclair State University, NJ

As the Russian language teaching situation in the United States has changed over the past decade, so has the need for placement instruments in the language. The vast majority of students in the typical Russian program were once "traditional" learners: students who had no previous experience with or exposure to the language, but who chose to pursue Russian for various individual reasons (interest in government service, love of literature, fascination with James Bond, or just plain curiosity). A small percentage of students began studying Russian in high school for the same reasons. Today, in many Russian programs, the typical student is much more likely to be a heritage speaker to one degree or another. We believe, based purely on anecdotal evidence, that many traditional students who once chose Russian for its exotic appeal are now drawn to languages that have been offered more recently such as Japanese, Arabic, or American Sign Language.

As programs deal with the changing student profile, they face two pressing questions: how best to place heritage students in traditional classes and whether and how to adjust the curriculum to best serve a changing student population. Programs tend to continue using placement tests geared to traditional/placed students. Heritage students tend to score very well on these tests, but the tests do not discriminate much between heritage students, whereas their actual proficiencies may be quite different. A need has developed for an instrument that will more accurately reflect heritage speakers' proficiencies and thus place them more effectively in the curriculum of a given program. At the same time, each program must determine whether its curriculum should be adjusted to reflect demographic changes. Should heritage speakers be offered separate sections to deal with their unique language-learning issues? Is such an option even feasible for a small program? Olga Kagan has asserted that heritage speakers do require a distinct type of instruction and that if offered heritage-specific instruction, they will progress much more quickly than traditional learners (Kagan, 2001). With that in mind, the specific context at Montclair State can be explored in depth.

Brandt, J. (2008). Placement within a changing curriculum: Russian heritage speakers at Montclair State University. In T. Hudson & M. Clark (Eds.), *Case studies in foreign language placement: Practices and possibilities* (pp. 89–98). Honolulu, HI: University of Hawai'i, National Foreign Language Resource Center.

Context of the program

Russian is one of 10 languages currently offered at Montclair, which requires a world language for each student, regardless of major. The text of the requirement is as follows:

> **World Languages: 3–6 semester hours**
>
> At a time when Montclair State University is committed to internationalizing the curriculum and when the public schools of New Jersey are under a state mandate to start world language study in the elementary schools, it is important to encourage students to pursue study of world languages.
>
> The World Languages requirement thus consists of a three to six semester-hour sequence in a foreign language, with emphasis on reading, speaking, and writing skills. The skills, valuable in themselves, will enhance an understanding of the ways in which language reflects cultural values and traditions.
>
> Students wishing to continue a language already studied in high school or elsewhere must demonstrate proficiency equivalent to completion of the third semester. Students who do not place at this level must take up to 6 s.h. of further study dependent upon their scores in the placement test (i.e., those who score at the second semester level must take 6 s.h., those who score at the third semester
>
> level must take 3 s.h.). Students who demonstrate proficiency equivalent to completion of the third semester of world language study must take one additional 3 s.h. course at a higher level in that language or a course in English about a foreign culture or civilization. Students wishing to begin a new language with which they have no experience must take two semesters (6 s.h.) of that language.
>
> Note: The entrance requirement for Montclair State University includes 2 years of a world language. As is the case with the current foreign language requirement, only elective credit is given for the first semester level of a language already studied in high school regardless of the placement score.

The only possibility for exemption from the world language requirement is to achieve a certain score on the New York University (NYU) Proficiency Test in a given language. This option is only recommended for students who already possess a fairly high level of fluency (based on a self-evaluation) in listening, reading, and writing.

The vast majority of students study a foreign language simply to fulfill the graduation requirement and thus stop taking the language once that requirement is filled. Many students (and their parents) feel strongly that a university education is useful only in so far as it will enable them to get "good" jobs, and language classes are seldom seen as anything more than a hurdle to overcome. Our students are primarily the first generation in their families to attend college, and most of them live at home and work while attending school. The student body as a whole is quite racially diverse, and approximately 40% of the students come from homes where one or both parents were not born in the United States. Some of these students have sufficient proficiency in a language other than English that they may be exempted from the language requirement by taking the NYU Proficiency Test. Allowing this option has political ramifications, however, because NYU only offers this testing in approximately 25 languages. Therefore, some students have the required level of skill in a language for which NYU does not have a test, and Montclair has no standard way of measuring their proficiency, so they cannot receive credit for this language skill.

The Office of New Student Experience (which handles orientation) and the registrar make it a high priority to have incoming students register for classes *before* they arrive in the fall, so students typically register during orientation, which is held in sessions throughout June and July, depending on major. This means that all basic skills testing should be completed before the students come for orientation. Incoming students may be scheduled to take their placement tests at any time after they have been accepted, but the majority of them test between March and June. This has presented various scheduling obstacles: because classes are still in session at the university, space is at a premium; also, most of the students are still in high school, and must either miss part of the day at school or come for testing after 3:00. Whenever possible, placement testing in foreign languages is scheduled to coincide with the Montclair State University Placement Test (MSUPT, a test of basic skills in math and English that all students are required to take). After completing the MSUPT, the students go to a room designated for the Russian placement test, which they have one hour to complete.

If students do not wish to take a foreign language in their first semester, they may wait to take the placement test. As a result, testing times are made available throughout the year on both a walk-in and a scheduled basis.

Course scheduling at Montclair is perceived to have had an effect on curriculum and instruction. The university is in the middle of an eight-year plan to increase enrollment from approximately 12,000 to approximately 20,000 students by the year 2008. At present, enrollment is between 16,000 and 17,000. Due to the rapidly growing student body, space has become more constrained, and while the university is building more classrooms, it cannot build fast enough. The solution to the problem has been to institute a uniform scheduling pattern, whereby all three-credit courses meet twice a week for 75 minutes each. Classes meet as early as 7:00am and as late as 10:45pm. It is commonly felt that a language cannot be acquired in so few course meetings, regardless of the fact that the contact hours remain the same as in a three-credit course that meets three days a week for 50 minutes. The faculty in foreign languages and mathematics feel that this approach is not conducive to the type of learning that takes place in their disciplines, but no studies have yet determined the impact, if any, on the students in these fields at Montclair.

Montclair State University offers few Russian courses but offers them consistently. The Russian department regularly offers beginning- and intermediate-level courses, but advanced-level courses are only offered when the demand is sufficient or when an instructor is willing to offer them as an independent study. The department offers a minor in both Russian and Russian Area Studies but no major. In 2004, the one full-time professor in the department retired and was replaced with a half-time line. Adjuncts do much of the instruction, and staff turnover has been considerable. Accompanying this turnover have been frequent changes in textbooks, and therefore, curriculum, but with limited overall coordination. Coordination among a group of part-timers is understandably difficult.

Many of the Russian students are heritage speakers of the language, but often with limited literacy skills. Some of them are part of the post-Cold War wave of Russian immigrants; thus, they were born in Russia, but left before attending school, so they may have some recognition of the alphabet, but no functional literacy in Russian. Others were born in the US and have grown up hearing Russian and speaking it somewhat but without exposure to the written language. These students often have apparent oral fluency, but very little accuracy (which can often be masked by eliding the inflected endings), and in fact, often are not aware of word boundaries.

Description of the process

Montclair's world language requirement dictates the placement process. Students who wish to continue studying a language with which they already have some experience must take a placement test in that language. In their acceptance packets, new students receive an explanation of the language requirement and instructions on how to register with the Office of Foreign Language Placement. All registration is done online through a website. Even students who are planning to study a new language are asked to fill out a questionnaire online so that we can keep track, at least informally, of the language choices students are making. The faculties of smaller language departments have historically believed that their programs benefit from the placement rule that states that students with at least two prior years of a language cannot take a 101 course for credit. The theory is that students who have been studying Spanish in high school and not enjoying it will be intimidated by the prospect of having to take Spanish 102 or higher, so they choose instead to begin a new language, such as German or Italian. Russian has seldom been the beneficiary of such choices, however, as it is still perceived as significantly more difficult to learn than the others.

The questionnaire that students complete asks for the number of years of experience they have with the language, particularly in high school. Students taking the placement test in French, German, or Spanish must complete a more detailed survey, including information about family members' use of the language, as part of the BYU WebCAPE test. For Russian, however, the survey is still quite basic and does not elicit enough information about students' home use of the language to make effective decisions about heritage speakers.

As mentioned above, the course options in Russian are limited, with beginning and intermediate courses being offered regularly, but advanced, only occasionally. As a result, classes are often adjusted to fit the students, rather than the students being moved into appropriate classes. Placement is more a question of timing than curriculum.

The current Russian placement test was most likely developed at least 10 years ago. The person who wrote it has retired, and the curriculum has changed more than once, with no change to the test. The test was written when the typical student was a traditional learner who would have had some formal instruction in the language in high school or at another university. It is a traditional paper-and-pencil test with three distinct sections: grammar, short answer, and three short reading comprehension passages. The test may be able to distinguish among traditional levels reasonably well, but the majority of current examinees are heritage speakers, and the test does not distinguish between them well at all. Students who are functionally literate in Russian tend to do very well, while those who are not cannot even take the test due to the orthographic knowledge required. No section tests productive language skills such as writing or speaking. Thus, a student who can read well but has no experience writing may be placed artificially high. Similarly, a student who has excellent speaking skills but little or no reading ability may be placed artificially low. The challenge is to develop a test that will address these issues. This may require developing a test specifically for the heritage population. Such an action may be costly, but it may be necessary as the heritage population continues to grow. Ideally, we may eventually want to use these improved placement results to justify creating a separate heritage-speaker track, as several other schools have done. At the very least, perhaps a separate course at the beginning level could be introduced for students who can speak well but do not know the alphabet or grammatical terms.

This leads to another difficulty in determining the best placement instrument for our students—the fact that the curriculum is so much in flux. Defining the goals or objectives of the program is very difficult. For example, the following is an excerpt from the undergraduate catalogue giving the course descriptions for Russian:

RUSS 101: Beginning Russian I 3.0

The fundamentals of grammar and pronunciation. Laboratory work. Meets Gen Ed 2002-World Languages. Meets the 1983 General Education Requirement (GER)-Foreign Language.

Prerequisite: Special fee.

RUSS 11: Beginning Russian II 3.0

The fundamentals of grammar and pronunciation. Laboratory work. Meets Gen Ed 2002-World Languages. Meets the 1983 General Education Requirement (GER)-Foreign Language.

Prerequisite: Special fee

RUSS 121: Intermediate Russian I 3.0

Continuation of Russian 101 and 112. Open to students who have acquired an elementary knowledge of Russian elsewhere. Detailed review of Russian grammar and pronunciation, more advanced conversation. Laboratory work. Meets Gen Ed 2002-World Languages. Meets the 1983 General Education Requirement (GER)-Foreign Language.

Prerequisite: Special fee.

RUSS 132: Intermediate Russian II 3.0

Continuation of Russian 101 and 112. Open to students who have acquired an elementary knowledge of Russian elsewhere. Detailed review of Russian grammar and pronunciation, more advanced conversation. Laboratory work. Meets Gen Ed 2002-World Languages. Meets the 1983 General Education Requirement (GER)-Foreign Language.

Prerequisite: Special fee.

RUSS 141: Advanced Russian I 3.0

Intensive study of Russian grammar, composition and translation, with assigned research in areas of special interest to individual students. Laboratory work. Meets the 1983 General Education Requirement (GER)-Foreign Language.

Prerequisite: Special fee.

RUSS 152: Advanced Russian II 3.0

Intensive study of Russian grammar, composition and translation, with assigned research in areas of special interest to individual students. Laboratory work. Meets the 1983 General Education Requirement (GER)-Foreign Language.

Prerequisite: Special fee.

The courses are described with the fewest possible definite terms and often only in relation to one another. The first and second semesters of each level appear undifferentiated, yet students can be and are expected to be placed into certain semesters (such as Beginning II), not just years (such as the first year). The individual instructors supply the real course goals or objectives in their own syllabuses, which they have almost complete freedom to develop. In some situations, maintaining a vague, circularly-defined description in the course catalogue may be an advantage because it can be interpreted to identify the goals of virtually any curriculum. Thus, textbooks may be changed, instructors may come and go, but the description need not be updated. Because the catalogue is only updated every two years, even if the entire program changes, the institution is protected from complaints that the course description is inaccurate.

Distinguishing features of the program

That the Russian program at Montclair is becoming dominated by heritage speakers does not distinguish it from other programs per se, but it does serve to frame the problem. While the department recognizes the changing needs of the students, it is limited in how it may address them. Even if it develops a better placement test for the heritage population, if it does not have other courses to place them into, or at least a more defined curriculum taking them into account, the efforts may be wasted.

Further complicating the curricular issue is the fact that the program is staffed entirely by part-timers, one who is considered a half-time faculty member and two adjuncts. Any time devoted to placement test or curricular development is time away from teaching, which is, of course, a precious commodity.

For the past year, the curriculum has revolved around a set of textbooks known as *Голоса* (*Golosa*) (Rubin, Evans-Romaine, Shatalina & Rubin, 2002). These books are considered to be communicative, though they do purport to emphasize all four skills; reading, writing, listening, and speaking. Beginning this fall, the department has adopted *Начало* (*Nachalo*) (Lubensky, Ervin, McLellan & Jarvis, 2002), which is also thought of as communicative though with a much more defined schedule. The development of any placement instrument will depend largely on a long-term commitment to a set of texts, materials, and a syllabus. If the curriculum is not defined any more specifically than it currently is, attempting to write a new test has very little point. Such an undertaking would require the cooperation of all current instructors, even though two of the three are adjuncts. The curricular backwash could be a great benefit to the program, however.

Current placement test

As discussed above, the current test consists of three sections: grammar, short answer, and reading comprehension. On closer inspection, however, the entire test may be seen as a reading test because reading comprehension skills are essential to the performance of each task (and each task is, in fact, simply choosing a response from a list of options). The following are the directions and some examples from each section:

Part A: Grammar

Directions: Each sentence contains a blank space. Below each blank are four choices. Select the choice that is grammatically correct and place the corresponding letter to the left of the number.

____ 5. ... она любит?

    A) кто

    B) кому

    C) кем

    Д) кого

____ 11. Вчера он должен был прийти, но не...

    A) приходил

    B) придёт

    C) пришёл

    Д) пришёлся

Part B: Short answers

Directions: In each of the following questions a certain situation is suggested. From the four choices given, select the response that is most likely to be made in the suggested situation and place the corresponding letter to the left of the number.

____ 29. Почему вы сегодня в шубе?

    A) Боря в рубашке

    B) Москва столица

    C) Моё платье старое

    Д) Холодно на улице

____ 38. Вы хотите снять номер в гостинице. Вы говорите:

    A) У вас есть свободная комната?

    B) Дайте мне последний номер вечерней газеты.

    C) Где находится номер 3 на этой улице?

    Д) Комната мне больше не нужна.

Part C: Comprehension and vocabulary

Directions: Read the following Russian passages carefully. Questions that follow each passage will focus on specific words from the passage to be translated or relate to comprehension of the material. From the four possible answers to each question select the most accurate and place the corresponding letter to the left of the number.

<u>Анна Каренина</u>, Л. Н. Толстой

    Все счастливые семьи похожи друг на друга, каждая несчастливая семья несчастлива по-своему...

    На третий день после ссоры князь Степан Аркадьевич Облонский - Стива, как его звали в свете - в обычный час, то есть в восемь часов утра, проснулся не в спальне жены, а в своём кабинете, на сафьянном диване.

____ 50. Похожи друг на друга

    A) friends look alike

    B) seemed to be friends to each other

    C) walked together

    Д) resemble each other

_____ 56. Почему Облонский спал в своём кабинете?

А) он спорил с женой

В) он долго работал ночью

С) у него нет спальни

Д) сафьянный диван уютный

The test presents a good mix of difficulty levels, including items that are representative of a typical curriculum in Russian, beginning through advanced. The questions range from asking discrete grammar points or specific vocabulary terms to speculation about the reason for or the outcome of a given situation. However, because the test is entirely multiple choice, an element of chance is always in each item; that is, a certain percentage of examinees will get the item correct simply by guessing. Such a test may be as much a measure of test-taking skill as it is of language ability. While nothing is inherently wrong with using multiple-choice items, whether they are truly providing the information needed to make placement decisions may be worthwhile to determine. One of the pressing questions is then whether a test of language should include a productive section, such as a formal speaking and/or writing sample. This type of question may depend largely on the curriculum, so certain curricular decisions should perhaps be made first.

A rough analysis of the placement test-takers in Russian for the last four years (2001–2005) reveals the growing number of heritage speakers, as 26 out of 33 examinees were heritage speakers. The scores were clearly divided, with all non-heritage speakers scoring below 23 and all heritage speakers scoring above 42. Test Analysis Program 4.2.5 (TAP) was used to analyze the results, and the test was shown to have quite high reliability, with a KR20 of 0.98. Basically, the test is doing what it is supposed to do: separating students into appropriate groups. The standard error of measurement is 2.58. TAP flagged three items that did not appear to be performing as expected, and when the test was analyzed with those three items removed, the overall reliability improved to 0.98. Those items should be reviewed to determine if the presentation of the questions, the item choices, or the answer keys are problematic. A quick glance at the items reveals that one is a very easy question, so nearly everyone answered it correctly. The next is a grammar question with a strong cultural component that, depending on the family, a heritage speaker may not have encountered. The third offers more than one possible correct answer—the question does not give enough context to determine the best answer.

No distracter analysis was performed on the test, though it could provide more information about the effectiveness of certain distracters. Because the test seems to work well, performing such an analysis does not seem necessary at this time. In fact, the test distinguishes remarkably well between heritage and non-heritage speakers. However, as the heritage population grows, distinguishing levels among heritage speakers is increasingly necessary.

Practical ideas for placement and future development

Perhaps the most important lesson to take away from this process is that one should not assume that a placement test is invalid, unreliable, or just plain bad simply because it is old or written by someone else. Such was the assumption in my attending the 2005 NFLRC workshop on placement testing, but the analysis has not born out that belief. What has been shown, however, is that a good test may not do all that you want it to do, depending on your curriculum. If a program is faced with an influx of heritage learners and developing courses geared toward heritage students is of interest, a traditional placement test may not provide quite enough information. In that case, scraping whatever has come before is not necessary; rather, a subtest could be developed to test a specific skill or skills that have been identified as vital for certain courses. This test could be administered separately to heritage students, after they have been identified through performance on the original test and a survey or questionnaire.

While the test is working well, and some degree of differentiation may be seen among the heritage speakers (perhaps enough to approximate cut scores), a test of a productive language skill could establish those differences more convincingly. When the curriculum is more firmly established, the exact type of productive skill test could be determined. A brief but formalized oral interview would be helpful to determine a student's comfort level with the spoken language. Likewise, a writing sample could identify students who may be able to pass as fluent but have no experience writing the language. This type of information about the students could enable the program to tailor its offerings more appropriately to the students involved. As a small program in transition, Montclair's Russian department may be in a unique position to do exactly that.

Another distinct challenge to placement test implementation, more than development, is that placement in six languages at Montclair is coordinated by a single person. At the moment, that person is a Russian specialist, but that is not likely to remain the case. Currently, the testing coordinator can conduct informal interviews with Russian heritage students to make placement decisions, but if that person leaves (as must happen someday), no procedure has been established for handling such students. During the summer, no faculty members in Russian are typically available, so a plan should be developed for working with these students.

In the coming years, Montclair and all of New Jersey's state colleges and universities will face a new challenge to foreign language placement. The high school graduation requirement in the state was reduced from two to one year of foreign language study, beginning with the freshman class in the fall of 2004. The state currently requires some amount of foreign language instruction in K-8, though this varies by district. Further, the state is working to implement a proficiency test that students may take in the eighth grade and that, if they pass, will exempt them from the high school requirement. Therefore, beginning in 2008, colleges and universities in New Jersey may begin admitting students who demonstrated some acceptable level of language proficiency in the eighth grade but have had no instruction in the ensuing four years. This will directly impact Montclair's current placement policy, which takes high school seat time into account in determining placement and credit.

Montclair is initiating a task force to re-examine the foreign language requirement and to consider implementing a proficiency-based requirement. Such a change would require a complete overhaul of the testing process and a thorough review of the curriculum in all languages. Given the scheduling system, which allows class meetings only twice a week, the task force will have to seriously consider the level of proficiency that students can reasonably attain. This situation may prove a double-edged sword for languages such as Russian—on one hand, heritage speakers may have an advantage in that their oral/aural skills tend to be quite advanced; on the other, the amount of time needed to achieve the required proficiency may be prohibitive to any students other than heritage speakers. As a result, Russian could gradually become exclusively a heritage-language program.

Conclusion

The Russian program at Montclair State University is facing many of the same issues as other Russian programs across the country. After shrinking during the last decade, the enrollments seem to have stabilized at a relatively low level. Likewise, high school Russian programs have been closing due to budgetary pressures. At the same time, Russian immigrant children from the 1980s are reaching college age, and new waves of Russian immigrants have been arriving.

Therefore, the student population at the college level has been changing, with a rising proportion of heritage speakers. These students pose new challenges to a traditional curriculum and to a traditional placement process. With the appropriate adjustments, Montclair's Russian program may benefit from the influx of heritage speakers because these students may be able to achieve a high level of proficiency relatively quickly. Before this can happen, some difficult curricular decisions must be made, and an assessment of productive skills should be added to the current placement test. These are not insurmountable hurdles and may very well result in growth, which would be welcome in most any Russian program.

References

Kagan, Olga. (2001). *Placing heritage speakers: A comparison of writing samples of heritage and non-heritage learners.* Paper delivered at American Association of Teachers of Slavic & East European Languages annual conference, New Orleans, December 2001.

Lubensky, S., Ervin, G., McLellan, L., Jarvis, D. K. (2002). *Nachalo.* New York: McGraw-Hill.

Rubin, R.M., Evans-Romaine, K., Shatalina, G., & Rubin, J.M. (2002). *Golosa: A basic course in Russian.* (3rd ed.). Upper Saddle River, NJ: Prentice Hall.

Placement Examination for a Heterogeneous Group of Russian Heritage Learners

Irina Dolgova
Yale University, CT

For many years, the student body in the Russian Program at Yale University consisted mostly of American high school graduates who elected to start studying a new language. Those requiring a placement examination were incoming freshmen who had one to four years of Russian in high school, a few transfer students, and occasionally one or two heritage learners wishing to be exempted from the institutional language requirement. Because the core material for first- and second-year Russian in terms of vocabulary and basal grammar was defined, a placement examination evaluating the knowledge of the most relevant subjects was not difficult to come up with. In rare cases, students were proficient above the intermediate-mid level and could be placed in third-year Russian or above. These cases were negotiated individually to provide students with the most appropriate upper-level courses. Some heritage learners were placed in the upper-level course required for literature majors. The curriculum included a grammar component and reading/writing essay activities. Even though these students were a minority in the class, they demanded more individual attention from the instructor and had to have different material prepared for them. The heritage learners with limited language abilities were placed in an individually tailored low-enrollment class focusing on improving their reading and writing skills. The course was called "Russian for Bilingual Students."

Context of the program

Student demographics

Since approximately 2002, the population of incoming students has changed drastically. Because many high schools nationwide have discontinued their Russian programs, the number of students taking a placement examination to be placed in the second semester of first-year Russian or higher has decreased significantly. At the same time, it has not been unusual to observe the classroom designated for the Russian placement exam being filled with freshmen casually chatting in Russian while waiting for the exam to begin. The department's traditional placement examination, which tests all of the four language skills with emphasis on grammatical accuracy and addresses a homogeneous student population, failed to meet this new challenge.

Dolgova, I. (2008). Placement examination for a heterogeneous group of Russian heritage learners. In T. Hudson & M. Clark (Eds.), *Case studies in foreign language placement: Practices and possibilities* (pp. 99–104). Honolulu, HI: University of Hawai'i, National Foreign Language Resource Center.

Only a reading comprehension component and a series of short-answer items proved to be valuable devices in measuring heritage learners' language skills.

The heritage learners received high scores in listening comprehension, demonstrated a wide range of results in reading comprehension, and produced non-ratable samples on a cloze test using various conversational and less commonly taught lexises. Almost all of the students scored poorly on short answer items, revealing unfamiliarity with writing in cursive and making multiple spelling and grammar mistakes.

Currently, American schools do not pay much attention to cursive writing, and students do not consider this skill to be a valuable one. Handwriting in Russia traditionally represents the level of education a person has received, and a note in printed letters would be taken for a rare case of illiteracy or some kind of learning disability.[1] Despite expanding computerization, mastering penmanship remains essential in Russia. In American colleges, it is taught in the beginning of first-year Russian and reinforced throughout the courses.

The grammatical errors and spelling mistakes made by the heritage learners were drastically different from the ones made by traditional students. An item analysis revealed several sets of problems:

- a lack of knowledge of the Russian orthographical system based on grammar. (Students' spelling was mostly phonetically based, which caused multiple mistakes; for example, students spelled *Всего хорошего!* as *Фсиво харошива!*, making six mistakes in a two-word sentence.)
- a vague notion of the Russian case system, materialized in systematically misspelled nominal and adjectival endings
- the scores on the verbs-of-motion items were surprisingly similar to the ones obtained by the traditional students and revealed poor command of this specific group of verbs

A ten-minute oral proficiency interview (OPI) helped to identify some patterned errors caused by English language influence and by different conditions of using Russian. The typical mistakes fall into several categories:

- using English syntax instead of Russian (*Мне нравится их* instead of *Мне они нравятся*, "I like them," *Я имею проблему* instead of *У меня есть проблема*, "I have a problem," or *В Нью Йорке много вещей делать* instead of *В Нью Йорке много интересиых мест*, etc.)
- using an English prepositional phrase model instead of a Russian one (*Я доволен с моей оценкой* instead of *Я доволен моей оценкой*, "I am satisfied with my grade" or *Я не уверен об этом* instead of *Я не уверен в этом*, "I am not sure about this," etc.)
- substituting Russian words with self-made English cognates to compensate for the lack of an abstract lexis. This phenomenon rarely occurs in traditional students' short answers on the test or in their essays.[2]

---

[1] Handwriting is believed by many to be a reflection of unique personal qualities. In 19th-century Russia, calligraphy was considered to be a valuable asset. Count Myshkin in Dostoevsky's *Idiot* was hired on the spot after demonstrating his "talent" in having beautiful handwriting.

[2] Heritage learners who make these quasi-substitutes by adding appropriate grammatical elements have typically been living in Russian communities and have gotten used to this language strategy of new

Even though some of the patterns were also typical for traditional students, the ones made by heritage learners, who generally have a significantly broader vocabulary, presented a more diverse picture of malformed syntactical structures. Existing course offerings could not accommodate this new population, which was significant (from 18 to 25 students) considering that the average Russian Language program enrollment from 2002 to 2005 was 97 students.

Yale University has a new language requirement. Students who start studying a new foreign language at the university are required to take three semesters of it. The Department of Slavic Languages and Literatures offers a minor (minimum three years of language study, at least intermediate-high proficiency) and a major in Russian language and literature (at least advanced-low proficiency).

Current placement test

The Russian courses affected by the placement procedures are as follows. Traditional beginners start with First-year Russian, R115, which is a two-semester sequence. The classes meet five times a week. Each of three sections is taught by a team of one experienced instructor and one teaching fellow (TF). R115a and b are video-based courses designed to develop all four language skills: reading, writing, speaking, and listening comprehension. They use dialogues, games, and role playing. In addition to readings in the textbook, students read original short stories and learn Russian songs and poems. They take oral and written examinations.

The next step in the sequence is Second-Year Russian, R122 (two semesters), which is taught five times a week by a team of one experienced instructor and a TF.

R122a and b expand students' knowledge of Russian grammar, vocabulary, phonetics, and stylistics; develop their skills in conversation, listening, reading, and writing; and acquaint them with Russian history, literature, and culture. Conversation practice is based on literary texts (Pushkin, Chekhov, and Lermontov), movies, and topics from everyday life. Students take written and oral examinations.

Students with talents for languages or those with a native Slavic language other than Russian are recommended to take an intensive two-semester course that covers the materials of first- and second-year Russian. Intensive Elementary and Intermediate Russian, R125, is a yearlong intensive course for students of superior linguistic ability covering the first year of Russian in the fall and the second in the spring. It includes intensive study of Russian grammar and practice in conversation, reading, and composition.

In 2003, a new course was designed to integrate heritage learners with their unique profiles into the Russian program. This course was designed to develop the language skills in which this group of students does not perform well, namely, reading and writing. To satisfy the language requirement, students have to demonstrate at least intermediate proficiency in all four language skills. Even though heritage learners' speaking proficiency and listening comprehension are usually rated high, according to the Department's regulations, students have to demonstrate an ability to read and write. Russian for Bilingual Students, R136a (fall) and R137b (spring), are designed to reduce or even to eliminate the gaps between speaking proficiency and reading and writing skills and build adequate abstract vocabulary. The first semester of Russian for Bilingual Students, R136a, focuses on general literacy—basic reading skills, a grammar overview with emphasis on cases, orthography, and cursive writing. R137b is a second-semester course that

---

emigrants (*У него не было иншурнса* instead of *У него не было страховки*, "insurance," *пять майлов* instead of *пять миль*, "mile," etc.).

continues developing reading and writing skills on higher levels and provides students with necessary knowledge of word formation, syntax, and punctuation. Successful completion of Russian for Bilingual Students, R137b (spring semester), with a grade of at least B− allows students to satisfy the language requirement and move on to higher-level Russian language courses.

Because the department's placement procedure is mostly geared towards traditional students who studied the language in an academic setting in high school or in another college, we need to develop a placement examination targeting specifically heritage learners of Russian.

Practical ideas for placement and future development

Overview

The format of the placement examination for heritage learners may be similar to the following example.

The test should take about one and a half hours and be designed to place students into one of three levels:

- R136a (fall semester), Russian for Bilingual Students;
- R137b (spring semester), Russian for Bilingual Students;
- R125, Intensive Russian, or any of the upper-level content classes taught in Russian or developing specific language skills (R136, Translation; R144, Russian Through Stage; R163, Russian Literature in Original; R164, Russian Prose and Poetry of the Twentieth Century; etc.).

Successful completion of the second semester of Russian for Bilingual Students, R137b, or Intensive Russian, R125a and b, with a grade above B− fulfills the university language requirement.

Test structure

Because students' levels of literacy may vary from zero to superior, all directions and reading comprehension statements in multiple-choice tests are presented in English.

Section 1: Short essay (12 sentences)

Imagine that you are writing your very first letter to a Russian pen pal. Introduce yourself, describe your appearance and personality, and ask the pen pal three questions about himself/herself. If you do not feel comfortable writing, please proceed to Section 3.

Comments: Students who are unable to score any points in Section 1 are placed in the first semester of R136a (fall semester), Russian for Bilingual Students. Writing skills are extremely valuable, and the students demonstrate a range of reading abilities. An interview with an instructor (Section 3) evaluates these students' speaking proficiencies. If they are intermediate-low or lower, they are recommended to take R125a and b, Intensive Russian, designed for students whose native languages are Slavic, and which concentrates on developing all four language skills.

Section 2: Reading and writing

Read the passage. If you do not feel comfortable reading, please proceed to Section 6.

Comments: Students who are unable to score any points in Section A are placed in the first semester of R136a (fall semester), Russian for Bilingual Students, because of the value of reading skills, even though they demonstrate a range of writing abilities. The interview with an instructor (Section 3) evaluates these students' speaking proficiencies. If they are intermediate-low or lower, they are recommended to take R125, Intensive Russian, designed for students whose native languages are Slavic, and which concentrates on developing all four language skills.

Text Characteristics: Finding an appropriate text for the reading section seems to be the most difficult task. The same reading passage is used for four separate sections of the placement test: multiple-choice reading comprehension, vocabulary/ability to guess a contextual meaning, short-answer reading comprehension/grammatical accuracy, and persuasive essay. Therefore, a reading passage must meet the following criteria:

- It must be written in a normative literary style reflecting the formal register of the language
- Its topic must be generally familiar to the students excluding the hot-house questions that are most likely being discussed at a family dinner table. This criterion is intended to eliminate situations when examinees have nothing to say about a problem in any language. On the other hand, some issues, especially ones that are important for their families, are so frequently addressed that coming up with an essay takes no time.
- Its content must present controversial information prompting students to produce a persuasive essay expressing and defending their opinions.

An ideal reading passage contains no English cognates, literary or cultural illusions beyond the students' reach, jokes, or word play.

For students' convenience, the text should be on a separate sheet of paper so that pages need not be flipped back and forth.

Using information from the reading passage, mark the most accurate statement.

This reading comprehension sub-section contains four items; each item prompts students to choose among three options. The first two items focus on details. The last two evaluate students' abilities to grasp the main idea.

Vocabulary. Using information from the reading passage, mark the most accurate definition of the word indicated.

Answer the following questions using one full sentence. Your answers must be based on information from the reading passage.

Comments: This section consists of five questions evaluating two different skills: reading comprehension, that is, the ability to detect nuances of the main idea and interpret the author's opinion correctly, and grammatical accuracy. An overall score, which includes a score for the grammar aspect, is used for each item.

Write an essay expressing your general attitude to the situation described in the reading passage. State your agreements and disagreements and explain the reasons. (15 sentences).

Comments: This section tests students' abilities to produce coherent texts and demonstrate a set of relevant skills: control over grammar and knowledge of necessary vocabulary, knowledge of writing mechanics (spelling and punctuation), abilities to use transitional phrases and write persuasively in the appropriate stylistic register, and so forth A student's performance is measured using an overall score, which grants different point values based on the relevance of specific items.

Section 3: Short OPI (maximum 10 minutes)

Comments: This section is designed to evaluate students' oral performances, identify their individual profiles, and learn about their motivations to take the Russian placement test. The evaluating scale is similar to the American Council for the Teaching of Foreign Languages (ACTFL)/Defense Language Institute (DLI)/York University standards, which use slightly more detailed ratings: N, NM+/-, NH+/-, IL+/-, and so forth. The scale has different values for the four cut scores of the placement test. This section has a decisive value for the cut score that differentiates students placing into R125a and b, Intensive Russian, and R136a, Russian for Bilingual Students.

Placement results

Four different cut scores place students in the appropriate classes. The separate section scores provide crucial information for the decisions. The main distinctions are as follows.

- R136a, Russian for Bilingual Students (fall semester): Low overall score on Section 1. (The performance ranges from an inability to write in Russian to writing in print using heavily contaminated syntax and lexis, systematic use of inaccurate nominal and adjectival endings, using a very limited vocabulary, etc.). Any score on the reading comprehension and writing section (most likely to be low). A short OPI score of at least intermediate-low.

- R125a and b, Intensive Russian: Low overall score on Section 1. (The performance ranges from inability to write in Russian to writing in print using heavily contaminated syntax and lexis, systematic use of inaccurate nominal and adjectival endings, using very limited vocabulary, etc.). Any score on the reading comprehension and writing section (most likely to be low). A short OPI score of intermediate-low or below.

- R136 b, Russian for Bilingual Students (spring semester): Median scores on sections 1 and 2 and a low to median score on Section 3 (read to write essay). A short OPI score of at least intermediate-high+.

- Several content classes designed to accommodate interests of different majors—R136, Translation; R145, Russian through Stage; R158, Reading Literature in Original; R163, Mass-Media in Russia; and so forth: High scores on Sections 1–2. Medium/high scores on Section 3. A short OPI score of at least advanced-low+. The choice of a particular course is negotiated individually at briefings after the total score is available.

Comments: The cut scores for placing students in R136a and R137b, Russian for Bilingual Students, and upper-level courses are determined empirically and depend on two conditions: the number of heritage learners, which uncontrollably varies from year to year, and institutional policy of canceling classes with enrollments of less than five undergraduate students.

Yet Another Test? Placement Issues in the Chinese Language Program at the University of Colorado, Boulder

Madeline K. Spring
University of Colorado, Boulder

Housed in the Department of East Asian Languages and Civilizations, the Chinese program at the University of Colorado (CU) offers four levels of modern Chinese and one year of classical Chinese. CU requires three semesters of a foreign language, but many students who take Chinese are not doing so to fulfill the requirement; often, they have studied another language. Generally, the Chinese program offers five sections of CHIN 1010, Beginning Chinese I (20-25 students per section); four sections of 1020, Beginning Chinese II; two sections each of 2110 and 2120, Intermediate Chinese I and II; two sections each of 3110 and 3120, Advanced Chinese I and II; and one section each of 4110 and 4120, Readings in Modern Chinese I and II. Generally, the students in the upper-level courses are Chinese majors or minors. The major in Chinese has two tracks. One focuses on Chinese language and literature and requires three years of the modern language and one year of classical Chinese. The other track focuses on Chinese language and civilization and requires either one semester of third-year Chinese or one semester of classical Chinese. A minor in Chinese is also an option for some students, although most of the students who decide to get one are from a school other than Arts and Sciences (e.g., Business, Engineering, or Journalism), and fulfilling all the college requirements for a regular major is not realistic for them.

Placement issues

Problem

Despite earnest efforts by some faculty members, placement in Chinese remains time consuming and less systematic than is ideal. On the whole, students are placed in appropriate classes, but the procedure depends on one or two faculty members, which makes scheduling problematic, particularly in the summer. Sometimes students are misplaced. Although we try to correct such errors within the first week of instruction, inevitably some students fall through the cracks. What is really needed is a comprehensive (four-skills), reliable test in Chinese that can be administered by departmental staff or teaching assistants (TAs), that is, one that is not dependent on the schedules of individual faculty members. Such a test is currently being field-tested at CU as part of a project through the Center for Acquisition of Second Languages at the University of Oregon. However, the chances that the university will purchase and use this test appear slim.

Processes: Departmental, institutional, and extra-institutional

Personnel and staffing of language courses
The Department of East Asian Languages and Civilizations (EALC) has offered majors in Chinese and Japanese for over 20 years; in recent years, it has also established minors and two years of instruction in Korean. Currently, Chinese language and literature has four full-time tenure track positions (two tenured), two tenured 50% positions in Chinese literature, and two full-time instructor positions. Japanese has four full-time tenure track positions and three full-time instructor positions. One instructor in Korean covers the Korean language courses. Eight TAs in Chinese are MA students, and three TAs are PhD students in comparative literature, whose teaching assignments are in EALC. The majority of these graduate students are assigned to work in the Chinese language program; others assist with teaching our large East Asian civilizations courses and classical Chinese, and occasionally a TA may assist with special pedagogical projects as determined by the full-time teaching staff.

The two full-time language instructors are for the most part responsible for teaching the first three years of Chinese, and they work closely with the TAs who help instruct these classes. All classes meet five hours a week; generally, instructors teach two to three hours of each section, and TAs handle the remainder of the instruction, individual tutorials, and most of the grading of homework assignments and some oral presentations. The fourth-year Chinese course is generally taught by a tenure-track faculty member or sometimes by visiting instructors, whose expertise generally lies more in the area of literature than pedagogy.

The instructor who is currently in charge of second- and third-year Chinese courses has been teaching in the department for several years and is fully committed to the program. A new instructor who will be on a one-year appointment will fill the second instructor position this year. This person will be in charge of the first-year Chinese language program and may or may not be hired for a longer-term position (a nationwide search will be held in the upcoming academic year).

Faculty involved with placement
Student placement in Chinese is mainly the responsibility of the director of the language program (DLP), who works in conjunction with the two language instructors. Given the high level of competence of the experienced instructor mentioned above, coupled with the fact that this individual is in direct contact with students in the second and third years, she should reasonably be involved with the placement of students who will likely be in these classes (roughly novice-high to intermediate-high level learners). Generally, the DLP handles more advanced students and any students who may pose unusual placement challenges. This arrangement is fairly successful, although the exact placement mechanisms are not as systematic and objective as is ideal.

Current practices for student placement
Students take one of three tests. Two of these are the final exams from CHIN 1020 and 2120, both of which focus on reading comprehension, translation skills, and writing. More advanced students are given a test created in the department that is roughly modeled on the Chinese proficiency test developed by the Center for Applied Linguistics in Washington, DC, and thus focuses mainly on grammatical competence and reading comprehension. The examiner meets with each individual who needs to be placed and estimates which test is at the appropriate level.

Although each of these tests has inherent problems that may impact placement, on the whole, they offer relatively good evaluations of key aspects of students' proficiency. In addition to taking a written test, students are required to participate in an oral interview, during which the examiner assesses the students' pronunciation, fluency, accuracy, and command of grammatical structures and vocabulary. Students are also asked to read passages from materials at the level that their test results indicate is appropriate (i.e., CHIN 2110, 3110, or 4110). Subsequently, the examiner decides which class is best suited to the student's proficiency level. In some cases, she may suggest that the student attend the first week of two different levels to see which is more appropriate. Students with extremely solid foundations in reading and writing (often this includes heritage students and speakers of Cantonese) are generally encouraged to take the fourth-year class (CHIN 4110) and/or CHIN 4210, Introduction to Classical Chinese. Students whose fluency in modern Chinese surpasses the level of CHIN 4110 occasionally are advised to take a graduate-level class, such as a seminar on modern Chinese literature. They can make an individual agreement with the instructor of that class so that they need not complete all work on the graduate level. Another option for highly motivated students who are entering the program with a high level of proficiency in Chinese is the joint BA/MA degree in Chinese. This degree offers selected, qualified BA students the opportunity to earn an MA degree using an accelerated undergraduate program in combination with a fifth year of study.

Profiles of students who need to be assessed for placement
Who are the students who come in for placement?

- heritage students (approximately 20–25% of the students in the Chinese language program)
- students who studied Chinese before college (high school, weekend schools, etc.)
- transfer students
- returnees from study abroad or summer intensive programs in the US

Language-specific considerations
Over time, the department has compiled a list of questions about students we place into modern Mandarin classes. The following are some of them:

- What are the language backgrounds of the students? Have they studied the language of Taiwan or the PRC? Do they know traditional or simplified characters? Are they Cantonese speakers?
- Are there discrepancies between the students' speaking and reading levels?
- What are the students' motivations? Are they concerned with fulfilling the language requirement (of three semesters) or hoping to be exempted from it?
- Once a student is placed in a class, moving him/her into another level may be difficult because of the student's schedule or restrictions on the number of students who can be accommodated in a particular class due to classroom size, limited personnel, and so forth. How can these moves best be effected?
- How can we accurately assess credit for study abroad, especially for students who attended non-CU programs, which may differ considerably in terms of academic viability and rigor?
- Considering that some students will inevitably self-place, how can these students be identified and advised appropriately and sensitively? Will all instructors (including

TAs, some of whom may not be experienced) be amenable to assessing a student's level after s/he is already in the class?

- How can we accommodate students who are between levels? If no class is at the appropriate level, how can the student continue with the language? Will his/her language atrophy? Is independent instruction an option?

Strategies for ensuring accurate placement of students

Every fall, the DLP and instructors conduct a three-day intensive orientation and training session for new and continuing TAs. This year, we decided to devote a separate section of this orientation to address the issue of placement and discuss strategies for recognizing when a student may be misplaced and what procedures TAs and instructors should take to advise the student to enroll in a more appropriate class. Given the predictable challenges that we face at the beginning of the academic year, overlooking placement issues is not unusual. Yet, once students have been in class for even a few days (each of the language classes meets daily, five hours per week), changing their schedules to take different Chinese classes may be difficult. If, for some reason, students end up in classes that are not appropriate for their levels of linguistic competency and this mismatch goes unnoticed, they are entitled to continue with the sequence of language courses throughout their academic career at CU. Thus, if a student with intermediate-level proficiency somehow were allowed to take an introductory-level course, s/he can legitimately expect to continue with the second semester of Beginning Chinese in the spring semester and so forth. In addition, given our increasing enrollments, many sections of our language courses are full or waitlisted, which may prevent students from changing levels once they are already in courses.

Another strategy to streamline the placement procedure is to maximize the on-going dialogue between the DLP, instructors, and TAs to consider the effectiveness of our efforts and brainstorm ways to improve the process in the subsequent semester and the next academic year.

Institutional issues: Procedures

At CU Boulder, incoming students (both freshmen and transfer students) are required to attend either an extensive two-day June or July orientation session or a large, three-day August session that begins immediately before classes begin. On the second day of these sessions, 50 minutes are allotted for foreign language placement (for the entire schedule, see http://www.colorado.edu/orientation/as/schedules.html). Students needing to be placed in French, German, Russian, and Spanish are required to take online tests (developed by Brigham Young University, focusing specifically on receptive skills), ideally before they come to campus. Students of Chinese and Japanese are required to meet with the faculty member in charge of placement for that session. Students need to be told what classes to sign up for at this time because they are required to register for all classes by the end of the orientation session.

Extra-university issues

Standards-based Measurement of Proficiency (STAMP) Project

For several years, I have been the academic director of a project to develop a standards-based, computer-adaptive proficiency assessment in Chinese of the Center for Applied Second Language Studies (CASLS) at the University of Oregon. CASLS has already developed online reading, writing, and speaking assessments in Japanese, Spanish, French, and German. Additional projects are being piloted in Hebrew and Turkish (reading and writing) and Japanese, Spanish, French, and German (listening comprehension). The pilot stage of the reading section of the test in Chinese is nearing completion, and the listening comprehension assessment is almost ready to pilot.

Below are some characteristics of the STAMP project.

- STAMP is a summative assessment designed for mid- to high-stakes testing.
- STAMP is a criterion-referenced test, that is, neutral with respect to textbooks and curricula.
- The items are verified through rigorous piloting and statistical analyses to assure that every student is fairly evaluated.
- The results are made available to educators, parents, and students in a clear, comprehensible, and usable format.
- Authentic tasks measure students' true proficiency.
- Computer-adaptive testing technology makes it possible to present individual, customized tests at students' levels of competency, reducing test time and students' frustration when forced to answer items above or below their proficiency levels.

One distinctive features of STAMP that makes it particularly effective as an assessment tool for Chinese is the use of benchmarks, which set minimum expectations for student performance. Regardless of curricula or teaching methodology, instructors can apply these benchmarks to chart the progress of their students. Rather than being limited to the three proficiency levels adopted by American Council for the Teaching of Foreign Languages (ACTFL), the STAMP benchmarks delineate six levels of student performance. This distinction is particularly important in Chinese and other more challenging languages that require more time for students to achieve higher levels of proficiency. Another advantage of using these benchmarks is that they specify particular topics and functions, whereas ACTFL guidelines are written in considerably more general terms.

STAMP is now being used by schools around the country to evaluate programs, place students, and provide accountability data. An impressive number of secondary schools and universities have adopted the STAMP and PLACE assessment tools (see http://www.onlinells.com/onlinells/users.asp for the complete list of current users).

Intersection of institutional and departmental mandates

During the spring semester of 2005, I met with the head of the testing office, who decides how placement testing for incoming students will be handled during freshman and transfer orientation sessions. The director of the Japanese language program and I presented an overview of STAMP and gave a detailed explanation of its strength in terms of validity, reliability, testing of the four skills, and so forth. Nonetheless, the decision was made to adopt the tests developed by Brigham Young University, which are relatively inexpensive and can be delivered online, even before students come to campus. This decision is problematic for two reasons. Because the BYU tests require an oral interview, instructors must be available to meet one-on-one with students, which, especially in languages such as Spanish and French, can be incredibly time consuming. Furthermore, the BYU tests are not available in Chinese and Japanese. Given that enrollments in these languages are at all-time highs, the attitude that instructors in these languages should just manage placement in their own programs by whatever means they devise is shortsighted and insulting.

Conclusions

The idea of creating yet another placement test overwhelms me with a sense of frustration. Certainly, the procedures our department currently has in place are inadequate; at best, they function as guidelines or approximations of students' levels. The interpretation of these tests largely depends on the time and expertise of an individual examiner. Such a personnel-dependent process can never really be entirely objective.

Effective placement testing requires considerable effort and careful planning so that the results will be consistently valid and reliable and that students will be ensured of placement at the appropriate level. These considerations are, in fact, what originally informed my decision to participate in the STAMP project and to elicit input from a select advisory board, comprised of nationally established leaders in the field of Chinese assessment and pedagogy. Having worked on the STAMP project for the past three years, I never considered the possibility that my own university would not be willing to purchase this assessment tool. Duplicating the process used in that project is certainly not time or cost effective. Drawing on the collaborative efforts of a team of item writers, graphic designers, computer experts, and statisticians, each STAMP item has been systematically evaluated. Furthermore, similar assessment tools developed by CASLS are already established and widely used in other languages, which confirms the efficacy and efficiency of the model. Suggesting that faculty members at any one university have the time or expertise to achieve similar results is simply not reasonable. Even if they did and were willing to work on such an endeavor, severe university-wide financial restraints would make financial compensation for their efforts unlikely.

Another concern specific to placement in Chinese extends to the broader Chinese language teaching profession. At a time when students are entering Chinese programs in increasing numbers with higher proficiency levels, having assessment tools in place is critical. Academic institutions need to consider the cost effectiveness of purchasing such credible assessment tools and reject the notion that placement is something individuals in departments should simply handle as part of their normal teaching activities. At the same time, instructors and teachers must move beyond the view that an assessment tool must be specifically created for and tailored to their own programs; instead, they should consider the benefits of using a standard that is objective and measurable. Ideally, in considering issues of placement and articulation, we should maximize ways to increase coherence in the community of Chinese pedagogy. In this way, we will truly benefit the profession and most critically, the students we teach.

Using a Web-Delivered Questionnaire to Improve Placement in Chinese

Rongzhen Li
Yale University, CT

Studying in an appropriate class can maximize a student's success in language study. Each year at Yale, on the first day of the fall semester, over 100 students need to be placed into appropriate Chinese language classes. Some of these are heritage students, some are study aboard returnees, some took Chinese classes in high school, and some traveled in China for a summer. Due to diverse language experiences and family backgrounds, placing each student quickly and accurately in an appropriate class has been very challenging and time consuming for all the instructors in our Chinese language program.

I will reflect on how to upgrade our current placement test by using the knowledge I gained from a workshop, Designing Effective Foreign Language Placement Tests, provided by the National Foreign Language Resource Center. I will explain the context of this program, test format, test content, test procedures, cut score of the test, decision making, and so forth. Hopefully, this case study will lead to the development of an effective placement procedure. At least, it should provoke discussion of what makes a good placement test.

Context of the program

Program

The Yale Chinese program belongs to the Department of East Asian Languages and Literatures (EALL). EALL offers language programs in Chinese, Japanese, and Korean, undergraduate degree programs in Chinese and Japanese Language and Literature, and PhD programs in Chinese and Japanese Literature. The goal of our department is to support the humanistic study of East Asian cultures through their languages and literary traditions, ancient and modern. The Chinese language program has 9 full-time instructors, 1 part-time instructor, and 10 teaching assistants. Teaching assistants are not allowed to give any lectures. They are only responsible for individual tutoring and grading students' tests or homework.

Li, R. (2008). Using a web-delivered questionnaire to improve placement in Chinese. In T. Hudson & M. Clark (Eds.), *Case studies in foreign language placement: Practices and possibilities* (pp. 111–117). Honolulu, HI: University of Hawai'i, National Foreign Language Resource Center.

Students

The first-year student enrollment each year is approximately 90. About 20-25 are heritage students, and about 20 are non-native English speakers from other countries such as Japan, Korea, and Thailand. The second-year student enrollment is approximately 70-80. About 20-30 are heritage students. The third-year student enrollment is approximately 50-60, and heritage students and non-heritage students comprise about 50% each. As the Chinese economy grows, more freshmen are in intermediate classes, which means that these freshmen studied Chinese in high school or that they are heritage students. The number of heritage students is growing, which is related to the increase in Chinese immigration after the 1980s. Therefore, quick and accurate placement is becoming more imperative.

Through the Light Fellowship, about 25% of the students from each level will go to China for a summer language program. Some students go to China for an internship without taking any regular Chinese classes. The students who attend summer intensive language programs in China are supposed to skip one level after they return. However, for various reasons, such as the quality of the programs, the dedication of the students, and so forth, most of these students need to take a placement test before they register for fall classes.

The students who take Chinese classes have very diverse majors, such as economics, political science, Asian studies, history, and music. Most of them are double majors. The students in the fourth- and fifth-year classes usually major in Asian studies, international studies, or Chinese literature.

The Curriculum

Each semester, the Chinese language program offers the 12 courses shown in Table 1.

Table 1. Chinese language courses each semester at Yale University

course #	course title
Chn115	Elementary Modern Chinese
Chn118	Modern Chinese Advanced Learner http://students.yale.edu/oci/resultDetail.jsp?course=20752&term=200501Elementary
Chn130	Intermediate Modern Chinese
Chn133	Intermediate Modern Chinese Advanced Learner
Chn145	Cantonese
Chn150	Advanced Modern Chinese
Chn153	Advanced Modern Chinese Advanced Learner
Chn155	Film Course (new course)
Chn156	Contemporary Chinese Texts
Chn160	Introduction to Literary Chinese
Chn161	Literary Chinese through Modern Chinese
Chn165	Chinese Composition

For the first three levels of classes, heritage and non-heritage tracks are offered. In Table 1, courses 115, 130, and 150 are non-heritage, whereas courses 118, 133, and 153 are the corresponding heritage courses. After the third year, only one track is offered. Starting in the fall of 2005, we offered a new course, 155, which is a film course. Besides language classes, EALL also offers about 10 classes on Chinese literature, Chinese modernism, middle Chinese phonology, Chinese poetry, and so forth. Those classes are taught in English by literature professors.

Existing placement process

In the existing system, the items on the placement test are not based on the curriculum of the program. We have no questionnaire that would enable the program to discover such information as the students' family backgrounds or previous language study. Information has been gathered in unsystematic oral interviews without the information being written down for subsequent evaluation. Several teams of two teachers conduct the oral interviews, and the teachers do not always teach the classes into which the students should be placed. Consequently, if students are placed into incorrect courses, the teachers have little information to consult to make course changes.

Description of the proposed placement process

Information needed for student placement

The following information needs to be collected from each examinee:

Family background
How many of his/her parents speak Mandarin?
Does s/he hear or speak Mandarin at home?
If his/her parents do not speak Mandarin, what Chinese dialect do they speak?

Language learning experience
If s/he is a heritage learner, did s/he attend school?
Has s/he studied, worked, or traveled in China or Taiwan?
Where did s/he study Chinese, for example, Chinese Sunday school, middle school, high school, or a summer program? For how long?
What textbooks has s/he used?

Language proficiency
How well can s/he express himself/herself in both written and oral contexts?
Approximately how many Chinese characters can s/he read?
Approximately how many Chinese characters can s/he write?
How much can s/he understand from listening to a dialogue or a short paragraph?
How much knowledge does s/he have of the core grammar patterns and vocabulary that are commonly covered in each level?
How much can s/he grasp the general idea of a given text with the assistance of a small vocabulary list?

Parts of the placement test

This placement test will be used to place students into three or four levels. Most of the examinees will be placed into the second- and third-year levels, which are classes 130, 133, 150, and 153. Therefore, the test will cover core grammar and vocabulary from the first-, second-, and third-year classes. To get all the examinees' scores quickly, except for those of an oral interview and character transcription, all the questions will be multiple choice. Within each section, 1/3 of the items will be from each of the first-, second-, and third-year levels.

Test sections:

Part 1: Questionnaire

Part 2: Character transcription (convert about five sentences from Pinyin to Chinese simplified or traditional characters)

Part 3: Oral interview

Part 4: Paper-and-pencil:

Section 1: Listening comprehension (20 sentences, 2 short passages, and 3 long passages). The students will hear all the passages and the test items and mark the answer for each question on a paper test. The audio will be online, and the students will be able to start whenever they arrive. Once the test starts, they cannot stop or go back to earlier passages.

Section 2: Grammar and structure (30 items)

Section 3: Word usage (30 items)

Section 4: Reading comprehension (10 questions based on three passages)

Placement procedure

Students will be required to take the placement test the day before class starts, which means that we have to finish all testing and scoring and notify each student at the end of the day of which class s/he should attend.

Step 1: Questionnaire

This will take three to five minutes. From the questionnaire, we will get information about each student's family background and language learning experience. To notify students of their placements, we will also need their personal contact information. The questionnaire is shown in Figure 1.

Directions : Please fill in all the fields to the best of your knowledge.		
Personal information	Last name	
	First name	
	Chinese name (Use pinyin, if any.)	
	Student ID (a temporary number is okay)	
	College/school	
	Phone	
	E-mail	
	E-mail confirmation (retype)	
Family language background	Parents	select
	Chinese used at home (Choose one.)	select
	If you selected "other" above, please specify.	
Chinese learning experience	I have studied Chinese in	select
	If you selected "other" above, please specify (in a few words).	

	Approximate length of Chinese study	select
Click "submit" when done.		submit

Figure 1. Questionnaire for collecting personal and language experience information.

This questionnaire will be filled out on the internet. We will receive an Excel worksheet including each examinee's information collected by a computer. The draft format is shown in Figure 2. Instructors will manually fill in the rest of the information after scoring the tests.

name	e-mail	Chinese parents	dialect	schooling	other schooling	schooling length	oral	character score	score on part 4	recommended class
Rongzhen Li	Name@yale.edu	both	Cantonese	weekend		3 years				

Figure 2. Draft of Excel worksheet: The shaded information is from the questionnaire and provided by the computer.

Step 2: Character transcription

We will give each student a sheet with five sentences in Pinyin and instructions to transcribe the sentences into Chinese characters.

Step 3: Oral interview

The interview will consist of three questions at different levels. For example:

> *Question 1*: "Please talk about yourself and your family" or "Please talk about your Chinese learning experience and why you study the Chinese language."
>
> *Question 2*: "What is your favorite book, movie, or city? Why do you like it so much?"
>
> *Question 3*: "What do you think is the most salient issue in China-USA relations?"

We will use a form to evaluate each student's oral performance. Two instructors as a team will interview each student for five to eight minutes and decide together which class the student should attend. If neither instructor is sure of a placement, they can send the student to the instructor who is charge of the recommended class. Figure 3 shows a draft of the oral evaluation form.

name	tone (5 of 20)	grammar (5 of 20)	vocabulary (5 of 20)	fluency (5 of 20)	total (x of 20)	recommended class

Figure 3. Draft of the oral evaluation form.

Step 4: Paper-and-pencil test (listening, grammar, vocabulary, and reading)

After finishing the character transcription, the students will receive Part 4, the paper-and-pencil test, which includes listening, grammar, vocabulary, and reading.

Step 5: Scoring

The instructors will grade the tests and score students' character transcriptions and Part 4. They will fill each score into the questionnaire form.

Step 6: Placement decisions

Once the form that has the questionnaire feedback and students' scores is completed, all instructors will discuss special cases. The total points will be 150. The cut scores are shown in Table 2 (to be revised after discussion with the other instructors).

Table 2. Cut scores for placement decisions

score	placement
0–20	118 (beginning-level advanced learner)
20–35	130 (intermediate level)
40–50	133 (intermediate-level advanced learner)
50–70	150 (advanced level)
70–100	153 (advanced-level advanced learner)
100–150	155, 156, 160, 161, or 165 (depending on the student's interest and schedule)

Step 7: Notification of each student of the class s/he should attend via e-mail

Distinguishing features

The Yale University program has several distinguishing features: a large number of heritage students, many high school non-heritage learners, and many study aboard returnees. The distinguishing features of the placement test will be that one test is used for all levels, the listening comprehension test is delivered via the web, the questionnaire is online to quickly find out students' family backgrounds and language learning experiences, decisions are made based on information received from each student that is clearly recorded in one consistent form, and instructors from each level are involved in making decisions in special cases.

Practical ideas for placement and future development

To save time, we can use a web-based oral proficiency test, which requires that the examinee use a microphone to answer each question. The questions can be the same questions that we use for our face-to-face interview. After a student submits the answers, we will receive a recording that is made by the computer. This can be done two or three days before the semester starts, leaving the instructors enough time to listen to and rate the recordings. This also allows the instructors from each level to score the recordings as a group to keep the scoring more objective. This type of oral test is also very good for special cases. If each group cannot have instructors from all levels, or if all of the instructors in a group have different opinions about the class a student should attend, the group can ask another group or the instructor who is in charge of one class level to listen to the recording. This is the advantage of a web-based oral proficiency test over a face-to-face interview.

Questions and conclusion

We will have one test for all of the levels as described above. However, at first, we were planning to create two placement tests. One would have been for the advanced level, and the other, for the intermediate level. Then, we realized that this could cause some complications:

a) Two placement tests will be more time consuming and involve more instructors.

b) We would need a quick and objective way to tell students which test to take.

c) We would need to determine how to differentiate two students' proficiency if, for example, one gets a 90 on the intermediate placement test and the other gets a 50 or 60 on the advanced placement test.

An equal number of items in each section come from each of three levels. For example, of the 30 items in listening comprehension, 10 are from the first-year class, 10 are from the second-year class, and 10 are from the third-year class. Is it appropriate to let students know this and tell them to stop wherever they completely cannot understand in each section instead of guessing?

To place over 100 students in appropriate classes within a day, this placement test will use selected-response format items. However, how much knowledge one has about a language does not necessarily reflect how well one can produce language. Reading over 100 essays within a few hours is very time consuming for one teacher, and the consistency of the scoring may be reduced if we ask all the instructors to read the essays. With this in mind, how can we test a language production skill objectively and quickly?

Developing a Chinese Placement Instrument in Response to the Diversity in a Student Population at the University Level

Song Jiang
University of Hawai'i at Mānoa

Placement is a very important issue in foreign language learning, teaching, and administration in institutions at the university level. In the case of teaching Chinese as a foreign language, almost every program at the university level in the United States at least claims to have some sort of placement procedure to find the best match between incoming students and the program. Such procedures can be easily found in a school's catalog, departmental statement, or course descriptions. Some schools have already begun to develop computer-based placement instruments in response to the increasing needs in Chinese language placement. Despite the importance of the placement test in a given program, very little literature either on the theoretical discussion or practical procedures for Chinese placement tests can be found in the field.

I will review the Chinese language program at the University of Hawai'i at Mānoa (UHM) from the language placement perspective to identify the diverse student populations and their special needs for Chinese language placement and to present some practical ideas and suggestions for placement design and future development.

Context of the program

The Department of East Asian Languages and Literatures (EALL) at UHM is the largest department of its kind in the US and includes programs in Chinese, Japanese, and Korean. The Chinese program in EALL offers five different levels of certificates and academic degrees: a certificate, minor, BA, MA, and PhD.

Chinese certificates are offered to any students who have earned a minimum of 15 credits from CHN 301, third-year Chinese, and above. Students who plan to declare minors in Chinese are required to complete successfully four semesters of language skill courses. A minimum of 15-17 credits from five courses in the Chinese language is an additional requirement for a minor.

At the undergraduate level, Chinese language skill courses are aimed at developing a high level of proficiency in both the spoken and written aspects of the language. The graduate program in Chinese is primarily designed to provide students with advanced professional training in language history, structure, pedagogy, and sociolinguistics.

The students who are taking Chinese language skill courses from EALL are from various places with different backgrounds and purposes. As one of the languages that can fulfill the general education core requirement for foreign languages, Chinese is among the most popular foreign languages at UHM. The majority of students who are taking CHN 101, 102, 201, and 202, the elementary to intermediate courses, are undergraduates from the general university student body, and most of them are aiming to fulfill their undergraduate language requirement. Given that people with Asian backgrounds are a majority of the population of Hawai'i, students with Asian family traditions, especially Chinese family traditions, make up a high percentage of the participants in these courses. International students and exchange students from various countries whose native languages are other than English form another significant proportion of these courses. A small percentage of the class participants are students without Asian or Chinese family backgrounds. Besides fulfilling their foreign language requirement, having personal interests, majoring in Chinese, and facilitating academic research are other top motivations and purposes for the students who are taking these courses.

In the upper-level Chinese language courses, namely, CHN 301, 302, 401, and 402, third- and fourth-year Chinese, most students are continuing from lower-level courses and plan to enter the workforce immediately upon completing their undergraduate studies, and many are graduate students who need to advance their Chinese study to use the language in research or graduate studies.

The numbers of students who are taking Chinese language courses at each level are summarized in Table 1. The enrollment numbers are based on statistics for the 2004–2005 academic year.

Table 1. 2004–2005 academic year Chinese language skill course enrollment

level of course (year)	fall 2004	spring 2005
100 (first)	84	60
200 (second)	73	76
300 (third)	52	55
400 (fourth)	17	16

Description of the curriculum, goals, and objectives

According to the EALL language program statement the mission of Chinese language skill courses is "developing a high level of proficiency in both the spoken and written aspects of the language." Two different tracks of Chinese language skill courses are available. One is a four-skills track that is aimed at developing comprehensive language competence in Chinese with equal instructional emphases on listening, speaking, reading, and writing. The target audience of the courses on this track is students who want to develop all four aspects of the language and plan to advance their Chinese study in the future. The other track is a speaking track that is aimed at developing listening and speaking skills only, with a special focus on oral performance and communication. The courses in this track are intended to reduce the burden of Chinese character recognition and writing during the learning process for some students, to increase the Chinese course enrollment, and to provide an alternative avenue to fulfill language requirements. The courses in both the four-skills track and speaking track are offered from the 100 (elementary) level up to the 400 (advanced) level. To compensate for the lack of reading and writing instruction on the speaking track, two 200-level reading and writing courses are included in our program. These two courses are also intended for Chinese heritage students who can handle daily conversation in Chinese but cannot read or write in the language. Our program also offers web-based online Chinese courses. The course levels include the first, second, and third years. The first two years of the program are intended to be comprehensive and address all four basic language skills. Of the two courses at the third-year level, one focuses on listening and writing, and the other, on reading and writing. Appendix A presents a detailed list of the Chinese courses offered at UHM.

For the four levels of instruction in the Chinese core program, namely, the four-skills core courses (CHN 101, 102, etc.) and the speaking-track courses (CHN 111, 112, etc.), proficiency-orientated syllabi are used. The instructional goals and objectives are outlined based on the American Council for the Teaching of Foreign Languages (ACTFL) Chinese Language Proficiency Guidelines. An effort has been made to directly map the different levels of the ACTFL Chinese Proficiency to the four levels of Chinese courses. The required features of linguistic competence and the functional situations under which a student is able to perform are both explicitly defined for the courses at each level. The general descriptions, goals, and objectives for CHN 101, 102, 201, and 202 are shown in Appendix B. Descriptions of the goals and objectives for the third-year (CHN 301 and 302) and fourth-year courses (CHN 401 and 402) are presented in Appendix C.

Current placement process and needs for improvement

We mainly use informal interviews with or without written exams for language placement. The oral interview has two parts: a language study background check and situational role-play. The situations are mainly based on the topics in the corresponding textbooks we are using in a target class. If the information gathered from an interview turns out to be inadequate in making a placement decision, a written exam is arranged to further assess the student's Chinese competence. The original final exams for each level are used as placement tests for determining students' language levels.

Although both methods mentioned above have worked in most cases, they can neither be considered scientific nor accurate. For the oral interview, a teacher's intuition plays a leading role in determining a student's language level. The student's background and self-assessment heavily influence the teacher's decision. For the written test, because no generic placement test exists that can be used to measure a student's level, we have to use our achievement tests (first- to fourth-year final exams). The problems with this approach are that a placement decision has to be made before the real placement testing because a teacher has to predetermine a student's level to provide an appropriate final exam and the content of these achievement tests is textbook-specific and usually lacks articulation with the student's previous learning experience. The real role of this type of written test is to confirm the teacher's intuition, rather than determine the student's language level.

Every semester, the EALL Chinese section has to administrate placement tests for about 30 newly enrolled students who have Chinese study experience from middle or high school or are heritage learners, transfer students, international students, study abroad returnees, or members of the military and assign them to the appropriate language classes. The current placement approaches obviously lack empirical validity, reliability, accuracy, and efficiency; therefore, they are inadequate for making placement decisions. Neither the instructors nor students are satisfied with the current placement procedures. We have an immediate need to develop a set of more comprehensive, objective, and standardized placement instruments, especially a set of written tests. Our goal is to standardize and formalize the Chinese placement procedures in the EALL and eventually make the necessary sections of the placement tests available online.

Distinguishing features of the program

A diverse student population is one of the distinguishing features of our program. The special groups of this population who need placement are as follows.

- *Students with experience learning Chinese* (in high school, middle school, or a private Chinese language school). Several public schools and most of the private schools in Hawai'i have Chinese language programs. The time the students have spent taking Chinese language courses in these schools can vary from one to six years. The curriculums in these schools do not align with that in the EALL Chinese program. This is the biggest concern in making a placement decision for this group of students.

- *Local heritage students without Mandarin learning experience.* These students are from local Chinese communities. The majority of this group comes from Cantonese-speaking families, although they may have had some exposure to Mandarin Chinese to varying degrees. Because of the differences between Cantonese and Mandarin Chinese, although these students may perform well on listening comprehension, most of them have no notable speaking or reading skills. Only a small number of students in this group are students at UHM.

- *Domestic transfer and exchange students.* This group of students normally has completed Chinese courses with course numbers or titles equivalent to those at UHM at universities on the mainland or local community colleges. Although they have completed courses equivalent to the ones at UHM, the content and language proficiency levels of these outside courses are not comparable to the ones at UHM. Those courses are significantly different from the ones offered by our program. The articulation problem between the programs must be addressed when making placement decisions.

- *International students.* This group does not make up a high percentage of the student population at UHM. The students are from various foreign countries, mainly in Asia and Europe. English is not their native language. They normally come to UHM through the school's official exchange program, study abroad, or individual arrangements. Pursuing Asian language studies and East Asian regional studies are major forces attracting them to Hawai'i. A large number of these students come from Japan, and their familiarity with *kanji* aides them in reading and writing but not listening or speaking.

- *Students with only online learning experience.* At UHM, new online courses can be taken to fulfill the language requirement; however, they differ significantly from the four-skills courses and the speaking-track courses in terms of curriculum design, course content and presentation, target skills to be covered, and teaching pedagogy. Assessment and placement decisions need to be made when the online students switch to the traditional classroom.

- *Advanced learners.* People in this group are graduate students majoring in Asian studies, Chinese studies, Asian or Chinese philosophy, history, sociology, or China-focused management of China-focused business management and administration. The majority of the students in this group have studied Chinese at other institutions with different curriculums, learning experiences, time periods, focuses, and interests.

- *Military students.* This group is mainly made up of Chinese linguists from the U.S. military stationed in Hawai'i. They all have completed two years of intensive Chinese language study at the Defense Language Institute. They are aiming at taking advanced Chinese language courses to pursue a certificate, BA, or MA in Chinese.

- *Study abroad returnees.* This group is composed of two different types of students. One type is returnees from the UH-sponsored study abroad program. This program is a clone of the current UH Chinese language courses from CHN 201 to 402. The study abroad courses use the same textbooks, syllabi, and schedules as the regular program. Therefore, these students have no special placement needs. However, another type of student is those who individually studied abroad or designed their own programs with the support of UHM faculty. This group of students needs placement.

Because our students have all these different backgrounds and learning experiences, the question is how to make our placement test serve all of their needs. This is the first question we should address when developing our placement instrument.

Another issue is how to deal with the articulation problem between the programs that students have attended and the one they are about to attend here at EALL. The Chinese course curriculums, objectives, and textbooks tend to vary significantly among the programs in different institutions. These differences usually have direct impacts on students' language competence. Finding the best way to fill the gap between the different programs is essential for making placement decisions.

Chinese characters are unique to the language. Unlike Japanese and Korean, in which the logographic characters can be taught separately from their phonetic writing systems, Chinese has no way to avoid the Chinese characters. Although the Pinyin writing system (a phonetic representation system for Chinese characters) can be used instead of characters in some speaking courses (as is done in the current speaking-track courses at UHM), students without knowledge of characters really cannot go beyond the intermediate level. Testing Chinese characters (both writing and recognition) is an important issue in placing heritage students and students from the speaking track into upper-level courses.

Practical ideas for placement and future development

In my experience, a placement decision cannot be made based on a single test. More information is needed in making each of the placement decisions. I feel that we may be able to make a better decision in each case if we have the following information.

- *Student language background information.* This includes family language background and Chinese language learning background information. For the family language background, the following are needed: native language/dialect, other languages/dialects spoken fluently, parents' and other family members' native languages/dialects, and language/dialect spoken at home. Substantial lengths of residence in Chinese-speaking countries should be included. The Chinese language learning background should cover information such as all Chinese language courses a student has recently taken at any university, college, or community college and in study abroad programs (including school, course title, instructor name, semester/year, and grade received), all other means by which a student has studied Chinese (e.g., high school, intermediate/elementary school, Chinese language school, or private tutor), and so forth.
- *Motivations, goals, and objectives for taking Chinese classes.* Second language acquisition research has showed that a student's motivation has an impact on his/her learning outcomes. Because we have three programs aimed at different student audiences (four-skills, speaking, and online), getting to know a student's motivations, goals, and objectives for taking Chinese courses will help us in recommending courses and making placement decisions. Eliciting

questions for this type of information may include "Why do you want to take Chinese? (To fulfill the undergraduate language requirement, for personal interest, graduate study, academic research, etc.)," "What's your ultimate goal in learning Chinese?" and "To what use do you expect to put your Chinese skills in the future?"

- *Self-assessment.* Student self-assessments can be useful references for us in making placement decisions. The questions may include "If you were allowed to choose a class from our program, in which class would you want to enroll?" "Considering the four basic language skills you have mastered so far, which skill is the strongest? Which is the weakest?" and "What aspect of the language do you think you will need to especially work on?"
- *Chinese language competence.* A paper-and-pencil test is needed to directly measure a student's language capability. The following aspects of the language skills should be addressed in the test: Chinese character writing and recognition, listening, speaking, reading, and composition.

A placement test can be arranged in two ways in an institution like ours. One way is to design a one-size-fits-all test. This test can be used to place students for all language courses offered in a program, namely, for elementary- to advanced-level courses. The other way is to make multiple tests and address the placement issue separately within divided environments. Considering the course arrangement and student population in EALL, we feel that two separate placement tests may better fit in our program and serve the needs of placement. One is a lower-division test that will serve the placement need for CHN 101, 102, 201, and 202. The other is an upper-division test for placement in CHN 301, 302, 401, and 402.

The reasons for this type of recommendation are that the student populations in the lower- and upper-division courses are different. Students' motivations for taking the courses are also different. Most of the lower-division students are undergraduates, and their goal is to fulfill their language requirement. Most of the upper-division students are majoring in China-related studies and graduates. Their goal is to use the Chinese language for their academic studies. We need to distinguish four levels in each of the two course divisions. For instance, for the lower-division courses, placement decisions need to be made for CHN 101, 102, 201, and 202. The same applies to the upper-division courses. Making one test to identify four instead of eight levels is more realistic, practical, and accurate.

Another issue we need to consider is how to select the discrete language points for the placement test. As we indicated previously, our course syllabi are very proficiency oriented. Before developing the test, we need to choose whether we will base it on textbook content or proficiency guidelines. However, based on our situation, we feel that an approach combining textbook content and proficiency guidelines can be adopted for the lower-division test. The reason is that although textbooks differ, a limited number of elementary and intermediate textbooks are used in classroom teaching, and the lower levels have more agreement on what should be taught and what students should be expected to master than do the upper levels. As for the upper-level tests, because the textbooks vary greatly and have less agreement on the course content, a proficiency-oriented test may better serve our needs.

The test format, length, and scoring method need to be decided before the writing test items. After the test is created, we suggest pilot testing with students who have enrolled in the corresponding courses during the regular semester. The results of the pilot testing can help us conduct a test-item analysis, revise the test items, identify the normal distribution of the test scores for each course involved in placement, decide how to interpret the scores, and then set a meaningful cut score for making placement suggestions.

Conclusion

Making a placement decision in a Chinese program in an institute like ours is a very complex process and needs to be based on more information than a simple placement test score. A student's language background, motivations, goals and objectives, personal interests and preferences, and so forth all need to be considered when making a placement decision. Further, reviewing the curriculum, comparing course goals and objectives, identifying student populations, and analyzing needs are essential in planning a well-designed placement instrument.

As the central part of placement instrument development, designing a good paper-and-pencil test for measuring language capability is complex. It requires close cooperation among the test designers, teachers, and students. I feel that placement instrument development should not be treated as a one-time investment. Once a placement system is established, to keep it running smoothly, continuous effort should be devoted to test maintenance. Monitoring test results and scoring procedures, making adjustments based on changes of curriculum and the student population, editing out-of-date content and supplementing it with new items, and so forth are crucial in maintaining the quality of an established placement test.

Appendix A: Chinese language courses offered at UHM

course title	CR	content	prerequisites
CHN 101 Elementary Mandarin	4	Listening, speaking, reading, writing, grammar. Meets one hour daily, Monday–Friday, plus daily lab work.	placement test
CHN 102 Elementary Mandarin	4	Continuation of 101.	101 or consent
CHN 103 Accelerated Elementary Mandarin	8	Content of 101 and 102 covered in one semester. Meets two hours daily, Monday–Friday, plus daily lab work.	placement test
CHN 111 Elementary Conversational Mandarin I	3	The purpose of this course is to offer the student the basic knowledge (listening, speaking, and grammar) of spoken Mandarin and to train the student to handle some familiar everyday topics.	None
CHN 112 Elementary Conversational Mandarin II	3	Continuation of 111.	111 or consent
CHN 201, Intermediate Mandarin	4	Continuation of 101 and 102. Meets one hour daily, Monday–Friday, plus daily lab work.	102, 103, or consent
CHN 202, Intermediate Mandarin	4	Continuation of 201.	201 or consent
CHN 204, Accelerated Intermediate Mandarin	8	Content of 201 and 202 covered in one semester. Meets two hours daily, Monday–Friday, plus daily lab work.	102, 103, or consent
CHN 211, Intermediate Conversational Mandarin I	3	The purpose of this course is to further strengthen the student's listening and speaking skills in Mandarin. The student is expected to be able to comprehend and produce speech at the paragraph level.	112 or consent
CHN 212, Intermediate Conversational Mandarin II	3	Continuation of 211.	211 or consent
CHN 251, Reading and Writing Chinese I	3	This is the first half of a year-long course designed for those who can handle daily conversation in Mandarin Chinese but cannot read or write in the language.	212 or consent
CHN 252, Reading and Writing Chinese II	3	This is the second half of a year-long course designed for those who can handle daily conversation in Mandarin Chinese but cannot read or write in the language.	251 or consent
CHN 301, Third-level Mandarin	4	Vocabulary building and extended mastery of sentence structures of modern Chinese through reading and related conversation. Meets one hour daily, Monday–Friday, plus lab work.	202, 204, or consent

CHN 302 Third-level Mandarin	4	Continuation of 301.	301 or consent
CHN 303 Accelerated Third-level Mandarin	8	Content of 301 and 302 covered in one semester. Meets two hours daily, Monday–Friday, plus daily lab work.	202, 204, or consent
CHN 311 Mandarin Conversation	3	Systematic practice on everyday topics of conversation. Lab work.	202, 204, or consent
CHN 312 Mandarin Conversation	3	Continuation of 311.	202, 204, or consent
CHN 313 Mandarin for Cantonese Speakers	3	For Cantonese speakers only. Competence in spoken Mandarin through comparison of Cantonese and Mandarin (pronunciation, Romanization, vocabulary, idioms, and syntax). Translation from Cantonese to Mandarin. CR/NC only.	placement test
CHN 314 Mandarin for Cantonese Speakers	3	Continuation of 313.	placement test
CHN 331 Advanced Chinese Listening and Writing	3	Web-based training in Chinese listening, reading, and writing to develop skills at the advanced level. Course activities combine independent work with communicative activities on the course website. Features language exchange with native speakers. Repeatable one time.	301 (or concurrent) or consent
CHN 332 Advanced Chinese Reading and Writing	3	Web-based training in Chinese reading and writing to develop skills at the advanced level. Course activities combine independent work with communicative activities on the course website. Ideal for in-service professionals seeking language development and maintenance. Repeatable one time.	301 (or concurrent) or consent.
CHN 401 Fourth-level Mandarin	4	Extensive reading on academic topics. Meets one hour daily, Monday–Friday, plus lab work.	302 or consent
CHN 402 Fourth-level Mandarin	4	Continuation of 401.	401 or consent
CHN 404 Accelerated Fourth-level Mandarin	8	Content of 401 and 402 covered in one semester. Meets two hours daily, Monday–Friday, plus lab work.	302, 303, or consent
CHN 411 Advanced Mandarin Conversation	3	Systematic practice on academic topics of conversation. Lab work.	302 or consent.
CHN 412 Advanced Mandarin Conversation	3	Continuation of 411.	411 or consent

Appendix B: Goals and objectives of Chinese language courses (adapted from EALL Chinese language course syllabi)

	CHN 101	CHN 102	CHN 201	CHN 202
general description	Students gain listening, speaking, reading, and writing skills in standard (Mandarin) Chinese, attaining approximately the novice-high level on the ACTFL/ETS proficiency scale. Specifically, students achieve the following:	Students gain listening, speaking, reading, and writing skills in standard (Mandarin) Chinese, attaining approximately the intermediate-low to intermediate-mid level on the ACTFL/ETS proficiency scale. Specifically, students achieve the following:	Students gain listening, speaking, reading, and writing skills in standard (Mandarin) Chinese, attaining approximately the intermediate-high level on the ACTFL/ETS proficiency scale. Specifically, students achieve the following:	Students gain listening, speaking, reading, and writing skills in standard (Mandarin) Chinese, attaining approximately the intermediate-high level on the ACTFL/ETS proficiency scale (1+ on the ILR/DLI scale). Specifically, students achieve the following:
listening	Ability to understand short, learned utterances and some sentence-length utterances, especially where the context supports understanding and the speech is clear. Comprehension of limited vocabulary and some simple questions/statements about family members, age, address, time, locations, interests, needs and daily activities.	Ability to understand sentence-length utterances that consist of combinations of learned elements in a limited number of content areas, particularly if strongly supported by the context. Ability to understand topics beyond a variety of survival needs. Comprehension areas include such basic needs as getting meals, lodging, and transportation and understanding simple instructions and routine commands.	Ability to understand paragraph-length utterances pertaining to a wide range of topics relating to daily life. (This includes lodging/living quarters, sending and receiving international mail, sports, traveling, transportation, communication, and events removed in space and time from the speaker, like past experiences, future plans, and current news events. Ability to understand the outline of the plot in episodes of soap operas and popular movies.	Ability to understand paragraph-length utterances and longer stretches of some connected discourse on a number of topics beyond basic survival needs. (This includes such topics as choosing one's major, commenting on current movies and TV shows, introductory Chinese culture and festivals, leisure activities, and personal opinions on a variety of social problems.) Ability to get the gist of some radio and TV news programs. Ability to understand some deliberate speech and discussion pertaining to such topics.
speaking	Ability to make short statements and ask simple questions, primarily by relying on memorized utterances but occasionally by	Ability to handle successfully a variety of uncomplicated, basic, and communicative tasks and social situations. Ability to talk simply	Ability to handle successfully a wide range of task-oriented and social functions pertaining to such topic areas as those mentioned above and	Ability to handle successfully most communicative tasks and social situations. Ability to talk in a general way about topic areas such as

	expanding these through simple recombinations of their elements. Ability to used vocabulary centered on areas such as common objects, places, activities, basic likes and dislikes, and terms for immediate family members.	about self and perform such tasks as ordering a meal, asking directions, and making purchases. Can ask and answer questions and participate in conversations on topics on the most immediate needs, for example, personal history, leisure time activities, and simple transactions.	participate fully in casual conversations. Can narrate, describe, compare, and contrast.	those mentioned above. Ability to support personal opinions using discourse strategies.
reading	Ability to identify a limited number of character components and high-frequency characters in areas of immediate need. Where specific characters and combinations have been memorized, ability to read standardized messages for instructional and directional purposes, such as some prices in stores, time/date on schedules, and simple public instructions.	Ability to read, for basic survival and social needs, simple connected, specially-prepared discourse for informative purposes and ability to puzzle out pieces of some authentic material with considerable difficulty and/or high-frequency oral vocabulary and structure. Ability to understand main ideas in material and puzzle out simple messages, personal notes, and very short letters that are written by a native speaker used to dealing with foreigners.	Ability to identify key facts and some details in descriptive material on daily life, news events, and carefully written personal communications. Can discern linkages among sentences in simple connected text. Ability to understand a wide range of authentic texts dealing with basic personal and social needs, such as signs, public announcements, and short, straightforward instructions dealing with public life.	Ability to read consistently with full understanding simple connected text. Ability to follow the narrative thread in more extended, specially prepared discourse. Ability to identify key facts and some details in some descriptions and narrations of several paragraphs, such as short stories, news items, social notices, and personal correspondence.
writing	Ability to write simple fixed expressions and limited memorized materials and some recombination thereof. Can supply information on simple forms and documents. Ability to write names, numbers, dates, own nationality, other simple autobiographical	Ability to meet a number of practical writing needs. Can write short messages, postcards, and simple letters and take down simple notes. Ability to create statements involving personal preferences, daily routine, everyday events, and other topics grounded in personal experience.	Ability to take notes in some detail. Ability to write notes and simple letters, brief synopses, summaries, and biographical data and of work and school experience.	Ability to write notes and simple letters, brief synopses, summaries, and biographical data of work and school experience in some detail. Ability to write narratives and descriptions of at least several paragraphs (more than 400 Chinese characters) on the

| | information, some short phrases, and simple lists. | Material produced consists of combinations of learned vocabulary and structures into simple sentences on very familiar topics. | | topics mentioned above. |

Appendix C: Goals and objectives of Chinese language courses (adapted from EALL Chinese language course syllabuses)

	CHN 301 & 302	CHN 401 & 402
general goal	Advanced level in listening, speaking, and reading and intermediate-high level in writing.	Advanced-high level in listening, speaking, and reading and advanced level in writing.
listening	Understand majority of face-to-face speech in standard Mandarin at normal rate and gain main ideas and most supporting details of reports on factual material and in non-technical prose, such as broadcast news, announcements, instructions/directions, and popular movies and TV shows.	Understand accurately the essentials of radio and TV news related to politics, international relations, economics, and science/high technology; understand accurately the essentials of talks and formal speeches or presentations; and understand advanced-level linguistic styles and forms within the cultural framework of the language.
speaking	Give simple narration and description in past, present, and future; make comparisons of a general nature; deal with social and transactional situations with complications; and give detailed instructions and simple reports.	Speak with fluency in a general way about the above topics. Express and support personal opinions using complex discourse strategies. Communicate with and interview Mandarin-speaking people from varied backgrounds. Give a speech or presentation on both formal and informal occasions.
reading	Understand main ideas and most supporting details of factual narrations and descriptions in non-technical prose, such as announcements, instructions/directions, newspaper and magazine articles, detailed correspondence, and factual reports.	Read, with consistent understanding and normal speed, longer items, editorials, academic or political debates, and various topics related to social, cultural, and current issues in China. Understand unfamiliar subjects and a variety of literary styles.
writing	Write social and basic formal correspondence; write summaries, descriptions, and narrations of several paragraphs; describe in detail with precision; and narrate in detail with precision.	Write accurate summaries based on original articles containing abstract ideas. Write articles of at least several paragraphs (1000 Chinese characters or more) on the topics mentioned above. Make drafts for personal talks and speeches. Summarize in written Mandarin accurately, including all pertinent detail.

Placement Assessment Issues for the Southeast Asian Studies Summer Institute

Robert J. Bickner
University of Wisconsin-Madison

The Southeast Asian Studies Summer Institute (SEASSI) was founded by a consortium of universities that pooled their resources to provide intensive summer instruction in the languages of Southeast Asia. The purpose of the institute is to help students and others develop the language skills they need for study and research focused on the peoples and cultures of the region. Summer was chosen as the timing for the institute so that instruction in these languages would be available to students from all universities and not just those with courses supported by National Resource Center grants.

Now in its 23rd year of operation, SEASSI is currently supported by a consortium[1] of academic institutions in North America. Various committees representing the administrative and pedagogical interests of the field meet at least yearly to provide oversight for the program and to help guide its development, while largely leaving the details of the operation of each session in the hands of the host university.

For much of its existence, SEASSI was at a host university for two years before moving on to a new site. These frequent moves were seen as a way of sharing the burden of organizing the institute and of providing both exposure and a sense of involvement for interested institutions. However well the rotation of the institute might have fulfilled these goals, it eventually became clear that the unfortunate cost was that limited attention was available to focus on pedagogical matters.

---

[1] The current members of the consortium are Arizona State University, California State University, Long Beach, Cornell University, Northern Illinois University, Ohio University, University of British Columbia, University of California, Berkeley, University of California-Los Angeles, University of Hawai'i at Mānoa, University of Illinois at Urbana-Champaign, University of Michigan, University of Washington, University of Wisconsin-Madison, and Yale University. Eight of these universities also receive summer Foreign Language and Area Studies Fellowship allocations from the U.S. Department of Education and voluntarily forward these funds to SEASSI to provide support for graduate students from a national pool of applicants. At various times, financial support has also been given by the Fulbright Visiting Scholars Program, the Henry Luce Foundation, and the Ford Foundation.

Bickner, R. (2008). Placement assessment issues for the Southeast Asian Studies Summer Institute. In T. Hudson & M. Clark (Eds.), *Case studies in foreign language placement: Practices and possibilities* (pp. 133–143). Honolulu, HI: University of Hawai'i, National Foreign Language Resource Center.

SEASSI no longer moves every second year because of a decision to experiment with a five-year commitment, with the University of Wisconsin acting as the first host site for that length of time. With this longer tenure at a single host institution, more intensive attention can be devoted to a variety of issues, among them, assessment and placement procedures for courses in the languages of Southeast Asia, which have not previously been the focus of intensive discussion and which do not have a body of research or literature.

Context of the program

SEASSI as an institution

Initially, SEASSI rotated through all of the consortium member universities that were interested in and able to act as hosts. Each site was responsible for developing an administrative and pedagogical structure, including recruiting and hiring instructional staff, publicizing the program and recruiting student applicants, and managing the awarding of Foreign Language and Area Studies fellowships. More mundane but often very complex internal arrangements included creating credit-bearing courses and finding ways to register students in them, locating temporary office space for approximately two dozen SEASSI faculty members, finding classroom space for approximately 150 students, and obtaining texts and teaching materials. The tasks proved to be formidable for each new site, and after two years, most hosts were happy to see SEASSI move on, to be recreated by someone else at another university.

The exposure that the arrangement provided each host institution and the sense of involvement that the work of hosting the institute might have fostered may have benefited the field, but the constant pattern of movement drew attention to administrative and logistic matters and inevitably reduced the energy available for pedagogical development. Following a policy decision put into effect in 1999, the consortium invited interested potential hosts to propose commitments of five years, with the goal of regularizing administrative processes and so bringing more stability and predictability to the institute. The shift toward a longer-term host arrangement has had clear administrative benefits in areas as diverse as international hiring and obtaining appropriate classroom space. At least equally significant is that the shift has allowed for more long-range planning in pedagogical matters.

SEASSI and the host site

The pattern of biannual moves, while well intentioned, had the unfortunate effect of erasing or rendering invalid nearly all institutional memory every two years. Each host had to devise new solutions to administrative issues. Finding an administrative staff in and of itself was a problem, as was locating and obtaining office and classroom space. The language supervisory and instructional staff changed with each move, severely limiting the possibility of maintaining continuity in teaching approach and quality. Problems surrounded the hiring of instructors from abroad and obtaining access to support facilities such as language labs and libraries at many sites. Despite these very difficult practical issues, the institute was seen by most members of the field as absolutely crucial.

The role of SEASSI in the context of Southeast Asian Studies was always of great concern. All of the languages offered at SEASSI are classified as "less commonly taught." Many are offered at only a very small number of universities, some only at the National Resource Center host universities, and others are not available during the academic year at all. The limited access to the languages of the region was seen as the single most significant block in the way of expanding the number of scholars who could hope to attain even limited proficiency in the languages of the region and thus, as the single most important block in the development of national expertise in the region.

Each year, the host institution was given the responsibility of addressing this critical need, but with only a two-year commitment, no long-range efforts could be undertaken to stabilize faculty, regularize teaching approaches, or develop resources. Rather than taking a long-term view of the situation, each host was forced to take an ad hoc approach to dealing with a transitory responsibility, one that would leave no mark on the home institution and on which the home institution would leave no mark. While instruction was being offered, and students were learning, larger goals could not be set, and the institute could not be stabilized over the long term.

To address these problems, the decision was made to locate the institute in a single institution for five years, with subsequent extensions of the stay or relocation to a new site to be considered following the first three years of the first five-year period. A decision to maintain the current site was subsequently made, and SEASSI is currently hosted by the University of Wisconsin (UW), with the summer 2005 session being the first year of a second five-year commitment on the part of SEASSI and UW to locate the program at Madison.

The advantages of a stable location have been great. The organizational advantages of retaining institutional administrative memory have made it much easier to organize classes and provide institutional support for the institute faculty, including a central location of classrooms, office space that is close to the assigned teaching space, and access to electronic media support. SEASSI is now a recognized administrative presence on campus, which has facilitated access to a variety of campus support units.

The advantages of retaining institutional instructional memory have been equally important. Faculty teams are now much more stable, with experienced teachers returning as coordinators for a number of years in succession. The inevitable changes that take place in faculty availability from year to year have been balanced by sufficient repeat faculty so that the memory of successful approaches to problem solving has become an important asset.

The retention of SEASSI at a single location has also facilitated the development of the instructional program. Having a stable core of coordinators and faculty has enabled focusing attention on developing the pedagogic aspects of the institute, moving instruction toward more modern approaches, and emphasizing team teaching focused on communicative and student-centered approaches to instruction. Workshops organized each year during the week before the eight-week instructional term have focused on a variety of aspects of teaching and curriculum development, allowing for concentrated work on shared problems.

Retaining SEASSI at a single location has also helped focus attention on a number of issues that stand in the way of developing the teaching of the languages of Southeast Asia. The lack of modern teaching materials for most of the languages and the complete lack of such materials for some of them has long been recognized, and steps have been taken by coordinators and faculty to address some of the most pressing problems.

Other issues that were not previously recognized as problems have come to light as coordinators and faculty have worked together over several years, in the workshop setting and during the period of instruction. One of those issues is assessment and placement, which has never been given concentrated attention, probably because it has been set aside after the rush of the beginning of each year's session. No body of published research on placement approaches exists for these languages, so each year, the instructional team is left to its own devices in deciding how to accomplish a complex task in a very limited time period.

Students

As might be expected, the student population for SEASSI is largely composed of academics with strong personal or professional interests in Southeast Asia.

The majority of the 175 or so participants in a given year are graduate students intending to do research in the region, meaning that they will need both speaking and reading skills of significant depth. A smaller number of students are undergraduates, some of whom are preparing to participate in study abroad programs soon after the end of their SEASSI sessions. Others are professionals (in law, social work, medicine, etc.), military personnel, and clergy, for whom speaking and listening skills are of paramount interest.

In recent years, the number of heritage students has grown significantly, ranging from a few in some of the language groups to a preponderance of the students in others. The heritage students represent a significantly different type of learner, bringing with them facility in oral skills but only limited or no literacy skills and often no mastery of the pragmatic differences between casual conversation in the home and the far more formal registers of speech required in the public sphere in Southeast Asia.

Languages, their placement needs, and placement strategies

The institute offers instruction in nine languages: Burmese, Hmong, Indonesian, Javanese, Filipino, Lao, Khmer, Thai, and Vietnamese. Instruction is offered for students at beginning, intermediate, and advanced levels, depending always on sufficient enrollment. Although the situation faced by the various language teams differs greatly, their placement choices are limited in part by the available personnel.

Classes meet for four hours per day, and each instructor is expected to have four contact hours per day. The remaining four hours of the official working day are given over to planning, office hours, and other needs as they arise. Coordinators may take on reduced teaching loads to observe classes offered by team members and to provide paired instruction or pull-out tutoring when needed.

For most of the SEASSI languages, the placement decisions for the majority of students have been straightforward if at least partly ad hoc. As a general rule, SEASSI has sufficient resources to provide instruction at three levels, and that is the most telling factor in the majority of placement decisions. Thus, those with no control of the language are placed in a beginning group or are assigned introductory-level tasks. Those who have the ability to converse at the question-and-answer level and have literacy skills at or near the level of deciphering but not yet to the point of real reading are placed in an intermediate group or are assigned intermediate-level tasks. Those who are able to converse with some fluency and whose literacy skills are at the level of true reading are placed in an advanced class or are assigned advanced-level tasks.

While the general picture appears at first glance simple and straightforward, many factors complicate it. First, the number of true beginners is smaller than it used to be, and even many of the students who need elementary-level instruction do come to SEASSI with some familiarity with the language. This familiarity is often gained from extended travel or residence in-country where an individual has picked up an agglomeration of words and phrases, frequently only poorly pronounced but deeply ingrained. For such students some time, often a considerable amount, must be devoted to unlearning poor habits.

Population changes in the US over the past two decades have also impacted the picture: the number of heritage students has risen, often significantly in recent years. Many of these students are appropriately thought of as false beginners because while their receptive skills, such as their abilities to recognize and differentiate between tones, are far beyond those of true beginners, they may have little practical control beyond their ability to use courtesy formulas or to mimic native pronunciation. Some are able to converse quite comfortably but have no literacy skills whatsoever and do not have more than rudimentary control over the levels of formality that are required outside of the family setting.

All of these details add great complexity to assessment and placement decisions. The instructional and placement issues faced by each SEASSI language team are explained in brief below.

Burmese

An average of about a dozen students study Burmese each year. Two or three instructors offer two and sometimes three levels of instruction, depending on the enrollment. Entry-level instruction attracts primarily true beginners, the majority of whom are monolingual speakers of English. Intermediate and advanced instruction is primarily for promoted students, so student needs tend to be predicable and uniform.

The intermediate and advanced levels vary significantly in size from year to year, and having sufficient enrollment for only one of these levels is not uncommon, sometimes for one and sometimes the other. The small numbers mean that often combining students of the two levels is necessary.

Of the 18 students in the 2005 program, 13 were true beginners and needed no testing, and 2 others were continuing students whose skill levels were known to the coordinator. Three students, therefore, needed to be placed. These students were asked to read a passage written in literary Burmese and then to retell the story in colloquial forms. They were then asked to respond to questions based on the passage and finally, to provide written answers to those questions.

Filipino

Two instructors generally teach Filipino to an elementary and an intermediate group of 6 to 10 total students. Each year's applicant pool includes a few true beginners in need of elementary instruction, with the balance being heritage students, some of them quite strong although lacking in control of formal language patterns. Occasionally, a heritage student will attend two consecutive summers, creating sub-groups within the intermediate class.

Assessment is conducted using a written test followed by an interview. The test first addresses comprehension by asking that students listen to a spoken passage and then select the most appropriate of four possible responses to each of ten written prompts. Knowledge of conversational Filipino is next assessed using two dialogues in which courtesy formulae are written and normal conversational items are illustrated, but with key items omitted. The instructions call for writing an appropriate and grammatically accurate utterance.

Hmong

Generally, about 30 students, the great majority of them heritage students, study Hmong each summer. Infrequently, demand is sufficient for a small class of true beginners. In 2005, for example, four such students made up a class, but it was the first in several years. The heritage students are all fluent speakers of Hmong but have been educated in the US, so they have varying degrees of skill and confidence in their use of Hmong.

Generally, two intermediate-level sections are formed, divided by both literacy skills and oral proficiency. In the 2005 SEASSI session, an advanced-level class was offered. All students in the class were heritage students, and they were promoted into the course based on demonstrated skill. This experimental course, now in its third year, uses English-language texts as a source of information for lectures and discussion in Hmong.

Placement is based on a written exam, promotion from one SEASSI session to the next, and oral interviews. Admission to the advanced-level class also requires an essay.

A dialect problem has surfaced this year: minority dialect speakers asserted a desire to be taught in their own dialect. Hmong is not a state-sanctioned language anywhere, so the disagreement over dialect preference is based on numbers without a geopolitical or intellectual component to bolster the preference for either of the dominant dialects.

Indonesian

From 25 to 30 students study Indonesian each year, most of whom are true beginners or promoted traditional students. SEASSI has little heritage demand for Indonesian. The script is based on Roman models, and the phonology closely resembles that of English, meaning that a mismatch between oral and written skills is seldom the problem that it is for other SEASSI languages. However, a significant number of U.S. programs feed students into the SEASSI classes, making placement and articulation significant concerns. Placement is based on a written exam for which two hours are allowed and an oral interview of 15 to 30 minutes. The directions for the written test indicate in English that conversational skills, reading comprehension, and writing will be covered and that skipping items that are too difficult is appropriate. Conversational forms are tested first using 10 prompts, each requiring the student to select the most appropriate response of four items. Two incomplete dialogs are presented next with directions to supply appropriate items for the missing sections.

The reading comprehension section begins with several pictures and asks the student to respond to questions based on the information in those pictures. The question formats are multiple-choice and short sentence responses. Written passages of different lengths are given next, with short-answer questions following each.

The grammar portion includes three sections. The first has 10 sentences that each have one position in brackets in which three possible wordings are included, only one of which is acceptable and is to be circled by the student. The next portion includes 10 prompts, each with four sentences, only one of which is correct. The third section is a passage of two paragraphs with several items in brackets; the directions in English ask for corrections if needed for each item in brackets.

The final section of the written exam is a prompt instructing the student to write a composition of 50 to 200 words on one of three topics.

The interview section includes a number of questions of increasing complexity based on the American Council for the Teaching of Foreign Languages (ACTFL) oral proficiency scale. Evaluations of speaking and listening are based on pronunciation, vocabulary, grammar, fluency, and comprehension.

Khmer

Two or three instructors use a modularized approach to teach about 12 to 18 students. The Khmer students are a mix of true beginners, promoted traditional students, placed traditional students, and heritage students. The non-heritage students are primarily graduate students planning on research careers; the heritage students are often undergraduates and less often graduate students, who have a mixture of cultural and academic aspirations.

The primary placement concern for the Khmer program is the heritage students, and the assessment procedure, created by Frank Smith, the SEASSI Khmer coordinator, includes a paper test and oral interview, followed by a meeting with the coordinator to create a study plan.

The listening section includes a pair of audio tracks for which the setting and questions are given in English. The student is allowed to respond in either English or Khmer so that the focus is on comprehension alone.

The reading section includes matching the content of a picture with the appropriate word and filling words into blanks left in a reading passage. Pictures of signs as seen in Cambodia are then followed by several questions in English to test the student's ability to interpret the signs properly. Responses may be in Khmer or English, again to keep the focus on comprehension.

A short reading in Khmer is followed by several questions in Khmer script, and for this exercise, responses must be in Khmer. A short written passage is also required, again in Khmer.

The student's mastery of speaking is determined in an interview with the instructors, with questions and prompts of increasingly difficulty, following the American Council for the Teaching of Foreign Languages (ACTFL) oral proficiency interview (OPI) approach.

Lao

An average of about 10 students study Lao each year with two instructors, although the types and numbers of the students vary greatly from year to year. In the 2005 group were three true beginners and nine heritage students.

Typically, Lao heritage students have strong listening and speaking skills but generally no literacy skills. Often, native speakers of Hmong are in the group, and they typically have non-native but very fluid control of Lao, often needing remedial work to correct fossilized pronunciation weaknesses. Like the true heritage students, they often lack literacy skills and must devote considerable time to the complexities of the Lao writing system. Complicating the picture further, the placed students often include native speakers of English who have varying control of both oral and written Thai, a sister language to Lao with very similar grammatical structures but a different tone system and considerable vocabulary differences.

Placement assessment includes a written examination and oral interview conducted by the instructors, based on the pattern of the Khmer program, in which the placement needs closely parallel those of the Lao program.

Thai

An average of about 30 students take Thai, including a dozen or more true beginners each year. The intermediate level is primarily composed of promoted students. The advanced level has some promoted students along with a somewhat larger number of placed students, some of whom have completed a study abroad year or have resided in Thailand as volunteer teachers or the like. Heritage students are generally at the intermediate level, with significant passive skills and limited productive skills, but generally with no command of the complex Thai script, which hinders their active participation with other students until they have mastered it.

True beginners are not tested and are placed together in an elementary group. All others are tested for listening, speaking, reading, and writing.

The listening portion of the assessment consists of recognition of items spoken aloud with potential answers presented in picture format. The student answers a question by choosing the picture that correctly represents the spoken prompt. Items begin with single words and increase in difficulty to the sentence level.

Next, a simple passage is read aloud, and the student answers questions about that passage presented in English. The answers may also be in English, focusing the exercise on comprehension rather than production.

The reading portion consists of items presented in Thai script, beginning at the word level and moving to the sentence level. Questions are presented in Thai, ranging from those asking for simple yes-no answers to more complex informational questions.

Reading comprehension for the more advanced student includes short passages in Thai script with questions on that passage. The questions are presented in Thai, and answers must also be in Thai. The questions are of a variety of types, including wh- questions requiring complex answers.

For the writing assessment, the student is asked to look at pictures and respond to them, beginning with lists of items found in the pictures and continuing on to describing activities seen in other pictures. Some pictures are also used as prompts for imaginative story writing.

The student's control of spoken Thai is evaluated using an oral interview. A specific set of questions is used with each student to elicit responses of a similar nature to facilitate grouping. During the interview, the student is also asked to read aloud short passages at different levels of complexity. The interviews are taped for later analysis, should that be necessary.

Vietnamese

An average of 30 to 35 students take Vietnamese each year, 8 to 10 of whom are true beginners. Four or five are promoted traditional students working at the intermediate level, and another four to five are placed traditional students, this latter group having had some experience living in Vietnam. Four to five heritage students with limited productive skills enroll each year, but because the script is based on a Roman model, it is a problem of limited scope compared to that of languages using a script derived from Devanagari, and it does not threaten to hold the student back from participation in intermediate-level work.

Dialect preference is a significant problem among heritage students because the majority of such students come from families that use South Vietnamese and have a strong political preference for that dialect and against the now politically dominant dialect of the north. Preparation for academic or professional work in Vietnam, however, demands command of North Vietnamese, so that dialect must be taught in the classroom.

The assessment includes a written examination and individual and group discussions with the instructors. Students who are above the true beginner level are given the same test, which includes two reading passages and an essay, and participate in an oral interview of 20 questions graded for difficulty.

The questions for the reading passages mix yes-no answers and informational answers that are designed to reflect student comprehension. No translation of the passages is required.

The oral interview is a series of questions intended to elicit informational answers of increasing length and complexity. The topics focus on the familiar areas of family, fields of study, travel, hobbies and interests, and the study of Vietnamese.

Placement is based on the results of the written examination and the oral interview. The intermediate-level group is composed of those who perform well on the first of the reading passages but not the second more difficult one and who can write an essay of about 100 words although with several mistakes. Those who can answer only up to the first 10 oral questions are also placed with this group.

The more advanced group includes those who do well on both reading passages and can write up to 200 words with few mistakes. These students are also able to answer some of the questions from the second and more difficult tier of questions in the oral interview.

Description of the process

As with all language programs, placement decisions must be made quickly and effectively, but the realities of the SEASSI session leave little time in which to make those decisions. In the months prior to each session, efforts are made by the program administrators to estimate from the number of applicants the number who will actually enroll at SEASSI and will study each language and at what level. The application materials ask that students describe any prior formal study of the language and in their personal statements to give details of additional experience, such as in-country employment, volunteer work, family use of the language, and so forth. This information can be helpful; however, as might be expected, applicant self-assessment is often uninformed and so may not accurately indicate the appropriate placement. Despite its inherent limitations, this information is what is available to estimate the number of students who will attend, which in turn dictates the number of faculty that the program will be able to hire and the number of groupings that will be available for classes.

As part of the week of preparation prior to the beginning of instruction, the language coordinators and faculty study the application materials to attempt to assess the placement decisions that they will have to make after the students arrive on site. Sometimes, the coordinators will attempt to reach each of the students by telephone before their arrival to gather further information. This process, however, is a significant burden on the coordinators' time.

The majority of the assessment and placement decisions are made on the first day of the summer session, which is always a Monday early in June. The morning begins with a general orientation meeting followed by meetings organized according to language group, during which the students are introduced to each other and to the faculty teams with whom they will work. The written and oral placement tests are administered for students who have some control of the language of study, and these are graded during the afternoon. Oral interviews are conducted during the written test and continue into the afternoon until all are completed.

Once all the examinations have been graded and the interview results evaluated, placement decisions are made. The class assignment for each student must be made by the end of the day on Monday so that room assignments are available for the beginning of instruction at 8:00am on Tuesday. Students then have until the end of the working day on Wednesday to complete online registration. Often, this entails dropping the course that the student originally thought was appropriate and electing a different one.

No commercial examinations are available for the SEASSI languages, so the assessment instruments are devised by each language group. The tests typically involve a variety of question types including true-false, multiple choice, fill-in-the-blanks, short answer, brief essays, and so forth. Oral evaluations are generally conducted as individual or small-group conversations. In some cases, a specific set of questions is used for each student. In others, a more generalized conversation format is used. Many SEASSI faculty members are trained in American Council for the Teaching of Foreign Languages (ACTFL) oral proficiency interview (OPI) techniques and use that information in these oral assessments, although the time and the number of trained testers are insufficient for a full proficiency interview for each student, especially for the languages with larger enrollments.

The final decisions regarding placement are generally straightforward for some students, but differing levels of mastery and numbers of students complicate the decisions for others. True beginners are placed together and registered in elementary courses. Promoted students, whether they have completed one or two years of prior study either during the academic year or at previous SEASSI sessions, are placed in either intermediate or advanced groups, depending on the students. In such cases, seat time is often an important part of the choice because having a student repeat a course for advancement toward a degree is not administratively possible.

Students who arrive at SEASSI with considerable mastery of the language gained outside of the university setting, for example, Peace Corps volunteers, generally are placed in advanced-level groups because they have significant facility in both oral and written forms of the language. In some cases, though, while they do have significant listening and speaking skills, they do not have control over the written forms. Depending on the complexity of the script for that language, such students may need significant amounts of time for individual work to bring their reading and writing in line with their listening and speaking skills.

Heritage students are increasingly common for a number of SEASSI languages and are nearly always well ahead of their peers in listening and speaking, so they should logically be placed in intermediate- or advanced-level courses. Depending on the script used by the language, however, these students may face a very difficult task. While they may have great facility in using the language, they may have very poor conceptual skills and difficulty keeping up with the approaches used by their peers who have been trained to think of the language as an object of study in and of itself. For these students, the script can be a major problem because without reading abilities, they cannot work successfully with others in either intermediate or advanced classes. In addition, while heritage students may be able to produce language that is phonetically quite native, they often are unfamiliar with pragmatic aspects of the language because they have experienced it primarily in home environments and not in the more formal setting of the classroom or in the even more formal imagined settings of the language exercises that they may encounter in the classroom.

Finally, some unique students do not fit any of these categories. Native speakers of languages other than English present additional problems for their teachers. For example, a native speaker of Japanese who is studying Thai, a native speaker of Thai who is studying Vietnamese, or a native speaker of French who is studying Burmese will encounter challenges in doing class work that are different from those of the majority of students, who are native speakers of English.

The false beginners, heritage students, and unique students are relatively few for most languages, but these students are the most difficult to place and increasingly need well-designed formal testing procedures.

Practical ideas for placement and future development

In moving toward a more stable host arrangement, SEASSI has an opportunity for development that was not possible when it moved every other year. One need that is increasingly apparent is for a more formalized assessment and placement process. Teachers of the languages of Southeast Asia, working with only limited resources, have not given this area of program development a great deal of attention, so they have no research to fall back on now that the need is increasing for more rigorous procedures.

Placement is not the same problem for SEASSI that it is for languages with large enrollments that have to place hundreds or even thousands of students each year. However, in working with our smaller number of students, SEASSI can still work toward more effective ways to assess the needs of its students. The study and application of placement testing theory will be a significant benefit for SEASSI and the field of less commonly taught languages in general.

Tools such as a more fully developed student self-assessment can assist in tentative student placement. Descriptions of what is involved in placement posted on a website can help students to help us by informing them more fully about, for example, what it means from a pedagogical perspective to be a heritage student. An accurate assessment and tabulation before the beginning of the summer session of how many students need remedial assistance with literacy skills can help in hiring decisions and in decisions about how to use pre-session preparation time.

Conclusion

SEASSI has moved into a new era of development, one that was not envisioned when purely administrative concerns governed the choice of location for its work. A number of pedagogical issues have been addressed in the years since it has moved to the University of Wisconsin, and the issue of assessment and placement is one of those now receiving attention. The issue has not previously been addressed in any systematic manner for the languages of Southeast Asia, and further development will be of use to all who are interested in the teaching of these languages.

Placement Issues in Study Abroad Programs: The Case of the Intensive Advanced Swahili Group Project Abroad

NFLRC

Masangu Matondo
University of Florida, Gainesville

Study abroad programs that bring together students from different institutions pose unique placement challenges. These challenges stem from the fact that the participating students are exposed to different curricula and backgrounds in their home institutions. This problem is especially pronounced in less commonly taught languages. The situation for African languages is particularly challenging because no proficiency guidelines or scales have been established to guide instructors. Thus, students who have completed similar lengths of African language training (e.g., four semesters of Swahili) at different universities often have significant differences in productive and receptive language skills. The problem is compounded by the fact that the majority of African languages are taught by non-professionals—native speakers who have no formal training in language pedagogy.[1] This creates a problem in study abroad programs that bring together students from different institutions because students might not be able to fit into the levels targeted by the programs. Articulation is thus often a critical issue in these programs. In general, the more diverse the potential participants are in terms of language background and training, the more difficult articulation becomes. Careful placement and screening of the aspiring participants must therefore be an integral part of any study abroad programs that involve heterogeneous student populations.

I examine the challenges posed by study abroad programs by using the Intensive Advanced Swahili Group Project Abroad (Swahili GPA)[2] as a case study. The Swahili GPA has had some

---

[1] The National African Language Resource Center (NALRC) at the University of Wisconsin-Madison has been running three- (and recently two-) week summer institutes for several years focusing on developing skills in teaching speaking, listening, reading, and writing for African language instructors in the US. While these institutes are essential and helpful, much needs to be done to professionalize the teaching of African languages in the US.

[2] The Swahili GPA is one of the three such study abroad programs for African languages. The other two programs are the Zulu Group Project Abroad administered by the University of Pennsylvania and the Yoruba Group Project Abroad administered by the University of Florida at Gainesville.

Matondo, M. (2008). Placement issues in study abroad programs: The Case of the Intensive Advanced Swahili Group Project Abroad. In T. Hudson & M. Clark (Eds.), *Case studies in foreign language placement: Practices and possibilities* (pp. 145–158). Honolulu, HI: University of Hawai'i, National Foreign Language Resource Center.

participating students who were unable to handle the intensive advanced materials and had to be placed into remedial programs while in the field, that is, Tanzania. Because students go through a placement process before they are admitted to the program, one can then question the placement tools and procedures that are used during the selection process. My main argument is that time-consuming misplacement (necessitating remedial programs while students are already in Tanzania) can be avoided if applicants undergo systematic and scale-based placement procedures before they are accepted to the program.

This paper is organized as follows. In Section 2, the context of the program is presented. A description of the Swahili GPA and the placement procedures involved are given in Section 3. In Section 4, the distinguishing features of the Swahili GPA are identified. I show that the main distinguishing feature of the program is the heterogeneity of the participants' proficiency levels, caused by their different language backgrounds and exposure to different curricula. Recommendations for improving the placement issues in the Swahili GPA program are given in Section 5. The last section summarizes the issues raised while emphasizing the critical placement decisions aimed at improving the program.

Context of the program

The Swahili GPA is an eight-week intensive advanced program in Tanzania. Any university student who is a U.S. citizen or permanent resident can participate in the program provided that s/he has completed three semesters of Swahili at the time of application. The program takes place in the summer, and participants are expected to have completed four semesters (i.e., two years) of Swahili at the start of the program. To participate in the program, applicants must demonstrate an interest in the African continent, and graduate students with research focuses on Africa are specifically encouraged to apply.[3] Annually, the number of participants has ranged from 12 to 18, and they usually come from U.S. universities that offer Swahili beyond the elementary level. To exclude participants with sufficient exposure to the Swahili language and culture, students who have spent six or more months in East Africa are not eligible. The program is sponsored by the United States Department of Education (DOE) and administered by different U.S. universities. Currently, it is administered by the African Studies Institute at the University of Georgia at Athens. In the 2005–2006 academic year, it was administered by Michigan State University.

Description of the process

As mentioned above, the Swahili GPA is an eight-week program involving five to six hours of daily intensive language instruction and interaction. It is part of the Fulbright-Hays Group Projects Abroad Program sponsored by the U.S. DOE. In the US, the program is coordinated by the Association of African Studies Programs (AASP) in consultation with the African Language Teachers Association (ALTA). While in Tanzania, the participants undergo cultural adaptation and orientation in their first week. At this time, they also visit various cultural centers in Northern Tanzania (e.g., Manyara, Ngorongoro, the Olduvai Archeological Center, and the United Nations Tribunal Center). In the remaining weeks (weeks 2–8), the students participate in intensive formal classroom instruction and undertake community research projects. In recent years, instruction has taken place at the MS Training Center for Development Cooperation in

---

[3] That the applicants must have an interest in the African continent implies that they are motivated to learn the language. However, this is not usually the case, particularly when dealing with undergraduate students whose academic focuses and emotional maturity are still issues.

Arusha. Participants also attend educational, cultural and historical site tours in Zanzibar, Dar-es-salaam, and Bagamoyo. In general,

The GPA Intensive Swahili Program is rigorous but very rewarding. Students participate five to six hours of daily intensive language instruction and community tours to practice their oral skills. Past experiences show that, by the end of the program, students are able to hold conversation with native speakers without much difficulty. Research projects conducted by the students in the community are presented at the end of the program.

Participants

As noted above, to participate in the Swahili GPA, an applicant must be a U.S. citizen or permanent resident. S/he also must be a junior or senior undergraduate or a graduate student in an institution of higher education and must have completed three semesters (or the equivalent) of Swahili at the time of application and four semesters (two years) when the program begins in summer. The applicant also must have a commitment to a career in a modern foreign language or African area studies. Participants can come from any U.S. university that offers Swahili beyond the first year. See Appendix D for an example of the required application forms.

Selection process

In considering the applicants, their overall previous academic performance in at least four semesters of university-level Swahili courses or equivalent and their promise of superior performance are considered.[4] Applicants must be enrolled in Swahili classes (including direct studies) at the time of application. Letters of recommendation that portray their academic strengths must be sent to the director of the program. Each student should write a statement of purpose and demonstrate a career commitment to the study of Africa and African studies development in the US.

A GPA committee member determines the applicants' levels of Swahili oral proficiency using a phone interview. This is the only placement technique that is used in the selection process. The main objective of the interview is to get a general picture of the applicant's Swahili oral proficiency. The applicant's performance is then judged on fluency, cohesion, and grammatical competency. Because African languages have no performance standards, the applicants' performances in these areas tend to differ significantly. An oversight committee comprised of members from AASP and ALTA makes the selections. The committee determines the final list of candidates and alternates that will be offered GPA fellowships.

Under normal circumstances, the number of interviewers has ranged from one to two and sometimes three. Unfortunately, the interview and the way it is administered are generally viewed as ineffective for placement even by the applicants themselves because the interview is either not long enough to give a true picture of the applicants' language competence or it covers elementary materials. In some cases, applicants were not interviewed at all. Yet in other cases, the applicants were told that they were already accepted in the program immediately after the interview and in some cases even before the interview. This gives the impression that the interview was only a matter of formality and is meaningless as a placement tool. The widespread notion is, therefore, that once you make it to the interview process, you are almost guaranteed acceptance in the program. Below is a representative sample of applicants' responses when asked if they were interviewed and if they thought that their performance on the oral interview was

---

[4] It is not clear what is considered "superior performance" and what specific tasks the applicants are supposed to perform to demonstrate it.

crucial in their acceptance in the program. A simple examination of these responses reveals the participants' dissatisfaction with the interview as the sole placement tool. The interview process clearly has problems.

> I was interviewed once by one interviewer over the phone, and the interview was basically a casual conversation in Swahili. Didn't last more than four minutes. The interviewer asked me things like what my educational plans were and the latest movie I had seen...

> I did get interviewed, by phone. Just one interviewer interviewed me. The interview was extremely short, just a little conversation. "Hujambo? Hali ya hewa ni nini? Unasoma nini?" I don't remember much about it, but *we were pretty much told were going before the interview actually took place* (my emphasis).[5]

> I did get interviewed, but only by one person, and it was very brief. I was asked about the weather, how I was, how my family was. Very basic stuff. *I had heard that several of the applicants weren't interviewed* (my emphasis).

Distinguishing features of the program

Like other study abroad programs of this sort, the Swahili GPA program brings together students with different language skills and backgrounds from different institutions. The situation, however, is more critical in Swahili and other African languages because African language teaching in the US is still a disorganized field with no clear proficiency guidelines or scales. Moreover, many African languages are taught by people who are not professionals in the field. Any native speaker of any African language is generally assumed able teach her/his language to American students even if her/his area of expertise is not language or linguistics and the person has never taught languages before. The lack of common proficiency standards and qualified teachers, among other things, causes critical articulation issues in a program like the Swahili GPA. The placement techniques that are used to select the participants in the program (e.g., an interview) must address these articulation issues to reduce the frequency of misplacement scenarios whereby misplaced students are discovered very late in the program (e.g., when they are already in Tanzania), thereby necessitating remedial programs. This is time-consuming and a burden to both the instructors and their students.

Practical ideas for placement and future development

From the discussion above, the Swahili GPA program faces the following four problems:

1. *The goals of the program are not clearly stated.* Thus, what the program accomplishes and what is expected of its participants are not clear. The major objective of the program is only stated as "to reinforce and enrich participants' knowledge of Kiswahili language and culture."

2. *African language programs in the US have no established proficiency standards and guidelines.* The field is not uniform, and every program sets its own proficiency standards (in speaking, listening, reading, and writing) and guidelines to achieve those standards. Thus, what students with the same level of training from different institutions are capable of doing is impossible to predict. This is clearly expressed by the following suggestion made by one of the participants.

---

[5] *Hujambo* ("How are you?"), *Hali ya hewa ni nini?* ("How is the weather?"), and *Unasoma nini?* ("What are you studying?").

I would suggest having different groups separated by skill or accepting students that are all at similar skill levels... But it really depends... I was a better with Swahili than some second years; some second years were better than third years.

3. *In some misplacement cases, students who are not ready to deal with the intensive advanced Swahili materials are admitted to the program.* This shows that the procedures used in the screening process, that is, the interview, have problems. Many participants who were interviewed clearly indicated that misplacement instances are common in the program and mentioned the measures taken by the instructors and coordinators to alleviate such instances.

There were definitely some students who lacked a solid foundation, and they were split up amongst the different groups in the beginning. However, by the end, they were placed in their own class where they could work at their own pace without the pressure of having more advanced students in their class.

One participant who was asked to comment on the program happened to be one of the students who found himself misplaced and his place in the program uncertain. Although his general view of the Swahili GPA program is strongly positive, his frustrations with the program are evident from the observations below.

> Yes, I was one of the students that felt like I didn't fit in well... The difficulty was that we were separated into smaller groups, but the teachers thought the weaker students would learn more if they were placed with the stronger students. Not so; the teachers didn't want to waste time helping and answering the questions of the weaker students, and the stronger students were bored... I don't think the material was too difficult, but the weaker students just needed a little longer to get through it... There was some difficulty with speakers who would talk as if we were all native speakers...
> Unfortunately, I don't think the weaker students were helped as much as they should've been. Sometimes we felt almost cast aside or ignored because we didn't know Swahili as well as the others... The same participant goes on to volunteer suggestions on how to improve the program.
>
> I would suggest having different groups separated by skill or accept students that are all at similar skill levels... But it really depends... I was a better with Swahili than some second years, some second years were better than third years... Another thing is that my program focused a lot on grades, which left many students a little stressed. The program should be more about fun, enjoying the language, and communicating with local people more than grades.

Another student (quoted below) explains the same problem with a more positive outlook. Although the student is optimistic, articulation problems are still evident. The observations made by this participant are important because they show that the participants are subjected to other placement exams (written and oral) when they arrive in Tanzania. One can then wonder why these placement exams are not administered while the students are still in the US as part of the admission process. This has the potential of bypassing most of the frustrations and negative attitudes that are caused by the articulation issues that students face while already in Tanzania.

For instance, we had three very distinct levels of students, although this was not influenced by how many years that they'd had. We were separated by levels and as we progressed, these groups were changed to reflect the progression, which I think was very effective. There was a lot of one-on-one if needed, and there was extra effort made to accommodate those students who were extremely advanced as well as the ones at the bottom. The problem was that they did a written placement test to put everyone in certain sections, and some people test very well but aren't able to translate that skill into actual use. So one student was great at taking tests and put in the advanced level, but couldn't speak. There was a lot of effort to get her to speak more, she was moved into a more appropriate class, but still refused to speak and in the end, while her comprehension wasn't bad (although she still struggled with it), her speaking was very little improved at all. Teachers can only do so much. Anyway, this problem was remedied by the staff at TCDC this year—they gave a written and an oral exam to place students.

4. *Although Swahili is the most taught African language in the US (excluding Arabic), in some years, the Swahili GPA program has faced a shortage of applicants to such an extent that applicants were sometimes admitted without being interviewed.* Although this may be caused by factors that GPA administrators cannot control (e.g., uncertainties about the availability and the late release of funds from the DOE, leading to late advertisement and hence, few applications to the program), its consequences are clear: it increases the potential for students who cannot handle the intensive advanced curriculum being admitted to the program.

Recommendations for improving the program

The Swahili GPA program is extremely important for our students, and every effort should be made to make it successful and more appealing to potential participants. Even though the organizers have done an excellent job over the years, a few critical areas need attention to make the program even more articulate for the benefit of our students. Below are a few recommendations that I believe, when implemented, will help in solving or alleviating some of the problems, particularly those involving articulation.

- What is the program meant to accomplish? What are the expectations from the students' point of view? The goals of the program must be stated clearly, and every potential applicant must have access to these goals. Without clearly stated performance goals, the success of the program is difficult to measure.

- Apart from clearly stating the program goals, a general consensus is needed on what language tasks the potential participants (with four semesters of Swahili) are expected to be able perform in speaking, listening, writing, and reading. This can be done if general language proficiency guidelines are adopted, for example, the American Council for the Teaching of Foreign Languages (ACTFL) proficiency guidelines (1986, 1999)[6] (see Appendices A–C). The participants' language performances must at least be intermediate-high in listening, speaking, reading, and writing and at level 2 of the Interagency Language Roundtable (ILR) scale (Appendix C).

- The GPA committee members who administer the interview must be certified to give oral proficiency interviews (OPIs).[7] If the interviewers are not OPI-certified, they must

---

[6] These proficiency guidelines were developed by ACTFL in 1986 and revised in 1999. While such guidelines for African languages are being developed by NALRC at the University of Wisconsin, the Swahili GPA can currently use the ACTFL guidelines to screen its potential applicants.

[7] The OPI is a standardized procedure used globally to assess functional speaking ability. It measures how well a person speaks a language by comparing his/her performance of specific language tasks with the criteria for each ACTFL proficiency level. The OPI involves a carefully structured conversation between a trained interviewer and an interviewee. A ratable speech sample is then elicited by an individually determined series of questions or comments.

use the same or similar sets of questions for their interviews. In any case, all interviews must be recorded and rated by at least one OPI-certified interviewer. This will make the screening process more professional and dependable and eliminate personal bias.

- Because Swahili is the most taught African language in the US, the Swahili GPA should not suffer from a lack of applicants. Efforts should be made to make the program transparent to all teachers of Swahili in the US. In turn, the teachers should encourage their students to participate in the program, knowing that every application will be treated equally and fairly through a thorough and transparent screening process. Because the program already has a very informative website, advertising it should not be a problem. This will prevent situations in which all applicants are admitted to the program without being interviewed due to too few applicants. Full participation and support from both teachers and students is essential to the success of the program.

- Teachers have a tendency to recommend students to the program even if they know that their students cannot be successfully articulated in the advanced intensive program. Swahili teachers in the US should be encouraged to provide candid evaluations of their students' abilities, highlighting their strengths and weaknesses in the major areas of language learning, namely, speaking, listening, reading, and writing. This will give the GPA selection committee a clear picture of every applicant's proficiency, leading to more informed decisions. This will reduce the instances of misplacement. The interview will then be used to confirm what the selection committee already knows about a particular applicant based on the candid evaluation provided by the instructor.

- Other forms of testing need to be introduced to supplement the interviews. This can be done by encouraging self-placement, for example, by asking students if they can linguistically survive in different language situations. The responses can be submitted in writing, and the applicants' teachers can administer the questions and submit them to the program director. The program director can also solicit information about the applicants from their teachers. If this is done at a personal level (e.g., by the director personally writing to the teachers to solicit as much information about each applicant as possible), teachers will be more likely to give candid evaluations of their students. This will give a clearer picture of the applicants' proficiency. A written component can be added to the oral interview.

- Applicants' emotional maturity must be addressed. Although it is not a language performance issue, it is directly related to students' success in the program. In some instances, students were emotionally drained, failed to cope with life in a new culture, and wanted to return home. A way is needed to assess applicants' emotional maturity and awareness, understanding, and appreciation of other cultures and the culture of the Swahili people in particular. Swahili instructors who personally know the applicants can be asked to candidly comment on the emotional maturity of their respective applicants.

- The DOE must be encouraged to release the funds and/or approval on time so that advertisements and preparations for the program can be made in a timely manner.

Conclusion

I have shown that study abroad programs that bring together students from different institutions pose serious articulation challenges by using the Swahili GPA as a case study. The situation is dire in African languages because no proficiency guidelines or clearly defined goals have been established that every instructor aspires to achieve. For a program like the Swahili GPA to avoid articulation issues, clear goals are needed that are backed by clear proficiency guidelines and scales for different levels. The National African Language Resource Center (NALRC) at the University of Wisconsin–Madison is developing proficiency guidelines and corresponding scales for African languages. This is a critical step for African languages, and NALRC should be commended for undertaking this important task. While this is being done, African programs like the Swahili GPA can use the ACTFL guidelines and their corresponding scales. The interviews should be designed to test the specific skills that a student who has finished the intermediate-high level is expected to be able to perform. This must be done by an OPI-trained GPA committee member. These interviews must be recorded and made available to another OPI-trained GPA member to rate the applicant. Moreover, the Swahili GPA needs to be better publicized to all students who study Swahili in the more than 40 U.S. universities that offer it.

The Swahili GPA is a great opportunity for our students to experience firsthand the language as it is used by its speakers. Every qualified student must be encouraged to participate in the program, knowing that his/her application is going to be treated fairly and equally using transparent placement parameters. This can be effectively done if the goals of the program and the proficiency guidelines and scales are well outlined. As summarized by the three participants below, the Swahili GPA is invaluable, and students' learning experiences should be enhanced and made as positive as possible. This can be achieved by using effective placement exams that can be administered to all applicants in the US before they are admitted to the program. The participants should not wait until they are in Tanzania to take these placement exams.

> I do think that GPA helped my Swahili skills immensely!! Especially because we were put in a situation where we were forced to speak a lot.

> The GPA helped my Swahili IMMENSELY! I was shocked at the improvements that I made…After a great teacher for my beginner's Swahili, going on Swahili GPA I advanced over a year's worth in language…GPA completely enhanced my abilities in language, as well as in a lot of other ways. It was absolutely invaluable.

> I think the GPA Program helped me significantly. It helped me to not be afraid to speak and to make mistakes. I didn't learn much in the way of grammar, but the constant opportunities to speak Swahili improved my vocabulary and my flow when speaking. I didn't realize how much I had learned until I came back and started taking Swahili classes again. I feel like I can express myself very well in Swahili, although I still need to work on understanding other people when they speak.

References

The American Council for the Teaching of Foreign Languages. (1983, revised 1985). *ACTFL proficiency guidelines*. Hastings-on-Hudson, NY: ACTFL Materials Center.

The American Council for the Teaching of Foreign Languages (1999). *ACTFL proficiency guidelines*. Hastings-on-Hudson, NY: ACTFL Materials Center.

Appendix A: ACTFL Proficiency guidelines in speaking, listening, writing, and reading for students who have completed intermediate level and that Swahili GPA can adopt

Intermediate-high (listening)

Able to sustain understanding over longer stretches of connected discourse on a number of topics pertaining to different times and places; however, understanding is inconsistent due to failure to grasp main ideas and/or details. Thus, while topics do not differ significantly from those of an Advanced level listener, comprehension is less in quantity and poorer in quality.

Intermediate-high (speaking)

Able to handle successfully most uncomplicated communicative tasks and social situations. Can initiate, sustain, and close a general conversation with a number of strategies appropriate to a range of circumstances and topics, but errors are evident. Limited vocabulary still necessitates hesitation and may bring about slightly unexpected circumlocution. There is emerging evidence of connected discourse, particularly for simple narration and/or description. The Intermediate-High speaker can generally be understood even by interlocutors not accustomed to dealing with speakers at this level, but repetition may still be required.

Intermediate-high (reading)

Able to read consistently with full understanding simple connected texts dealing with basic personal and social needs about which the reader has personal interest and/or knowledge. Can get some main ideas and information from texts at the next higher level featuring description and narration. Structural complexity may interfere with comprehension; for example, basic grammatical relations may be misinterpreted and temporal references may rely primarily on lexical items. Has some difficulty with the cohesive factors in discourse, such as matching pronouns with referents. While texts do not differ significantly from those at the Advanced level, comprehension is less consistent. May have to read material several times for understanding.

Intermediate-high (writing)

Able to meet most practical writing needs and limited social demands. Can take notes in some detail on familiar topics and respond in writing to personal questions. Can write simple letters, brief synopses and paraphrases, summaries of biographical data, work and school experience. In those languages relying primarily on content words and time expressions to express time, tense, or aspect, some precision is displayed; where tense and/or aspect is expressed through verbal inflection, forms are produced rather consistently, but not always accurately. An ability to describe and narrate in paragraphs is emerging. Rarely uses basic cohesive elements such as pronominal substitutions or synonyms in written discourse. Writing, though faulty, is generally comprehensible to natives used to the writing of non-natives.

Appendix B: Relationship between levels of ACTFL and ILR proficiency scales

The ILR scale was originally developed by the United States Foreign Service Institute, and is still known as the FSI scale. As shown here, it is a set of descriptions of abilities to communicate in a language. It consists of descriptions of five levels of language proficiency. Swahili GPA participants are suggested to at least be at level 1+ of the ILR proficiency scale. Applicants must also be screened to make sure that they can at least function at the limited working proficiency as outlined in Appendix C.

ILR scale	ACTFL scale	definition
5	Native	Able to speak like an educated native speaker
4+ / 4	Distinguished	Able to speak with a great deal of fluency, grammatical accuracy, precision of vocabulary and idiomaticity
3+ / 3	Superior	Able to speak the language with sufficient structural accuracy and vocabulary to participate effectively in most formal and informal conversations
2+	Advanced Plus	Able to satisfy most work requirements and show some ability to communicate on concrete topics
2	Advanced	Able to satisfy routine social demands and limited work requirements
1+	Intermediate-high	Able to satisfy most survival needs and limited social demands
1	Intermediate-mid	Able to satisfy some survival needs and some limited social demands
1	Intermediate-low	Able to satisfy basic survival needs and minimum courtesy requirements
0+	Novice-high	Able to satisfy immediate needs with learned utterances
0	Novice-mid	Able to operate in only a very limited capacity
0	Novice-low	Unable to function in the spoken language
0	Novice-low	No ability whatsoever in the language

Appendix C: ILR working proficiency for potential Swahili participants

Limited working proficiency is the second level of five in the Interagency Language Roundtable (ILR) scale of language proficiency, formerly called the Foreign Service Institute (FSI) scale. This level is sometimes referred to as S-2 or level 2. A person at this level is described as follows:

- able to satisfy routine social demands and limited work requirements. Can handle with confidence, but not with facility, most social situations including introductions and casual conversations about current events, as well as work, family, and autobiographical information.

- can handle limited work requirements, needing help in handling any complications or difficulties; can get the gist of most conversations on non-technical subjects (i.e., topics which require no specialized knowledge), and has a speaking vocabulary sufficient to respond simply with some circumlocutions

- has an accent which, though often quite faulty, is intelligible, can usually handle elementary constructions quite accurately but does not have thorough or confident control of the grammar

Appendix D: Application forms for the Swahili GPA

APPLICATION
Summer 2005 Intensive Advanced Kiswahili GPA
(June 17–August 9, 2005)

1. **Contact Information**

   _____
   (Last)   (First)   (Middle)

   _____
   (Street Address)

   _____
   (City)   (State)   (Zip Code)

   _____
   (Day Telephone)   (Night Telephone)

   _____
   (Email)

2. **Additional Information**
   Social Security Number: _____
   Date of Birth: _____/_____/_____ mm dd yy
   Gender: _____ male _____ female
   Race: _____
   Citizenship: _____ U.S. citizen
                _____ Permanent Resident with _____ Citizenship

3. **General Background**
   Undergraduate Education
   Institution: _____
   Degree: _____ Date: _____
   Major: _____ Minor: _____

   Graduate Education
   Institution: _____
   Degree: _____ Date: _____
   Major: _____

4. **Kiswahili Language Study:**
   1st year: _____
                   (where)   (when)   (instructor)

   2nd year: _____
                   (where)   (when)   (instructor)

   3rd year: _____
                   (where)   (when)   (instructor)

   4th year: _____
                   (where)   (when)   (instructor)

5. **Statement of purpose:**
   Type below (or on another sheet) your statement of purpose for this program (not more than 500); include the following key aspects:

   a. Your previous academic or professional work and experiences, including course work, non-course educational experiences, teaching or other relevant employment, and future professional career plans that you believe specifically qualify you for a summer Fulbright-Hays Group Projects Abroad. Fellowship to study advanced Kiswahili.

   b. Current academic work & accomplishments highlighting work or research in African Studies, including any publications you have had and awards or honors received including a list of African Studies courses, or courses with substantial African content.

   c. Africa related activities such as service learning and outreach in you community or in Africa, participation in cultural awareness programs (state what you specifically did), other campus Africa related activities.

   d. Professional objectives and the relevance of the intensive GPA program to your career development.

6. **Career commitment:** What are your plans beyond the GPA program?

7. **Previous visits to East Africa:**
   If you have lived or traveled in East Africa for more than a few weeks, indicate where and when that visit occurred and how long you were in that country. If you spent more than 6 months in the country, explain why you did not gain a conversation mastery of Kiswahili as part of that experience

8. **Letters of reference**
   Send the attached copies of the Letter of Reference form to your Kiswahili instructor and to two other people who are well acquainted with your education and abilities. Provide your referees with a stamped envelope addressed to the Director. Give the names and addresses of these referees:

   1. Name: _____ Address: _____
      Position _____ _____

   2. Name: _____ Address: _____
      Position _____ _____

   3. Name: _____ Address: _____
      Position _____ _____

   4. Name: _____ Address: _____
      Position _____ _____

LETTER OF REFERENCE
2005 Intensive Kiswahili Group Project Abroad

To be completed by applicant

Name of Applicant: _____

Optional) I hereby waive my rights to access this confidential recommendation as provided in the Educational Rights and Privacy Act of 1974.

Signature: _____ Date: _____

Instructions to the referee

Please state below your opinion of the applicant's ability to carry on advanced study and capacity to pursue a successful career in his or her field. Also address the student's interpersonal, and group-living skills, and their ability to live in Tanzania. Please include how long you have known the student, known commitments to area studies and future plans in area studies. If the student is a graduating senior, do you have knowledge of their plans for graduate school? Use the reverse side if necessary. If the applicant has signed item (2) above, the confidentiality of this letter of reference is assured.

Among approximately _____ students I have known in this field in recent years, I would rank this applicant in the upper _____%.

Printed Name: _____

Position: _____

Signature: _____ Date: _____

Institution and Address: _____

Please return this evaluation to:

University of Georgia
African Studies Institute
Attn. Ms. Loretta Davenport
321 Holmes/Hunter Building
Athens, GA 30602
Fax: 706-583-0482

Placement Testing For a Large Spanish Program With Separate Tracks for Heritage- and Second-Language Learners

Derek Roff
University of New Mexico

I describe some features of the lower-division Spanish program at a western land-grant state university. I sketch the structure of the instructional program, outline the tests used, and describe the test administration. I delineate perceived problems with the testing and placement program.

Context of the program

The main campus of the university has an undergraduate enrollment of roughly 15,000 students and nearly 10,000 graduate students. Undergraduates make up the vast majority of lower-division Spanish students, but some graduate students are also enrolled. For about a decade, parallel heritage-language and second-language tracks have been available for the first four semesters of instruction. The heritage track has about 300–400 students enrolled, and the second-language track has about 1400–1600. The university uses the semester system, and lower division is four semesters of instruction, 101, 102, 201, and 202. The College of Arts and Sciences has a four-semester language requirement. Most other colleges have no language requirement.

The campus is considered commuter, with a fairly small percentage of campus residents. The student body includes many non-traditional students, with a reported average age of above 30 years. Many students take less than a full class load. Many have full-time jobs and families. A majority of the students come from in-state high schools.

Heritage students are defined for placement purposes as those who grew up hearing Spanish in the home and who have lived or spent substantial time in a Spanish-speaking country. Most of the heritage students are from Hispanic families who have lived in the state for many generations. Few of these have had any formal education in Spanish. Also represented in the heritage classes are relatively recent immigrants, primarily from Mexico and Central America. Some of these have received formal education in Spanish, and some have not.

Roff, D. (2008). Placement testing for a large Spanish program with separate tracks for heritage- and second-language learners. In T. Hudson & M. Clark (Eds.), *Case studies in foreign language placement: Practices and possibilities* (pp. 159–166). Honolulu, HI: University of Hawai'i, National Foreign Language Resource Center.

Two placement tests are used, one for the heritage track, developed in-house, and another for the second-language track, which was purchased from BYU. The tests are taken by more than 2,000 students each year.

Description of the process

All students registering for any undergraduate Spanish classes are required to take a placement exam or show a college transcript with a Spanish class. The decision to make this requirement universal was made largely for practicality. Given the large number of students in the program, we believed that if exceptions were allowed, more time would be spent on handling exceptions than testing. The large number of students tested makes practicality a major factor in all testing decisions. Limiting the required staff and faculty time per student is a necessity.

While many of the students who would self-place into 101 express frustration at being required to take the test, 101 is the most important target group to discriminate for placement. Before the placement exams were adopted, many students with some Spanish skills self-selected into the 101 level. This made instruction very difficult and led to discontent among teachers and students. True beginners were intimidated by the presence of more competent students, while the false beginners tended to be bored and shocked if they received grades lower than an A. An important goal of the placement program is to move false beginners up into a more appropriate class level. If students who rate themselves as beginners were to be exempted from the placement test, we believe that most of the false beginners would opt out of the test and again self-select for 101.

This is a low-stakes testing situation. Students cannot place out of the language requirement, nor can they receive back credit through these tests. Therefore, they have little incentive to score artificially high through artifice. Placing properly into a higher class level will allow a student to finish the language requirement sooner, giving him/her the opportunity to take more electives or to work on a major or minor sooner. The perceived incentive of an easy grade in 101 remains for the false beginner who places artificially low. We attempt to combat that through discussion with examinees of the likelihood of boredom and receiving a lower than expected grade.

Anecdotal evidence from exam proctors indicates that cultural programming may be working to our advantage in this regard. Proctors report that some students state at the outset of the test that they intend to do poorly so that they can get into 101. As they are taking the test, their years of striving to score well on tests seem to take over. When they receive a placement score for 102 or higher, most of these students express acceptance. We speculate that the students' sense of doing better than expected on the test combines with the official confirmation that their Spanish knowledge exceeds the beginning level to overcome the expressed desire for an easy class.

Regulation versus reality

As previously stated, all students are required to take the placement exam before registering for a Spanish class. However, we have no mechanism for directly enforcing this requirement. Students can, in fact, use a computerized system to register for whatever classes they wish, regardless of requirements, regulations, or pre-requisites. Students are informed in the schedule of classes, through their advisors, during orientation, and by other means that they must take the test. Still, a significant fraction either remains unaware or chooses to ignore the requirement.

On the first day of class, all teachers request a placement exam score card from each student. Those who do not have cards must take the test. This leads to many tests given during the first week of class. Some students try passive resistance, attempting to wear down the resolve of the teacher. The department has been successful in insisting that everyone take the test or be disenrolled. We still give a few tests during the second and third weeks, but students are beginning to learn and the student grapevine confirms that students cannot get out of taking the test.

Spanish students who do not take the placement exam before the first week of classes tend to be very resistant to changing levels. (Currently, no other language at this university requires a placement exam.) They protest that they cannot fit different classes into their schedules. We are fortunate to have a large number of sections available, which increases the chances that a student can move up to 102 or higher. However, the need to change registrations at the last minute is a significant problem for students. I suspect that this leads to fewer re-placements than are pedagogically appropriate.

Late examination remains a problem area for the program, which we hope to resolve after the incoming administrative computer system is fully operational. We are promised a lockout in the class registration computer system, which will prevent student registration for a Spanish class until the placement exam has been taken. Coordinating this procedure may be very challenging.

Logistical details

All exams must be taken on campus at the Language Learning Center. This was decided both to allow some level of oversight and because the chosen testing instruments were not available in a web-accessible version at the time of the decision. Most of the exams are administered by work-study students. The center has 90 computers available for student testing, soon to expand to 120. This has always been sufficient. However, during the first week of classes, testing has conflicted with other uses of the Center. This would be prevented if we were able to enforce our requirement that testing occur before registration.

The on-site requirement is difficult for some students, especially those that live outside of the city. This is usually handled through phone conversations with individual students. Students are advised to register for the levels that they feel are most appropriate and to take the exam as soon as they come to campus. We have had few major difficulties over this issue. If the promised future registration lockout system is implemented, this approach will no longer work. Changes in the testing procedure will be required. A web-based test, accessible from off-campus, is the solution currently supported by faculty discussing this question.

Students completing the placement exam receive a score card, referred to as the "orange card." These are collected by teachers on the first day of class. Any student without an orange card must take the exam or get a duplicate card. Students losing their cards has not been a major problem, but it is a time-wasting annoyance for all concerned. The cards are used by the department to track student progress. At the end of a semester, orange cards must be given to successful students, to be given to their teachers on the first day of their next Spanish class. This aspect of the system satisfies no one. The department is looking for more efficient ways to handle the verification of continuing students.

We have no formal mechanism for guiding students to the heritage exam vis-à-vis the second-language exam. Students are told that the heritage exam is for those students who grew up hearing Spanish in the home and those who have lived or spent substantial time in a Spanish-speaking country. They are warned that heritage students who take the second-language exam often place too high, due to their passive knowledge, and then are unsuccessful in the class. We emphasize that the heritage track is well tailored to the needs of heritage speakers, while the regular track may not be a good fit. Each student then selects the exam to take.

This is a problem area. Many students are very hesitant to take the heritage exam. They deny any ability in or knowledge of Spanish. We point out that the 101 level in the heritage track assumes a beginning level, just as does 101 in the second-language track. Still, for a variety of social and cultural reasons, many students for whom the heritage track is intended choose to avoid it. This is a problem that we do not know how to address.

Heritage exam

The heritage exam was developed by two professors in the department more than 15 years ago. Both professors have now left the university. The exam was originally pencil-and-paper, with a listening component played from an audio tape, while the students noted their answers on a paper answer sheet. The test has five parts: listening discrimination, listening comprehension, reading comprehension, grammar, and writing (or essay). About five years ago, the first four sections of the exam were converted to a computer-delivered version, with the essay remaining pencil-and-paper. The main motivation was to simplify administering the exam.

All items are multiple choice except the essay. Each section of the exam is scored separately. The computer provides a raw score for each section. Those scores and the essays are passed on to an evaluator, usually the coordinator of the heritage program or one of the senior heritage-track TAs. That person evaluates the essays, integrates the scores from the other exam sections, and provides each student with a level recommendation and an orange card.

Second-language exam

The second-language exam is the stand-alone version of BYU's Spanish Computer Adaptive Placement Exam (S-CAPE). This exam has question types internally titled grammar, vocabulary, and reading. Students do not see these labels (although test administrators can check them in the student results report), and the question types are mixed in the presentation. All questions are text-based and multiple choice. The adaptive feature of the exam uses a computer algorithm to attempt to find a student's level using relatively few questions from a large question bank. After each correct answer, the student is presented with a more difficult question. Incorrect answers lead to simpler questions. In this way, the student's level can be found fairly quickly.

Beginning students may see only six or eight questions before being given a raw score of 0. This may take as little as five minutes. Most students will be given a raw score after 15–25 questions. This takes an average of about 20 minutes. A student sees the raw scores on his/her computer screen. An exam proctor explains where the raw score falls in the class-level ranges. For example, raw scores of 0 to 237 indicate 101 as the recommended class level. A proctor then fills out a placement-exam score card (orange card) and gives it to the student. The class level ranges were established by testing many sections of our students while we were norming the test.

Perceived problems with the placement testing program

Aspects of the placement testing program have been criticized by members of the faculty and staff. Initiatives have been taken on several occasions to replace aspects of the program. A lack of resources, particularly time, knowledge, and training in choosing or creating alternatives, has been the brake on the initiative to change.

Parts of the administrative system are cumbersome and/or time consuming. Some of the desired data is not easily available. Tracking student progress is difficult. The available data cannot be used flexibly for analysis, comparison, or research. These aspects were not perceived as issues when the program was set up. They now loom large among our desired improvements. I recommend careful consideration of these factors for anyone considering developing a placement system.

The lack of an effective way to distinguish between heritage students and second-language students is an ongoing frustration.

Exam fit

I critically examined each exam for aspects that do not seem to reliably test the factors that we wish to emphasize in our program. A lack of resources has prevented a more careful analysis of this and related questions. We have not been able to track the number of student complaints about placement levels, the number of re-placements, nor the success of placed and re-placed students in comparison to promoted students. We have no data on how closely the test scores correlate to student performances in the classes. All of these factors would be very useful in evaluating the effectiveness of our testing program.

S-CAPE issues

Selecting an exam from an outside vendor has led to some predictable and some unexpected problems. In the norming phase, we tested multiple class sections from each of the lower-division class levels, near the end of a semester. We found that the range of scores among the students in each class was very wide. In fact, some successful students in 101 got scores higher than the average for 201, while some 202 students would not qualify for 102 under our final cut scores. In the end, our norming led us to divide students on a range of scores that is much narrower for each level than the range of scores measured among successful students in those same levels. This is not entirely surprising because the exam is not based on any of the specifics of our curriculum. However, it does call into question our placement decisions.

We do not have a list of the questions in the question bank nor information on the scoring and adaptive algorithm. We cannot check or modify any aspect of the test. We are somewhat concerned that students may be given raw scores after answering as few as six questions. Students are concerned when they answer perhaps 15 questions and are given raw scores of 0. In fact, most students who receive scores of 0 are upset, especially if they have studied Spanish before. They don't mind being placed in 101, but they don't want to be told that their skill levels are "0." A student may be mystified when the person sitting next to him/her is finished within a few minutes, while s/he labors for 20 minutes and get a similar or identical score.

With some frequency, students take the test twice in succession. They may be wishing for higher scores or lower ones. Because this is an adaptive test, they will not necessarily see any of the same questions twice. Successive scores often place students in different class levels and not always in the directions that the students desire. The test seems to be very sensitive to contamination from other Romance languages. A student who has never studied Spanish but has had a few years of French or Italian will be placed in 201 or 202.

We are concerned about the validity of some test items. Faculty members taking the test as an experiment have noted questions that they feel offer two correct answers, no correct answers, or insufficient information for deciding on a correct answer.

Heritage exam issues

Concerns about the heritage exam are of a different nature. The exam is not adaptive, and all of the questions are known and potentially modifiable. The structure of the test is wider than the S-

CAPE exam in that it includes two listening sections. Concerns center around the validity of the questions and of the different sections' success in testing the intended skills.

The first section, listening discrimination, contains 16 similar items. It is intended to test the student's ability to hear differences between similar Spanish phonemes. Each question presents the student with a sentence in Spanish that has one word (or short phrase) missing. Shown below it are three similar alternatives for filling in the blank. Clicking a button allows the students to hear the sentence read by a native speaker. Students can hear the sentence only once, and they are supposed to listen for the missing word and choose the correct answer.

The first item presents the sentence *Tengo que* _____ *las tortillas*. The answer choices are *a ser*, *acer*, and *hacer*. Spanish speakers will observe two problems with this item for testing listening discrimination. First, the correct answer is easily deduced from the grammar of the sentence, so listening to the audio file is not necessary to answer correctly and with certainty. The second problem is that the three alternatives are homophones. In spite of the spelling variations, they are all pronounced the same. Therefore, the sound file provides no information that could be used to make a correct choice via listening discrimination. Distinguishing between homophones using their grammatical functions is, of course, a necessary skill for writing standard Spanish. However, grammar is not the stated goal of this section of the test.

The first problem affects all the questions in this section. Listening is not necessary. The second problem affects half the questions, which present pure homophones. The other eight questions present alternatives that are phonetically distinct but include variants that are phonemically identical for the predominant dialect of Spanish in the area. Dialectical spellings are offered among the alternatives. These factors reward the student with standard academic training and penalize the heritage speaker. I consider this to be counterproductive on a heritage exam.

The second section, listening comprehension, contains five questions. For each question, a sound file presents a narrative, followed by four answer choices. The students see no text for these questions and must work entirely from listening. I see two problems with this section. One is item difficulty. The narratives range from 25 to 35 seconds, with a similar time given to reading the alternatives. They use some vocabulary beyond the 202 level and ask about subtle elements of the narratives. Because of their length and complexity, most of the students tested are guessing on every question. Not only is the level of discourse too high for most of the students being tested, but this length of the audio material makes it a test of memory skills as well as language. Our experience is that the better heritage students correctly answer a couple of the items. High scores (four or five correct) are only attained by those fluent speakers, generally immigrants in our case, who place above the 202 level—that is, beyond the intended scope of the test.

These questions do not discriminate well among the students that we are trying to place into 101-202. This leads to a statistical problem. The questions are so challenging that our 101 and 102 students are guessing randomly. Random guessing will lead to most students getting one or two correct. In fact, doing the math indicates that 68% of those who guess randomly will get one, two, or three correct answers. Some of our 200-level students will be able to understand enough that they won't be guessing randomly. For them, the distractors will actually distract. Getting two or three correct would be the expected result. Thus, we cannot distinguish between the 100-level students, who guess randomly, and the 200-level students, who show some understanding of the questions.

Section 3, reading comprehension, contains nine questions. While some adjustment of the readings and questions would probably improve the reliability, this section is not considered a problem.

Section 4, grammar, contains 17 questions. The first six questions ask the student to fill a gap in a sentence with the proper word or phrase. These questions will be easy for a student who has heard much standard Spanish. They may not discriminate effectively between a student who has great familiarity with dialectical Spanish and a student who knows little Spanish of any sort.

The remaining 11 questions of this section ask the student to identify items within sentences using standard grammatical terminology such as "verb," "adjective," and verb tense names, including "present," "present perfect subjunctive," "present," "future," and "past subjunctive," "imperfect," "future," and "conditional." Many students who can converse comfortably in Spanish get most or all of these wrong. This is not surprising to me because few of our heritage speakers have had any instruction in the terminology of standard grammar (in English or Spanish) nor in identifying Spanish parts of speech and verb tenses. This section of the exam seems to me to discriminate against the skilled heritage speaker. It rewards only academic, structural knowledge and does not evaluate awareness of and facility for producing correct grammatical usage in spoken Spanish. Therefore, this section of the exam does not help us divide the skilled heritage speakers from the less skilled ones.

Section 5 asks the students to write as much as they can in Spanish within 10 minutes. They are asked to write an essay on *La importancia de una educación*. Many students are intimidated by this request and say that they cannot write at all. We try to coax them, and sometimes we find that they can write a great deal. Sometimes helpful is suggesting that they write what they can in Spanish and use English words for any words that they do not know in Spanish. This helps some of the students who are code switchers. Still, the majority lack confidence in their Spanish abilities and are very hesitant to even try. The tremendous variance in student confidence in their writing abilities leads to increased variability in the essay results. I am not sure how we can address that problem. That we have used the same essay topic for more than 15 years opens the door to students preparing in advance. We have not observed a problem in this regard, perhaps due to the low-stakes nature of the test and the predominance of the desire to score lower, rather than higher.

Conclusison

Our experience in test development and administration shows that we were not able to anticipate and address many important issues. Improvements are needed in many areas to improve the efficiency and accuracy of our placement-testing program. The large size of our testing program requires more time-efficient administration in several areas, especially tracking student progress and integrating placed and promoted students in registering for classes each semester. We must find a more effective way of separating heritage students from second-language students. We must improve the reliability of our test items, the overall test design, and the fit of the tests to our curriculum. Finally, our recognition that ongoing placement-test management, analysis, and improvement is a central part of our placement program must be matched by sufficient resource allocation to accomplish these tasks.

The large size of our program confers some advantages, as well. We have large sample sizes and can expect normal distributions. We have an opportunity to do many kinds of analyses yielding results with statistical significance. We can pilot, norm, and see the results of any changes quickly. This gives us some opportunities in developing, improving, and maintaining a placement-exam system that are not available for less commonly taught languages.

Asterix in Testland:
Can a Large Department Resist Tests as a Part of Its Placement System and Get Away With It?

Francoise Sorgen-Goldschmidt
University of California, Berkeley

While hyperactivity might characterize test creation, with a particular focus on placement testing, one large department in a well-known university does not use any placement tests for placing students into the first four semesters of language. A little like Asterix, the Gallic hero whose village managed to resist invasion by the Romans, the French Department at Berkeley has kept a simple and barely quantitative system for placing its students that relies mostly on self-placement according to published guidelines. Are students placed successfully using this method?

Context of the program

This is a traditional program in a more commonly taught language, with multiple sections for first- to fifth-semester courses. The overarching goal is to "prepare students for the kinds of reading, critical analysis, and writing expected in our upper-division courses." See Appendix C for the goals and objectives of the second-year program. The fifth-semester course is the first upper-division course and a prerequisite for all other upper-division courses.[1] Articulation between the different levels (along with textbook discussions) is a frequent subject for informal and formal discussions among the teaching staff and is viewed as more of a problem than potential misplacements.

Two semesters of college-level language study or the equivalent are required. The requirement can be satisfied by three years of high school language study, a score of 550 on an SAT II, or an Advanced Placement (AP) score of 3 or above. Some majors under the aegis of international and area studies, such as peace and conflict studies or political economy of industrial societies, require three or even four years of college-level foreign language instruction.

The goals and objectives of the first-year program (see Appendix B) are primarily presented in terms of proficiency ("an ability to...") and occasionally in terms of knowledge.

---

[1] University of California courses are divided into lower (numbered 1 to 99) and upper divisions (numbered 100 to 199) and graduate courses (numbered 200 to 299).

Sorgen-Goldschmidt, F. (2008). Asterix in Testland: Can a large department resist tests as a part of its placement system and get away with it? In T. Hudson & M. Clark (Eds.), *Case studies in foreign language placement: Practices and possibilities* (pp. 167–175). Honolulu, HI: University of Hawai'i, National Foreign Language Resource Center.

The goals and objectives of the second-year program (see Appendix C) emphasize "the integrated development of speaking, listening, reading, and writing abilities, vocabulary expansion, grammar development, and cultural knowledge." Individual objectives within each skill are described in terms of "ability to..." and include more details and examples than the description of the first-year goals: specification is indeed more crucial in second year, when decisions will be more department-specific than in the more standard introductory year. A memo on the second-year goals specifically addresses the issue of articulation between the first- and second-year programs.

The first four semester courses are taught by graduate student instructors (GSIs) and experienced lecturers; the fifth-semester course is taught by lecturers and professors.

Heritage students are rare. Their situation is comparable to that of students returning from a year-long immersion program abroad, that is, they tend to possess very good to excellent oral/aural skills that are not necessarily matched by their writing abilities. They place into advanced courses (sixth semester and above).

With the development of new options in the University of California's study abroad programs, returnees now include a new cohort of students who have attended shorter programs, non-immersion programs, or programs in English that include language courses.

Description of the placement process

The placement system consists of the following elements:

- *Self-placement according to published guidelines.* The placement process essentially relies on self-placement based on the student's language background. Guidelines (see Appendix A) are published on the department website: they consist of a combination of seat time and AP test scores. One year of high school French is equal to one semester of college French. Generally, students with 1-2 years of high school French go into the first semester at Berkley; 2-3 years, into the second semester; and so forth. Students with AP scores of 3 go into the third semester; scores of 4, the fourth semester; and 5, the fifth semester.

- *Consultation via e-mail or in person* with a lower-division advisor when a student is unsure as to where s/he belongs.

- *One placement exam* determining in-coming students' abilities to start directly in the fifth-semester course, which is the gateway to the other upper-division courses. Only one specific upper-division course can be taken concurrently with this gateway course. The placement exam consists of 35 fill-in-the-blank, non-contextualized sentences testing four grammar points and one essay with a choice of two different topics, both based on the same literary excerpt. Students who take it usually hope to place out of second-year courses, either to avoid having classes every day or because they intend to major in French and do not want to delay their entry into upper-division courses. This is especially the case for transfer students from community colleges.

- *Re-placement when necessary.* The university's rules allow students to add and drop for up to five weeks.

Distinguishing features of the program

All courses are taught in the target language from the very first day (although contemporary textbooks always include some English). This occasionally causes difficulties with placed students, whether from high schools or community colleges, especially concerning grammar explanations.

While different types of texts are discussed and analyzed, including films (see the goals of the second year in Appendix C), the emphasis of the department's advanced courses is on literature.

Practical ideas for placement and future development

Advantages and disadvantages of the current system

The primary placement methods we use are seat time and AP tests. AP tests are more reliable than seat time for first-year students, given the wide variation in the quality (and methodologies used) in high school programs. We occasionally hear the names of teachers who we recognize as regularly producing the best language students. This admittedly is not a scientific method for placement, but experience indicates that when available, it may prove more reliable than seat time. Requiring an AP test is probably not feasible.

Our consensus is that in spite of its extreme simplicity, the system works, with only a few re-placements necessary each semester. This consensus may denote too high a degree of self-satisfaction, but I would argue that the reported success of our placement system could be attributed to a shared consensus on (a good sense of) what the different levels entail. Some of the specific factors that build this shared sense include

- constant communication between lower-division advisors,
- clear directions from lower-division advisors to the lecturers and GSIs whom they supervise,
- a well-structured program whose goals are well defined (see Appendices B and C),
- thorough supervision of GSIs with more attention given to new ones, and
- encouragement of oral participation and early written assignments to allow early re-placement.

With all instructors on the same page and extremely close supervision of new GSIs, an understanding of the program by all insures quick evaluations of whether students are well placed.

A simple placement system can free up time and resources for more urgent priorities. If we accept that we will never teach homogeneous classes and thus accept fairly approximate tools as placement tests whose feasibility is thus high, we free up time to concentrate on the curriculum, assignments, in-class tests and exams, feedback from tests, congruence between curriculum and exams, and so forth; in other words, we can directly help our students learn better in our classes rather than expend energy before they enter them. Drawbacks are discussed below.

Problems with the placement system

The first problem is a dearth of information, that is, we would like to know what is missing due to the absence of a placement test.

For teachers

No placement test means no overall profiles of students before they start their classes: instructors do not know what individual students can and cannot do and know or do not know, which would help them target their teaching toward what needs to be emphasized if course goals are to be met. We are assuming here that promoted students know and can do certain things that they were taught in previous courses, which is not always the case: learning and mastering are not synonymous, and language is no exception to this important difference, often to the chagrin of instructors who are convinced that their teaching of a given point implies that their students "know" it.

For students

In a best-case scenario, a placement test that is congruent with the department's curriculum would give some advance information to students as to the abilities and knowledge they will be working on in their courses. A well-designed placement test can be a formative, summative assessment. A placement test might help reduce the gap between placed and promoted students.

One colleague (the newly arrived coordinator for the second-year program) wrote the following about the shortcomings of self-placement:

> My concerns with self-placement are as follows: since students can place themselves, it is possible that they could take a class that was too easy for them (either out of laziness or without knowing), and this can lead to great disparity in the classroom, and the other students are intimidated. Also, students may be placed at a level that is too difficult, and newer instructors may not be able to recommend a lower class for them in a timely manner (students may drop out of the class and leave French all together, or they may be placed in a lower class rather late.)

She then raised the question of the comparative validity of self-placement and a placement test, wondering whether placement tests insure more reliable placement.

The self-placement could be refined to include questions on the student's ability to do certain tasks, perhaps using an adapted version of the Common European Framework Global Scale from the Council of Europe (2001); but would this more refined process place students differently? This would have some of the advantages of a placement test in terms of giving instructors some sense of their students' abilities in different skills and/or domains and giving students a little preview of what will be expected of them in the program.

The existing placement test, even if it "does the job" of placing students in second- or third-year courses, has many shortcomings (partly due to its age) that reflect badly on our department and might discourage students from taking our courses.

Future developments

The precision of the goals and objectives for the first and second year (in Appendices B and C) seems to be crying out for a placement test that would determine which goals entering students are already meeting; as a colleague from the 2005 NFLRC workshop said: "With such good objectives, you could really build a placement test!" (and probably better class assessments) for at least some of the items in the description of the goals. Using the concepts of Wiggins and McTighe (2005) in *Understanding by Design*,[2] creating a placement test would be a matter of aligning the assessments to the goals, with possible repercussions on the curriculum if it does not truly reflect the goals. The department is not about to develop a placement test for semesters one to five in the near future, but some relatively painless improvements on the current system could be implemented:

---

[2] This seminal book presents "backward design." In backward design, standards are the organizing principle, and standards-aligned assessments drive instructional activities.

- Write a new placement exam for screening readiness for upper-division courses.
- Refine the self-placement (from a self-placement with an optional consultation to a guided self-placement with an optional consultation): Publish the first- and second-year objectives on the departmental website and/or discuss them with students who come for consultation regarding their placement.
- Require individual conferences from students returning from short programs abroad: their abilities will often be different from those of students who have learned most of their French in the United States (at UC Berkeley or elsewhere, including high schools and community colleges.) They need special attention: they are a population we should not discourage from continuing their language studies through improper placement (too high or too low), when they may be among our more enthusiastic learners.

Conclusion

Placement is fairly painless and fairly successful in the Berkley French program. Building placement tests properly involves a great amount of work. Many tests are flawed, for a variety of reasons. One must guard against ever increasing possibilities of cheating. The difficulty of constructing tests may lead to greater reluctance to change or revise the curriculum. Given all these difficulties and the circumstances I have described, I would leave well enough alone for now. I do not believe that a placement test would generate much less misplacement or provide a better way to cope with the problem of students wanting to be placed in lower-level courses to improve their GPAs. Instead of working on producing a state-of-the-art placement test, the department has started to seriously look at articulation issues with a view to smoother transitioning from first to second and from second to third year. It should also reexamine how well assessments reflect what is taught and how it is taught and the uses and misuses of computers for testing. After this reexamination is well on the way to reform, it might be useful and advisable to devise a placement test that is congruent with the clear goals and reexamined assessment methods of the courses.

References

The American Council for the Teaching of Foreign Languages. (1983, revised 1985). *ACTFL proficiency guidelines*. Hastings-on-Hudson, NY: ACTFL Materials Center.

The American Council for the Teaching of Foreign Languages (1999). *ACTFL proficiency guidelines*. Hastings-on-Hudson, NY: ACTFL Materials Center.

Council of Europe. (2001). *Common European framework of reference for languages: Learning, teaching, assessment*. Cambrige: Cambridge University Press.

Wiggins, G., & McTighe, J. (2005). *Understanding by design* (2nd ed.). Alexandria, VA; Association for Supervision and Curriculum Development.

Appendix A: Placement guidelines from catalogue and department website

French 1
If you have never studied French before, or you have taken 2 years or less of high school French, sign up for French 1. Enrollment is limited. If you cannot get in on Tele-BEARS, sign up on the waiting list and attend the course.

French 2
Sign up for French 2 if you have a passing grade in French in a first-semester college French course, or three years of high school French. If you are unsure of your ability to take this course, see one of the department's lower division placement advisors.

French 3
Sign up for French 3 if you have a passing grade in French 2 at UCB or four years of high school French. New students, who have taken second- or third-semester college French courses elsewhere or received an AP Literature score of 3, should also enroll in French 3; they will be screened for appropriate placement during the first week of classes. If you are unsure of your ability to take this course, see one of the department's lower division placement advisors.

French 4
Open to students with a passing grade in French 3 at Berkeley. New students who have taken a fourth-semester college French course elsewhere or received an AP Literature score of 4, should also enroll in French 4. They will be screened for appropriate placement during the first week of classes. If you are unsure of your ability to take this course, see one of the department's lower division placement advisers.

(...)

French 102
Open to students with a B- grade or above in French 4 at UCB. New and transfer students who have taken the equivalent of a third-year college-level French course elsewhere, or who have AP Literature scores of 5, should enroll in French 102 via Tele-BEARS. Students will be informed of screening procedures at the first class meeting.

French 103A-B
Open to students who have completed French 102 at UCB or who are enrolled in that course concurrently. See above information for French 102.

Transfer students intending to declare a major in French should consult the Undergraduate Assistant in French early in their first semester at Berkeley.

Appendix B: Goals of the first-year French language program

Speaking
- ability to describe objects, people, routine activities, and events in the present, past, and future.
- ability to express ideas, thoughts, and feelings in the present, past, and future.
- reasonable fluency.
- knowledge of the sound system—reasonable pronunciation.
- ability to ask questions.
- ability to make maximal use of limited vocabulary (i.e., overcome or compensate for gaps in lexical knowledge).
- ability to participate in a conversation.
- good command of common formulae of greeting, leavetaking, requesting, thanking, and so forth.
- ability to use *tu* and *vous* appropriately.

Writing
- ability to describe objects, people, routine activities, and events in the present, past, and future.
- ability to express ideas, thoughts, and feelings in the present, past, and future.
- good command of French spelling (including accents).
- maximum use of limited vocabulary.
- ability to write compound sentences (use coordination, subordination, etc.).
- ability to use punctuation correctly.
- ability to write a summary of a text.
- ability to use pronouns.
- ability to formulate a simple argument in French.

Reading
- ability to comprehend (gist—not every word) texts at the level required in the beginning of French 3.
- ability to identify a main idea and supporting details.
- ability to summarize a text.
- ability to critically evaluate ideas/information presented in a text.

Listening
- ability to understand directions and other relatively simple French spoken at normal speed.
- ability to capture the gist of orally presented material.
- ability to understand grammar explanations in French.
- ability to understand discussions of reading materials in French.

Appendix C: Goals of the second-year French language program

The curricular goal of the second year program is to prepare students for the kinds of reading, critical analysis, and writing expected in our upper-division courses. The program emphasizes the integrated development of speaking, listening, reading, and writing abilities, vocabulary expansion, grammar development, and cultural knowledge.

Speaking
A major goal is to foster students' abilities to elaborate the expression of their thoughts in speech (moving them towards producing what ACTFL calls "paragraph length" discourse). Speaking is highly integrated with all learning activities and with the development of reading, listening, and cultural awareness. Practice includes focus-on-form activities, discrete-point drills, open-ended communicative activities tied to textbook themes, and discussions of films and readings. Pronunciation is explicitly addressed in class activities.

Listening
A major goal is to foster students' abilities to comprehend not only classroom speech but also "outside" contexts of spoken French (e.g., films and songs). In French 3, students engage in listening comprehension and practical phonetics. For example, students continue to learn the final consonant rules to distinguish masculine and feminine endings and to identify tenses by what they hear. They practice comprehension through dictations and listening activities. These elements are reinforced in class and tested on quizzes and exams. In French 4, brief phonetic reviews are integrated into the class lessons (e.g., the letter "l" day one *il s'appelle*, "r" when reviewing future and conditional tenses, and intonation and rhythm). Listening is tested in French 3, but not in French 4.

Reading
A major goal is to foster students' abilities to read a range of literary and non-literary texts analytically and critically. French 3 moves students from reading for comprehension towards reading for analytical purposes. Students read 1–2 texts per week (newspaper/magazine articles, literary extracts, short stories, fairy tales, fables, songs, and web-based articles on cultural/historical topics). French 4 focuses more intensively on literary texts and their interpretation.

Writing
A major goal is to foster students' abilities to write coherent, well-organized, and grammatically correct essays on both literary and non-literary topics. Students regularly write analytical compositions on texts and films, as well as journals, general and creative writings, and midterm and final exam essays. A process approach is used to teach students systematically what analysis entails (across genres), and students peer-edit and rewrite their essays to improve content, organization, style, and grammar. Writing instruction also includes work on rhetorical organization, thesis statements, introductions, and conclusions. Students are introduced to some canonical French forms of academic discourse, with the idea of expanding their rhetorical repertoire and preparing those who will participate in the Education Abroad Program. French 4 has a particularly intensive focus on argumentative writing methodology.

Vocabulary
Continued expansion of vocabulary in both written and spoken contexts. In French 3, thematic vocabulary lists are presented in each lesson. In both French 3 and 4, vocabulary is developed through reading and discussion. Vocabulary development includes a specific focus on literary terms.

Grammar

French 3 includes an expanded review of key structures presented in the first year, plus the presentation of new tenses such as *plus-que-parfait, conditionnel passé, futur antérieur, passé simple, passé du subjonctif,* and *infinitif passé,* structures such as *faire causatif,* ordering of multiple pronouns, and temporal expressions. Rather than being treated as a separate topic unto itself, grammar is highly integrated into all aspects of the class (reading discussion, exercises, conversation, film viewing, etc.). French 4 continues this grammar review in greater depth. In both French 3 and 4, the emphasis is on solid mastery in spoken and written use of major tenses and structures, rather than a dispersed familiarity with all structures including minor exceptions. Grammar is reviewed at home following inductive presentation in class.

Culture

In French 3, each lesson is grounded in a cultural aspect of France or the francophone world. High-interest topics engage the students in discussions (the French educational system, immigration, transportation, TV and film, folk traditions, family structures, and the European Union). In French 3 and 4, literary texts and films are linked thematically (childhood and school days, colonization, reinterpretation of traditions, and exploration of gender roles and sexual identity).

Articulation with French 2

Because students in the past sometimes complained that the "jump" to literary analysis in French 3 was too abrupt and too exclusively literary, French 3 has been modified to have a broader appeal and smoother articulation with the first-year program by including a wider variety of text types, by diversifying the kinds of writing done, and by approaching analysis from a broad semiotic perspective.

The Challenge of Placing Hindi Heritage Students

Rakesh Ranjan
Emory University, GA

Hindi is a less commonly taught language. It has been taught in the United States for the last thirty years. It used to attract graduate students from social sciences who wanted to study about India. However, in recent years, many universities have started teaching Hindi on the demand of student organizations, and Hindi has shown a substantial growth in enrollment at the undergraduate level. One of the main reasons for this high number is the enrollment of students of South Asian origin, that is, heritage learners. This population has changed the characteristics and dynamics of Hindi classes by introducing new challenges. What are the new challenges? How are these problems different from the problems of other heritage learners? To answer these questions, understanding the linguistic complexity of South Asia/India is very important.

Multilingualism in South Asia

South Asia is a land of staggering linguistic and cultural diversity. Four language families 22 official languages and hundreds of other languages and dialects make the linguistic spectrum in India very complicated. The four language families and 22 official languages are as follows:

Indo-Aryan (15): Assamese, Bengali, Dogri, Gujarati, Hindi, Kashmiri, Konkani, Maithili, Marathi, Nepali, Oriya, Punjabi, Sanskrit, Sindhi, Urdu

Dravidian (4): Kannada, Malayalam, Tamil, Telugu

Tibetan-Burman (3): Bodo, Manipuri, Santhali

Austro-Asiatic (2): Kharia, Khasi

Hindi is one of the 22 official languages. Though spoken in northern India, it is the most widely spoken and understood language throughout India. Hindi is written in the Devanagari script, which is also used to write Sanskrit, Marathi, and Nepali. Modern Standard Hindi has developed from Khari Boli, a dialect of Hindi spoken around Delhi and Meerut. Hindi literature consists of all genres, such as poetry, drama, short stories, novels, and essays. Urdu,[1] the official

---

[1] Urdu is widely used in the Hindi belt and has an official status in the states of Bihar and Uttar Pradesh.

Ranjan, R. (2008). The challenge of placing Hindi heritage students. In T. Hudson & M. Clark (Eds.), *Case studies in foreign language placement: Practices and possibilities* (pp. 177–185). Honolulu, HI: University of Hawai'i, National Foreign Language Resource Center.

language of Pakistan, is also spoken in areas where Hindi is spoken. Hindi and Urdu share the same grammar and conversational vocabulary and expressions, though they use different scripts.

Hindi is the primary language of entertainment, media, and journalism in India. The Bollywood film industry – the largest in the world with about 800 movies every year– together with Hindi songs have particularly popularized Hindi at home and abroad. Hindi movies, songs, and modern pop music are highly popular with Indians settled around the world, including those in America, Canada, England, Fiji, Mauritius, Surinam, Trinidad, parts of Africa, and many countries of the Middle East. Singing and dancing to the tunes of Hindi songs are the most popular parts of cultural programs of the linguistically diverse Indian communities in diaspora.

While Hindi is used as a medium of instruction in schools in the northern states of Bihar, Haryana, Madhya Pradesh, Rajasthan, and Uttar Pradesh, other Indo-Aryan languages are used in other regions; for example, Gujarati is used Gujarat, Marathi in Maharastra, and Punjabi in Punjab. Among the Dravidian languages, Kannada is used in Karnataka, Malayalam in Kerala, Tamil in Tamil Nadu, and Telugu in Andhra Pradesh. Hindi is taught as a second language in the Indo-Aryan area, but it is not compulsory to study it in the Dravidian area. However, Hindi movies are very popular in this region, too. These linguistic regions are culturally diverse. Different festivals are celebrated in different regions in India.

Heritage-learner issues

Who are heritage learners of Hindi?

Indian communities inherit the same linguistic and cultural diversity in diaspora. The linguistic composition of these Indian communities varies. The main linguistic groups in the Indian communities in the USA are Gujarati, Hindi, Punjabi, Tamil, and Telugu speakers. Speakers of Bengali, Marathi, and Malayalam constitute a part of the Indian communities, too.

Hindi is taught as a foreign language at many university campuses in the United States. Students learn it for academic, business, and/or personal reasons, though the majority of undergraduates of South Asian/Indian origin want to learn Hindi to explore their cultural roots. Their linguistic and cultural backgrounds are diverse, but Hindi has emerged as the most commonly taught language among the South Asian languages. Hindi has also become a mark of Indian identity. Does this Hindi learners' population form one homogeneous group as Hindi heritage learners in diaspora or must it be subdivided? The linguistic and cultural diversity of this population makes it hard to believe that it could be uniform.

Categories of Hindi heritage learners

If we consider their linguistic backgrounds, we may divide the learners into the following four groups:

Group A: These learners have learned Hindi formally either in India or in the United States. They have speaking, listening, reading, and writing skills, and they can use the language fluently. They may not know grammatical terms, but they use Hindi accurately. They want to learn Hindi to improve their literary skills.

Group B: These learners have backgrounds in Hindi from using it with their parents/grandparents, but they have never learned Hindi formally. Although they can speak and understand Hindi well, they cannot write or read it. Groups A and B share the same cultural background.

Group C: These learners have backgrounds of other Indo-Aryan languages like Gujarati, Punjabi, Marathi, and Bengali. These languages are considered cognate languages for Hindi learners because they share the grammatical features of Hindi and have some common vocabulary. These learners cannot speak Hindi but may understand simple constructions. They share some cultural features with groups A and B, and most of them have grown up watching Hindi movies.

Group D: These learners do not have any background in Hindi or any Indo-Aryan languages. The languages they know are considered non-cognate languages. They may have speaking and listening skills in Dravidian or other Indian/South Asian languages but not in Indo-Aryan languages. They may share some cultural background with groups A, B, and C, and these learners may have grown up watching Hindi movies.

Hindi program at Emory

Structure of the program

The Hindi program at Emory is very young. South Asian student organizations increasingly demanded the introduction of Hindi at Emory in the mid 1990s. The administration finally introduced Hindi in 1996 by hiring a part-time teacher. In 1999, a full-time teacher was hired because the number of students was increasing. Emory also introduced a one-year language requirement as a part of its general educational requirement. Students of South Asian origin make up 16% of the Emory population, and they constitute the majority in Hindi classes. The Hindi program offers the following courses:

Elementary Hindi (101 & 102): Two sections (18 students in each)

Intermediate Hindi (201 & 202): One section (15 students)

Advanced Hindi (301 & 302): One section (10 students)

Directed Study in Hindi (375)

The Department offers a minor in Hindi, which requires four courses beyond Elementary Hindi (Hindi 101 & 102).

The linguistic background of Hindi students at Emory is presented in Table 1.

Table 1. Hindi students at Emory, 2002–2004

linguistic background	2002 (%)	2003 (%)	2004 (%)	3-yr. total
Elementary (101–102)				
Gujarati	9 (50.0)	7 (38.8)	7 (38.8)	23
Telugu	3 (16.6)	3 (16.6)	2 (11.1)	8
Punjabi	2 (11.1)	2 (11.1)	3 (16.6)	7
Hindi	2 (11.1)	2 (11.1)	3 (16.6)	7
true beginner	2 (11.1)	3 (16.6)	3 (16.6)	8
others (Marathi)	0	1 (5.5)	0 (0.0)	1
total	18	18	18	54

cont...

Table 1. Hindi students at Emory, 2002–2004 (cont.)

linguistic background	2002 (%)	2003 (%)	2004 (%)	3-yr. total
Intermediate (201–202)				
heritage	9 (81.8)	7 (87.5)	10 (83.3)	26
true learner	2 (18.2)	1 (12.5)	2 (16.7)	5
total	11	8	12	31
Advanced (301–302)				
heritage	6 (75.0)	0 (0.0)	3 (75.0)	9
true learner	2 (25.0)	2 (100.0)	1 (25.0)	5
total	8	2	4	14

The diversity of the linguistic backgrounds shown in Table 1 indicates the heterogeneity of Hindi classes, particularly at the elementary level. The elementary class includes not only heritage learners but true beginners and speakers of non-cognate languages. The heritage-learner group is also heterogeneous because it includes speakers of Hindi and other cognate languages.

Present placement assessment

Hindi students form a very heterogeneous group, and unfortunately, we have no proper placement test. In fact, no placement test is available for Hindi, and instructors use their own methods to place the students. Placement in the Hindi program at Emory is based on a conversation. The Hindi instructor talks to a student in person, and based on the proficiency level, s/he is told to join Elementary or Intermediate Hindi. If the student has formally learned Hindi, s/he is placed at the intermediate or advanced level. Heritage learners do not have a separate class.

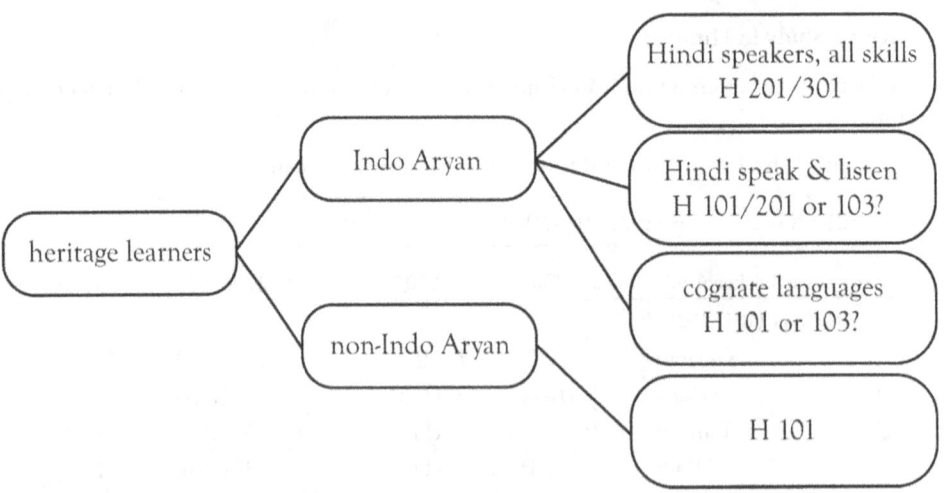

Figure 1. Heritage learner placement: H 101=Elementary Hindi, H 103=Accelerated Hindi (a proposed course), H 201=Intermediate Hindi, H 301=Advanced Hindi

Is the placement system working well at Emory without a placement test? Placing true beginners and non-cognate speakers in Elementary Hindi 101 seems logical, and it works out well.

Students who can speak, understand, read, and write are placed into the intermediate or advanced class depending on the level of their proficiency. This looks good. However, what happens to the students who speak and understand Hindi but have no literary skills? How are speakers of cognate languages placed? Figure 1 shows the placement of heritage learners.

The placement of speakers of Hindi and cognate languages is the main problem. Should these students be allowed to join Elementary Hindi 101 with true beginners, or should they be placed at the intermediate level with students who know to read and write Hindi well? Do we need to start a separate class like Accelerated Hindi especially for those Hindi learners who can speak and understand? This class may include the Hindi learners who can speak cognate languages like Gujarati, Punjabi, Marathi, or Bengali. In the absence of a proper student language profile and a proper placement test, placing students is very difficult.

What needs to be done? In a program like Hindi at Emory that has an extremely diverse population, developing a systemic placement assessment is important. We have no documentation at present, and it must begin as soon as possible. The following must be developed to ensure proper assessment: a student language profile, a placement test, and a new course for heritage learners.

Keeping a profile of each student's language proficiency is useful. An example form is presented in Appendix A.

In terms of developing a placement test, we recently became involved in developing a placement test for Hindi through the South Asian Languages Resource Center using the Standards-based Measurement of Proficiency (STAMP) with the help of the Center of Applied Second Language Studies at the University of Oregon, Eugene. STAMP is a test based on a set of standards consistent with the American Council for the Teaching of Foreign Languages (ACTFL) Proficiency Guidelines (American Council for the Teaching of Foreign Languages, 1986). It uses computer-adaptive testing technology to identify students' proficiencies from novice-low to intermediate-high. It is already in use for online reading and writing assessment for French, German, Japanese, Spanish, and Turkish. The reading assessment for Hindi is in an early stage. Appendix B gives the benchmark for the reading items.

Finally, because of the high percentage of heritage learners in the Hindi classes, the department has been offering a new course, Accelerated Hindi 103, starting in the spring semester of 2006. This is a fast-paced, one-semester course for learners who have prior exposure to Hindi. That is, the learners are able to understand basic conversational Hindi and may be able to express themselves in survival situations but have minimal or no literacy skills. In the first part, students build up their listening and speaking skills, acquire basic reading and writing skills, and enrich their vocabularies. By the end of the semester, students can read and discuss straightforward written texts on general topics found in newspapers and magazines with the help of a dictionary. Students develop explicit knowledge of grammar and sociocultural rules that help them monitor their own language performances. Students go to Intermediate Hindi 201 after completing this course.

Conclusion

The increase in enrollment of Hindi students clearly shows a growth of Hindi studies. However, Hindi studies are also clearly facing new challenges. These new challenges are not only in terms of using new technology but also from the high enrollment of heritage learners. I have discussed the complexities related to Hindi heritage students and the challenges that have developed in a new situation. Though Hindi teaching lacks a standard curriculum, textbooks, placement tests, and other tools, the growing interest of heritage learners has drawn the attention of instructors, administrators, and institutions, and scholars have begun discussing relevant issues. I have discussed the heterogeneity of Hindi heritage learners to understand the complexities of placing them and the steps that have been taken to face these new challenges.

Reference

American Council for the Teaching of Foreign Languages. (1986). *ACTFL Proficiency Guidelines.* Hastings-on-Hudson: ACTFL Materials Center.

Appendix A: Student language profile

Hindi Language Program
Department of Middle Eastern and South Asian Studies
Emory University

You are violating the Emory University Honor Code (Article 4 (d)) if you "intentionally give false information to professors or instructors for the purpose of gaining academic advantage." By not providing full information regarding your Hindi education and/or by placing yourself in a Hindi course that is not at your level, you are violating the Honor Code.

1. Name _____
2. Emory Student ID _____
3. Major _____ Minor _____
4. Telephone _____
5. E-mail ID _____
6. Address: _____

Please provide information about your proficiency levels in Indian languages (mark the appropriate columns):

language	speaking			listening			reading			writing		
	nov*	mid	high	nov	mid	high	nov	mid	high	nov	mid	high
Hindi												
_____												
_____												
_____												

* nov (novice): minimal ability; mid: some fluency; high: very fluent

8. Please provide the following information regarding your previous Hindi education:

type of program	name & location of school/program	duration of program	hours per week
elementary school			
middle school			
high school			
Hindi school			

9. What language(s) do you use

   a. with your grandparents? _____
   b. with your parents? _____
   c. while visiting India _____

10. Have you had other opportunities to speak or listen to Hindi or any other Indian language?

11. What are your reasons for studying Hindi? _____

12. Please mark the items that you can do with some effort:
    - ☐ Understand some Hindi while watching a Hindi movie
    - ☐ Understand some prayers during services
    - ☐ Read prayers
    - ☐ Recite prayers/Hindi songs
    - ☐ Initiate simple conversations with your family members or friends
    - ☐ List some simple words/kinship terms that you can write in Hindi.

_____   _____
            (signature)   (date)

Appendix B: Hindi literacy benchmarks for reading assessment

Level 1 Novice-low	self calendar classroom family season/weather pets/animals food	signs (traffic, commercial) lists of words and phrases schedules menus	–skim for gist –extract details
Level 2 Novice-mid	clothing time friends home daily routines places	advertisements simple notes and messages labels phonebook instructions/directions	–skim for gist –extract details
Level 3 Novice-high	community leisure/activities school stores/shopping festivals	brochures maps simple rhymes announcements invitations	–skim for gist –extract details
Level 4 Intermediate-low	health occupations travel/vacations transportation	postcards letters simple narratives aphorisms and proverbs descriptions of persons, places, and things	–skim for gist –extract details
Level 5 Intermediate-mid	future plans religion history political system geography career-related fields	simple literary texts simple non-fiction texts simple magazine and newspaper articles simple poems	–skim for gist –extract details
Level 6 Intermediate-high	(no new topics)	literary texts academic texts magazine and newspaper articles poems	–skim for gist –extract details

A Case Study of Thai Language Program Placement Testing: Incorporating News Articles Into the Thai Placement Process

Chintana Y. Takahashi
University of Hawai'i at Mānoa

Each language program has its own explicit standards to meet. For the Thai language program at the University of Hawai'i at Mānoa (UHM), the goal is for students to become literate users of the Thai language. Hence, emphasis is placed on acquiring reading and writing proficiency. Creating a syllabus that will lead to a certain level of proficiency requires that students start at a comparable ability level within each course, and therefore, effective placement screening is necessary. The Thai language program has traditionally been small, which has allowed instructors to conduct placement testing individually. Candidates come in for oral interviews, read from a chapter of the textbook or material used for instruction at different levels, and write short paragraphs in Thai to summarize the content. The assessment is subjective and based entirely on the instructor's impression of the candidate.

I propose a uniform reading and writing placement test using online Thai news articles that will screen for students whose proficiency is above Level 200. I selected this particular level to reflect the real need for students to develop high levels of reading and writing competency to do research in their chosen graduate fields. Furthermore, a number of graduate students required to take the Thai language at the 300 level (and above) typically have had instruction from a variety of institutions, used different textbooks, and gone through different curricula.

Context of the program

The Thai language program at UHM offers courses through the Department of Hawaiian and Indo-Pacific Languages and Literatures, in the College of Languages, Linguistics and Literatures. The department contains other programs in Southeast Asian languages: Cambodian (Khmer), Indonesian, Ilocano, Filipino (Tagalog), and Vietnamese; Pacific Islander languages: Hawaiian, Maori, Samoan, Tahitian, and Tongan; and Arabic and Sanskrit. In addition to languages, courses are offered related to various aspects of these languages by the department and other departments and are coordinated by the Center for Southeast Asian Studies in the School of Hawaiian and Indo-Pacific Studies.

Takahashi, C. (2008). A case study of Thai language program placement testing: Incorporating news articles into the Thai placement process. In T. Hudson & M. Clark (Eds.), *Case studies in foreign language placement: Practices and possibilities* (pp. 187–195). Honolulu, HI: University of Hawai'i, National Foreign Language Resource Center.

Most departments at UHM require two years of foreign language study for undergraduate programs, which generates a demand for foreign languages. Students who take Thai can be divided into three groups. The members of the first group usually enroll in Thai out of curiosity, necessity, or simplicity. Students who have visited Thailand, have one or two Thai parents, or want to stay away from the more commonly studied Chinese, French, Japanese, and Spanish make up the majority of students in the beginning level. A number of these students have some oral proficiency but no reading or writing knowledge, while the remaining students are total novices.

However, in fall 2006, a Thai 107 course was created for heritage Thai students to eliminate the disparity of oral proficiencies in entry-level Thai classes. In years past, a few heritage Thai students always enrolled in the beginning class, which inevitably caused some easiness among non-Thai-speaking students. However, the number was too small at that time to warrant a separate class.

The second group of students enrolling in Thai consists mostly of graduate students who must fulfill the 300- and 400-level Thai language requirement and on rare occasions, a small number of undergraduates who are too advanced for the first two levels because they are heritage Thai learners or have spent some years growing up in Thailand due to their parents' professions. Within the graduate student population are military officers, who are often assigned to study Thai for their specialized field, and students who have returned from Thailand after spending two years on religious missions.

The third group of students consists of those who know some Thai and think that studying it will be the easiest way to fulfill the language requirement. Members of this group, more often than others, are the first to drop the course when faced with challenges beyond their expectations.

About the language

Thai is the official language of Thailand, a country on the Southeast Asian mainland, sharing borders with Malaysia, Myanmar, Laos, and Cambodia. Over 63 million people throughout Thailand speak the language; some do so in addition to other regional Thai dialects. Thai belongs in the Tai language family, which includes languages spoken in Assam, northern Burma, Laos, Northern Vietnam, and the Chinese provinces of Yunnan, Guizhou (Kweichow), and Guangxi (Kwangsi).

The Thai language is tonal and alphabetic. Thai script was developed in 1283 A.D. The typical structure of a Thai sentence contains a subject, a verb, and an object, similar to that of Chinese. The Thai language does not have inflections, subject-verb agreement, or verb conjugations. Tense distinctions in sentences are determined by either context or adverbs and expressions of time. Loan words, particularly those derived from Pali-Sanskrit languages and to a lesser extent, Chinese, have been integrated into the Thai vocabulary. The Thai language taught at UHM is standard Thai, spoken in the central region of Thailand.

Degrees and language certificate program[1]

Students who wish to earn a BA in interdisciplinary studies with a concentration in Thai must consult advisors from the Interdisciplinary Studies Program and Department of Hawaiian and Indo-Pacific Languages and Literatures to develop a program of interest. A minimum of 36

---

[1] More information on the program can be found at http://www.hawaii.edu/thai/.

credits of courses on Thai language and culture are required beyond the 200 level of the Thai language courses.

Students can acquire a certificate for Thai by earning 15 credits from Thai language or literature courses. Of the 15 credits, 6 must be from Thai language courses beyond the 200 level. In addition, a student must maintain a minimum GPA of 3.0 for all courses required for the certificate.

Description of the process

The Thai language program offers four levels of instruction and other special courses that are tailored to the interests of students, such as Thai 415: Thai in the Media. Each level starts in the fall and ends in the spring. Beginners are not allowed to enroll in Thai 102 in the spring because it is a continuation of the instruction in the fall. Students who have some knowledge of Thai must contact instructors before the start of the semester to be tested for placement. Students are recommended to self-assess by filling out a form on the UHM Thai language program website.

Students may use elementary and intermediate-level Thai courses, Thai 101-202, to fulfill the foreign language requirement for all bachelor's degrees at UHM. Thai 201-202, 301-302, and 401-402 are designated as "writing intensive" courses, which satisfy the writing-intensive focus requirement for the UHM undergraduate core curriculum. The two highest-level courses being offered regularly are Thai 415, Thai Language in the Media, and Thai 461, Readings in Thai Literature.

At UHM, students are expected to master Thai script in the beginning level courses, Thai 101 and Thai 107. Incoming students who have no reading or writing proficiency must be in these classes regardless of their speaking fluency. After this level, students are promoted to the levels appropriate to their reading and writing abilities. Oftentimes, these students are placed in Thai 202 so that they can learn reading strategies and writing skills. Real beginners who join the program from Thai 101 are usually promoted systematically.

Starting from the 200 level, all Thai courses are considered to be writing intensive. Undergraduate students who take these courses receive both language and writing credits as required by the UH core curriculum. Students are taught reading strategies and are expected to write essays and keep weekly journals. At the conclusion of Thai 202, students are assumed to be at the intermediate-low level. Most students leave the program after having fulfilled the two-year foreign language requirement. Those who continue on to the upper levels do so because they need to acquire skills. Therefore, they are highly motivated to master the language.

Students in the third and fourth levels are usually of varied backgrounds, and instructors try to accommodate their abilities and needs. With limited resources, ensuring that all students can make progress at the same rate is vital.

In addition to the four regular levels of language instruction at UHM, students who are very advanced can take specially designed courses, while others who need to move to the upper level as soon as possible may be able to enroll in a variety of language programs at universities in Thailand during the summer months.

The Thai language proficiency standards for listening, speaking, reading, and writing are a series of modifications of the American Council for the Teaching of Foreign Languages (ACTFL) guidelines. Member universities of the Consortium for Advanced Study of Thai[2] (CAST) held a meeting in Bangkok in August 2003 to review the ACTFL criteria and tailored those criteria to suit the features of the Thai language. See the Appendix for details of the guidelines.

Students who wish to be placed in the 300 level should be able to read at the intermediate-mid/high or advanced level and write at the intermediate-mid or advanced level, as defined in the Appendix.

Students who can read and write at the advanced-plus or superior levels will be placed in the 400 level.

The following are the objectives for each level of the Thai courses and two 400-level courses at UHM.

Thai 100

At the end of the semester, students are expected to be able to

- carry on a conversation in Thai using vocabulary and structural patterns in *Thai Language and Culture for Beginners* (Hoonchamlong, 2007) and appropriate language introduced in class;
- read simple phrases and sentences written in Thai script with correct pronunciation; and
- take simple dictation of words, phrases, and sentences using the Thai writing system.

Thai 200

At the end of the semester, students are expected to be able to

- converse with accurate pronunciation and sufficient fluency about passages and stories read;
- answer questions based on passages and dialogues read or recorded on tapes;
- explain and describe, orally and in writing, events, places, objects, and ideas; and
- write in Thai script answers based on the stories read, simple original narratives, descriptive paragraphs, and short essays.

Thai 300

At the end of the semester, students are expected to be able to

- read and express, orally and in writing, their comprehension of passages read;
- summarize, in Thai script and orally, what was read;
- discuss and comment on the topics of materials read, orally and in writing; and
- write in Thai script original short narratives and expository essays.

Thai 400

At the end of the semester, students are expected to be able to

---

[2] Consortium members: Arizona State University; University of California, Berkeley; University of California, Los Angeles; Cornell University; University of Hawai'i; University of Michigan; Northern Illinois University; Ohio University; University of Washington; University of Wisconsin; and Yale University.

- read and express, orally and in writing, their comprehension of passages read;
- summarize, in Thai script and orally, what was read;
- discuss and comment on the topics of materials read, orally and in writing; and
- write academic expository essays in Thai script.

Thai 415

By the end of the semester, students are expected to be able to

- read and express, orally and in writing, their comprehension of print media of various types and genres;
- view and/or listen to and express, orally and in writing, their comprehension of various types and genres of broadcast news items or programs;
- summarize, in Thai script and orally, information from media introduced in class; and
- discuss and comment on the topics of materials covered.

Thai 461

Throughout the course, students are expected to be able to

- understand, summarize, and evaluate selected works in Thai contemporary prose literature;
- in oral and written Thai, discuss, critique, and express opinions on stories read;
- write critical reviews (in Thai) of stories read; and
- give oral presentations on stories read.

The placement process in the 100 and 200 levels does not pose a major problem because students are still learning to read and write and hence have limited abilities. However, after one year of writing at the 200 level, students begin to show different aptitude levels.

Another reason for administering a well-planned placement test after the 200 level is the opportunity for students to win fellowships to study advanced Thai in Chiang Mai, Thailand. This fellowship, the Advanced Study of Thai in Chiang Mai (AST Program), is administered by the University of Washington and given annually to students who can pass a telephone oral proficiency interview after submitting a written essay in Thai. The program is intensive and requires a high level of reading and writing proficiency. Students who have taken a placement test will be able to gauge their readiness to apply for this fellowship.

The ultimate goal in Thai language instruction at UHM beyond the 200 level is to improve the reading and writing proficiency of students. An advanced reading ability in Thai is a prerequisite. The writing ability of students should improve after going through extensive readings in class. Therefore, placing students in the right level after the 200 level is very important.

Distinguishing features of the program

The Thai language and Thai related studies are offered in several departments at UHM. However, Thai resources and instructors are scarce. Thai studies are generally a part of Southeast Asian Studies. Hence, no faculty specialize in Thai *per se*. Students who are doing graduate work in Southeast Asian programs often consult their Thai language instructors about resources in their respective fields. For this reason, in an attempt to assist these students, the curriculum for the upper-level Thai classes is tailored toward providing knowledge of the Thai language in fields such as history, literature, and anthropology. To design a class in such a manner for a small group of varied graduate students, teachers ascertain that all students meet the standard requirements of reading and writing proficiencies. How can one determine what level a certain student belongs to when an e-mail such as this arrives?

> I am a prospective graduate student to the MA Southeast Asian Studies program starting this fall. I was encouraged to contact you regarding my previous experience with Thai and future language goals.
>
> I have obtained fourth year Thai as an undergraduate student. My language competency was gained though (sic) a variety of both domestic and overseas experiences. Altogether, I have spent almost 3 years in Thailand as a student, intern and tourist.
>
> My first and second year Thai was studied at Payap University and my third year was obtained though (sic) the SEASSI program at the University of Wisconsin-Madison. Finally, I completed my fourth year Thai though (sic) the AST program at Chiang Mai University. I have also studied abroad though (sic) CIEE at Khon Kaen University...
>
> My biggest weakness is writing...

The above student is not an exception but rather the norm. Each year, the Thai language program receives similar e-mails and telephone calls inquiring about the possibility of entering the program from the 300 level and up. The students are as varied in their past training as they are in their language learning styles. To complicate the situation, military officers who attend UHM graduate schools may have learned Thai at the Defense Language Institute in Monterey or the Thai Military Officer Institute in Thailand, whose curricula are different from those of college language programs.

In general, students at this level tend to underestimate their abilities, resulting in misplacement because of inadequate scrutiny of their reading and writing proficiencies. With resources as limited as they are, meeting the needs of these students is a challenge.

As mentioned above, from the 300 level and up, courses are tailored to meet the needs of students. In the 300 level, students must acquire the skills to read a variety of Thai fonts and words with Indic roots, that is, Pali-Sanskrit words and royal language. For this reason, reading materials are selected from various fields, topics, and sources to increase the vocabularies of students.

In the 400 level and beyond, students are expected to acquire Thai reading proficiency equivalent to that gained in a Thai post-secondary education. The materials used for this level are similar to those used by students in Thai universities.

Practical ideas for placement and future development

Because reading and writing proficiency is the most important aspect of language learning in the Thai department, a placement test that requires candidates to exhibit reading strategies and writing ability will encompass the expected knowledge acquired through the completion of the 200 level courses.

Typically, a comprehension test is administered to students to test their reading knowledge of target languages, but in doing so, their integrative writing ability is reduced to finding information in a reading passage. A more complex task of reading and summarizing selected prepared passages or synthesizing multiple texts will enable students to demonstrate their comprehensive language competence. Multiple texts designed to assess knowledge of structures and vocabulary must be developed.

One obvious problem that will arise from using a summary task and synthesizing texts for a placement test is rating. How can summaries and synthesized writing be rated without being subjective and biased?

One solution is to lay down explicit guidelines for raters. What exactly must the rater look for in the finished product? In the same manner, the instructions for candidates must stipulate what the rater will expect to see in the work.

The following guidelines will help to minimize foreseeable problems for raters.

The writing must

- contain a stipulated number of main ideas,
- be logically organized into paragraphs, and
- be of an appropriate length.

The test candidates should be instructed as follows.

Their text must

- include all the main ideas,
- present the ideas in an essay format (cutting and pasting text is unacceptable), and
- be of the specified length.

A problem that stems from relying completely on online news is that news articles do not contain sufficient targeted vocabulary or idiomatic expressions. For this reason, it may be necessary to implement the assessment using material with content specific to different graduate programs.

Conclusion

For a small program like the Thai language program at UHM, developing a placement test may seem like a waste of time and effort. However, in developing a good placement test and using it regardless of the number of students, instructors will be able to pinpoint and focus on the skills that need work. At the same time, students who do not make the cut can be advised to attend programs that are available in Thailand in the summer and can be retested to join the program during the academic year. A reading and writing placement test will show the importance the UHM Thai language program places on literacy in the Thai language.

References

Hoonchamlong, Y. (2007). *Thai language and culture for beginners, volume 1.* [text + DVD] Honolulu: University of Hawai'i Press.

Appendix: Thai proficiency guidelines[3]

Reading

Intermediate-high

Able to read consistently with full understanding simple connected texts dealing with basic personal and social needs about which the reader has personal interest and/or knowledge. Can get some main ideas and information from texts at the next higher level featuring descriptions and narrations. Structural complexity may interfere with comprehension; for example, basic grammatical relations may be misinterpreted, and temporal references may rely primarily on lexical items. Has some difficulty with the cohesive factors in discourse, such as matching pronouns with referents. While texts do not differ significantly from those at the advanced level, comprehension is less consistent. May have to read material several times for understanding.

Advanced

Able to read somewhat longer prose of several paragraphs in length, particularly if presented with a clear underlying structure. The prose is predominantly in familiar sentence patterns. Reader gets the main ideas and facts and misses some details. Comprehension derives not only from situational and subject matter knowledge but from increasing control of the language. Texts at this level include descriptions and narrations such as simple short stories, news items, bibliographical information, social notices, personal correspondence, routine business letters, and simple technical material written for a general reader.

Advanced plus

Able to follow essential points of written discourse at the superior level in areas of special interest or knowledge. Able to understand parts of texts that are conceptually abstract and linguistically complex and/or texts that treat unfamiliar topics and situations as well as some texts that involve aspects of the culture. Able to comprehend the facts to make appropriate inferences. An emerging awareness of the aesthetic properties of the language and of its literary styles permits comprehension of a wider variety of texts, including literary. Misunderstandings may occur.

Superior

Able to read with almost complete comprehension and at normal speed expository prose on unfamiliar subjects and a variety of literary texts. Reading ability is not dependent on subject-matter knowledge, although the reader is not expected to comprehend thoroughly texts that are highly dependent on knowledge of the target culture. Reads easily for pleasure. Superior-level texts feature hypotheses, argumentation, and supported opinions and include grammatical patterns and vocabulary ordinarily encountered in academic/professional reading.

Distinguished

Able to read fluently and accurately most styles and forms of the language pertinent to academic and professional needs. Able to relate inferences in the text to real-world knowledge and understand almost all sociolinguistic and cultural references by processing language from within the cultural framework. Able to understand a writer's use of nuance and subtlety. Can readily follow unpredictable turns of thought and author intent in such materials as sophisticated editorials, specialized journal articles, and literary texts such as novels, plays, and poems and in any subject matter area directed to a general reader.

---

[3] Thai Language Proficiency Guidelines, developed by CAST, verified by the Council of Teachers of Southeast Asian Languages (COTSEAL).

Writing

Intermediate-high
Able to meet most practical writing needs and limited social demands. Can take notes in some detail on familiar topics and respond in writing to personal questions. Can write simple letters, brief synopses and paraphrases, and summaries of biographical data, and work and school experience. Some precision is displayed in expressing time and aspect. An ability to describe and narrate in paragraphs is emerging. Only rarely uses deletion and basic cohesive elements such as pronominal substitutions or synonyms in written discourse. Writing, though faulty, is generally comprehensible to natives used to the writing of non-natives.

Advanced
Able to write routine social correspondence and join sentences in simple discourse of at least several paragraphs in length on familiar topics. Can write simple social correspondence, take notes, write cohesive summaries and resumes, and write narratives and descriptions of a factual nature. Has sufficient written vocabulary to express self simply with some circumlocution. May still make errors in spelling symbols. Good control of the most frequently used syntactic structures, for example, common word order patterns, coordination, and subordination, but makes frequent errors in producing complex sentences. Accurately uses a limited number of cohesive devices. Writing may resemble literal translations from the native language, but is understandable to natives not used to the writing of non-natives.

Advanced plus
Able to write about a variety of topics with significant precision and in detail. Can write most social and informal business correspondence. Can describe and narrate personal experiences fully but has difficulty supporting points of view in written discourse. Can write about the concrete aspects of topics relating to particular interests and special fields of competence. Often shows remarkable fluency and ease of expression, but under time constraints and pressure, writing may be inaccurate. Generally strong in either grammar or vocabulary, but not in both. Weakness and unevenness in one of the foregoing or in spelling may result in occasional miscommunication. Some misuse of vocabulary may still be evident. Style may still be obviously foreign.

Superior
Able to express self effectively in most formal and informal writing on practical, social, and professional topics. Can write most types of correspondence, such as memos and social and business letters, and short research papers and statements of position in areas of special interest or in special fields. Good control of a full range of structures, spelling, and a wide general vocabulary allow the writer to hypothesize and present arguments or points of view accurately and effectively. An underlying organization, such as chronological ordering, logical ordering, cause and effect, comparison, and thematic development is strongly evident, although not thoroughly executed and/or not totally reflecting target language patterns. Although sensitive to differences in formal and informal styles, still may not tailor writing precisely to a variety of purposes and/or readers. Errors in writing rarely disturb natives or cause miscommunication.

Challenges in Placing Korean Heritage Learners: Validity, Heterogeneity, and the Foreign Language Requirement

Seungja Kim Choi
Yale University, CT

Context of the program

Curriculum

The Korean language program at Yale, which started in 1990, is in the department of East Asian Languages and Literatures along with the Chinese and Japanese language programs. Currently, the program has three levels with two semesters at each level: Elementary Korean (K115, a first-year course for true beginners), Intermediate Korean (K130, a second-year course for continuing true beginners), Intermediate Korean for Advanced Learners (K133, a first-year course for heritage learners), and Advanced Korean I (K150). Advanced Korean II, a web-based fourth-year course (K154) will be offered in 2007; interactive web-based learning material is being developed. Students with no background (i.e., true beginners) are placed in K115 and promoted to 130 after completing it. The challenge with placement tests is to adequately place heritage learners into K133, K150, and K154. The total number of students enrolled in all three levels averages around 40 each year, and approximately 20–25 students take the placement test every year.

Center for Language Study

The Center for Language Study provides leadership and support for pedagogical innovation, professional development (including workshops and informal seminars offered in collaboration with language programs), and implementation of new methodologies in language programs offered at Yale. Currently, Yale offers 53 foreign languages, which are part of academic departments or area studies councils. One unique feature of foreign language education at Yale is directed independent language study (DILS), through which students can study a language on their own and meet with a native speaker once a week. Currently, many languages, such as Urdu or Tibetan, which cannot be offered regularly, are studied through DILS. The Center is now in the process of developing web-based language testing software and has encouraged all language program directors to develop online placement tests. In terms of administrative and course management and for students, offering language placement tests before students arrive on campus is good. Another advantage of online placement testing is that useful data on students can be collected and then analyzed.

Foreign language requirement

The three most important features of the foreign language requirement at Yale, implemented in the fall of 2005, are as follows:

- All students are required to study a foreign language while enrolled in Yale College. This is in contrast to the old requirement in which students who passed the intermediate level of department placement tests were not required to study a foreign language.
- Students who matriculate at Yale with no previous foreign language training must complete three terms of instruction in a single foreign language. This requirement is fulfilled by the completion of courses designated L1, L2, and L3.[1]
- Students who have taken an Advanced Placement examination in a foreign language and who present scores of 4 or 5 are recognized as having completed the intermediate level of study. Scores of 6 or 7 on the International Baccalaureate Advanced-Level examination are also accepted as evidence of intermediate-level accomplishment. Students at this level can fulfill the language distributional requirement by completing one course designated L5. Alternatively, they may successfully complete instruction in a different foreign language through the level designated L2.
- Students who have studied a foreign language before matriculating at Yale but who have not achieved a score of 4 or 5 on the AP test must take a placement test offered by the appropriate language department.

In short, two changes have been made to the old requirements. First, all students with intermediate-level foreign language skills must study their chosen language for one semester at the L5 level or explore another foreign language for two semesters. Second, in principle, students can be placed into L1, L2, and so forth. The placement test is the key factor for determining into which semester students are placed. This is in contrast to the old requirement, in which students were placed into a certain level by year, not semester.

Challenges

Heritage learners

The source of difficulty in placing heritage learners is two-fold: the heterogeneity of the linguistic backgrounds of students and the differences between the spoken and written language abilities of individual students. Sometimes this difference creates unusual cases (i.e., a student with high oral proficiency and very low or zero literacy).[2] Typical characteristics of most heritage learners are high listening abilities and low literacy. Although students' communicative abilities in the spoken language vary, they can be roughly divided into two groups: those who can maintain predictable face-to-face conversations (with hesitations and pauses) and satisfy limited social demands (ILR level 1/1+) and those who have high oral proficiency (ILR level 2 and above).

---

[1] L1, L2, L3, L4 indicate the first- through fourth-semester levels of language study. The level beyond the fourth semester is labeled L5.

[2] In the case of traditional foreign-language learners, the tendency often is the opposite (i.e., high literacy with low spoken language ability).

Given the mismatches of spoken language and literacy levels within some learners, a question arises: should we use spoken or written language ability as the criteria for placement? What should we do with exceptional cases (i.e., students who have advanced spoken language abilities and zero/very low literacy)?

Validity

Validity is the central concept in testing and assessment. However, what does it mean when one says that a test or assessment is valid? Should one say that this test score or interpretation of the score is valid? In perhaps the most significant work on validity since the 1970s, Samuel Messick (1989:20) wrote

> Traditional ways of cutting and combining evidence of validity, as we have seen, have led to three major categories of evidence: content-related, criterion-related, and construct-related. However, because content- and criterion-related evidence contributes to score meaning, they have come to be recognized as aspects of construct validity. In a sense, then, this leaves only one category, namely, construct-related evidence.

Thus, Messick sets the validity framework in a unified way in which the traditional three types of validity (content, criterion, and construct), which are closely related, are a single concept. He described validity as

> an integrated evaluative judgment of the degree to which empirical evidence and theoretical rationales support the adequacy and appropriateness of inferences and actions based on test scores or other modes of assessment.

Messick fundamentally changed the way in which validity was understood. In this view, "validity is not a property of a test or assessment but the degree to which we are justified in making an inference to a construct from a test score (for example, whether '20' on a reading test indicates 'ability to read first-year business studies texts), and whether any decisions we might make on the basis of the score are justifiable." (Fulcher and Davidson, 2007:12). Furthermore, test validation is "the process of accumulating evidence to support such inferences" (American Educational Research Association, American Psychological Association, & National Council on Measurement in Education, 1985:9). With the understanding of validity in this framework, consider what construct a placement test is designed to measure and what pieces of information are needed for placement test validation.

Construct

The construct to be measured in a placement test is language ability. However, language ability must be defined for this particular situation in precise terms to distinguish the language knowledge that is required for students to function in Advanced Korean I (K150) because currently only two courses are available for starting heritage learners, K133 and K150.

Earlier, we raised the question as to whether the primary criteria for placement should be spoken or written language ability. Although not the only criterion, literacy plays an important role in placement in the Korean program. Because the curriculum of Advanced Korean I does not include the teaching of basic Hankul (Korean alphabet) reading and writing, and the course includes an authentic reading component, an intermediate level of reading and writing ability is necessary. Thus, general placements are as follows.

Students with zero or very low literacy (e.g., frequent errors in basic spelling such as particles and verb stems) are placed into K133. However, students with high levels of communicative ability in the spoken language who are functionally illiterate are occasionally not placed into K133 because the goal of the course includes the improvement of oral skills from the elementary to intermediate level, and those students have little to learn in this area. In the past, students in this category have been placed in K150 with a hope that they can quickly catch up with reading and writing skills, but it has not worked. What is needed is the development of online self-teaching material for mastering basic literacy skills for these students; they can be placed into K150 after mastering basic literacy skills.

Students who are illiterate or very low in literacy and have low (ILR level 1/1+) communicative ability in speaking are placed into K133. Such students have difficulty in using complex sentences and in handling daily routine topics but have considerable listening abilities.

Students with intermediate levels of literacy and intermediate (ILR level 1+/2) speaking abilities are placed into K150.

Students with high levels (ILR level 2/2+) of proficiency in literacy are placed into K154.

New challenges

More L5-level courses

Under the foreign language requirement, students who complete the intermediate level of a foreign language must take an L5-level course in that language or study a new language for two semesters. For those students who need to take an L5 course, a fourth-year online course has been developed and will be offered in the 2007–2008 academic year. However, more diverse L5 courses must be developed.

Construction of new placement test

The current placement test consists of a written test, which assesses writing, vocabulary, and grammar, followed by an oral interview of 20–25 minutes. This test is designed only to differentiate those students who will be placed into K133 from those placed into 150.

The Center for Language Study, together with the Yale College Dean's Office, supports the development of new placement tests to align placement mechanisms with the demands of the foreign language requirement. For example, all placement tests must now yield one of exactly five possible results: L1, L2, L3, L4, and L5. A new, more detailed online test for upper-level content is needed. Online tests are web-based and designed to assess reading, vocabulary, grammar, and listening ability in a selected-response format (multiple choice, matching, and true/false). They will be criterion referenced. The purpose of the tests is to differentiate groups among L5 students to be placed into the Advanced I and Advanced II courses.

In addition to online tests, supplementary handwritten tests are needed for writing. Although a placement test measures literacy, not every taker of the Korean placement test will be capable of typing in Hankul. Thus, a computer-based test can create problems unrelated to language abilities. To reduce the margin of this type of error, writing skills should be assessed on paper, while speaking ability can be assessed either via a computer or a face-to-face interview. Because the number of examinees should be small (about 20–25), structured face-to-face oral interviews should be conducted to assess speaking abilities, and follow-up conferences during the first and second weeks of the semester can be conducted to ensure reliable placement decisions.

Future tasks
- *Accumulation of evidence for validation.* Data collection on correlations between placement test scores and class performance
- *Process of validation.* Item analysis → Revision of test items

- *Norm-referenced test.* For setting cut scores, a norm-referenced test would be desirable. However, to analyze items for difficulty and discrimination, collaboration with other institutes is needed because the number of test-takers each year at Yale is only 20-25.
- *Steps for actual construction.*
    1. test content: Course textbooks and materials
    2. class objectives, authenticity
    3. articulation of courses: Inventory of important items in each course and tasks/functions derived from mastery of each course
    4. test format/items/time
    5. scoring system
    6. interpretation of scores/information/placement
    7. placement test guidelines on web

References

American Educational Research Association, American Psychological Association, & National Council on Measurement in Education. (1985). *Standards for educational and psychological testing.* Washington, DC: American Psychological Association.

Fulcher, G. & Davidson, F. (2007). *Language testing and assessment: An advanced resource book.* London: Routledge.

Messick, S. (1989). Validity. In R. L. Linn (Ed.) *Educational Measurement* (3rd ed., pp. 13-103) New York. American Council on Education-Macmillan Publishing Co.

Pragmatics & Language Learning

Pragmatics & Language Learning ("PLL"), a refereed series sponsored by the National Foreign Language Resource Center, publishes selected papers from the biannual International Pragmatics & Language Learning conference under the editorship of the conference hosts and the series editor. Check the NFLRC website for upcoming PLL conferences and PLL volumes

PRAGMATICS AND LANGUAGE LEARNING VOLUME 11
KATHLEEN BARDOVI-HARLIG, CÉSAR FÉLIX-BRASDEFER, & ALWIYA S. OMAR (EDITORS), 2006

This volume features cutting-edge theoretical and empirical research on pragmatics and language learning among a wide-variety of learners in diverse learning contexts from a variety of language backgrounds (English, German, Japanese, Persian, and Spanish) and target languages (English, German, Japanese, Kiswahili, and Spanish). This collection of papers from researchers around the world includes critical appraisals on the role of formulas in interlanguage pragmatics and speech-act research from a conversation-analytic perspective. Empirical studies examine learner data using innovative methods of analysis and investigate issues in pragmatic development and the instruction of pragmatics.

430 pp., ISBN(10): 0-8248-3137-3, ISBN(13): 978-0-8248-3137-0 $30.

NFLRC Monographs

Monographs of the National Foreign Language Resource Center present the findings of recent work in applied linguistics that is of relevance to language teaching and learning (with a focus on the less commonly-taught languages of Asia and the Pacific) and are of particular interest to foreign language educators, applied linguists, and researchers. Prior to 2006, these monographs were published as "SLTCC Technical Reports."

CHINESE AS A HERITAGE LANGUAGE: FOSTERING ROOTED WORLD CITIZENRY

AGNES WEIYUN HE, & YUN XIAO (EDITORS), 2008

Thirty-two scholars examine the socio-cultural, cognitive-linguistic, and educational-institutional trajectories along which Chinese as a Heritage Language may be acquired, maintained and developed. They draw upon developmental psychology, functional linguistics, linguistic and cultural anthropology, discourse analysis, orthography analysis, reading research, second language acquisition, and bilingualism. This volume aims to lay a foundation for theories, models, and master scripts to be discussed, debated, and developed, and to stimulate research and enhance teaching both within and beyond Chinese language education.

280pp., ISBN 978-0-8248-3286-5 $40.

PERSPECTIVES ON TEACHING CONNECTED SPEECH TO SECOND LANGUAGE SPEAKERS

JAMES DEAN BROWN & KIMI KONDO-BROWN (EDITORS), 2006

This book is a collection of fourteen articles on connected speech of interest to teachers, researchers, and materials developers in both ESL/EFL (ten chapters focus on connected speech in English) and Japanese (four chapters focus on Japanese connected speech). The fourteen chapters are divided up into five sections:

- What do we know so far about teaching connected speech?
- Does connected speech instruction work?
- How should connected speech be taught in English?
- How should connected speech be taught in Japanese?
- How should connected speech be tested?

290 pp., ISBN(10) 0-8248-3136-5, ISBN(13) 978-0-8248-3136-3 $38.

CORPUS LINGUISTICS FOR KOREAN LANGUAGE LEARNING AND TEACHING

ROBERT BLEY-VROMAN & HYUNSOOK KO (EDITORS), 2006

Dramatic advances in personal-computer technology have given language teachers access to vast quantities of machine-readable text, which can be analyzed with a view toward improving the basis of language instruction. Corpus linguistics provides analytic techniques and practical tools for studying language in use. This volume provides both an introductory framework for the use of corpus linguistics for language teaching and examples of its application for Korean teaching and learning. The collected papers cover topics in Korean syntax, lexicon, and discourse, and second language acquisition research, always with a focus on application in the classroom. An overview of Korean corpus linguistics tools and available Korean corpora are also included.

265 pp., ISBN 0-8248-3062-8 $25.

NEW TECHNOLOGIES AND LANGUAGE LEARNING: CASES IN THE LESS COMMONLY TAUGHT LANGUAGES

CAROL ANNE SPREEN (EDITOR), 2002

In recent years, the National Security Education Program (NSEP) has supported an increasing number of programs for teaching languages using different technological media. This compilation of case study initiatives funded through the NSEP Institutional Grants Program presents a range of technology-based options for language programming that will help universities make more informed decisions about teaching less commonly taught languages. The eight chapters describe how different types of technologies are used to support language programs (i.e., Web, ITV, and audio- or video-based materials), discuss identifiable trends in e-language learning, and explore how technology addresses issues of equity, diversity, and opportunity. This book offers many lessons learned and decisions made as technology changes and learning needs become more complex.

188 pp., ISBN 0-8248-2634-5 $25.

AN INVESTIGATION OF SECOND LANGUAGE TASK-BASED PERFORMANCE ASSESSMENTS

JAMES DEAN BROWN, THOM HUDSON, JOHN M. NORRIS, & WILLIAM BONK, 2002

This volume describes the creation of performance assessment instruments and their validation (based on work started in a previous monograph). It begins by explaining the test and rating scale development processes and the administration of the resulting three seven-task tests to 90 university level EFL and ESL students. The results are examined in terms of (a) the effects of test revision; (b) comparisons among the task-dependent, task-independent, and self-rating scales; and (c) reliability and validity issues.

240 pp., ISBN 0-8248-2633-7 $25.

MOTIVATION AND SECOND LANGUAGE ACQUISITION

ZOLTÁN DÖRNYEI & RICHARD SCHMIDT (EDITORS), 2001

This volume—the second in this series concerned with motivation and foreign language learning—includes papers presented in a state-of-the-art colloquium on L2 motivation at the American Association for Applied Linguistics (Vancouver, 2000) and a number of specially commissioned studies. The 20 chapters, written by some of the best known researchers in the field, cover a wide range of theoretical and research methodological issues, and also offer empirical results (both qualitative and quantitative) concerning the learning of many different languages (Arabic, Chinese, English, Filipino, French, German, Hindi, Italian, Japanese, Russian, and Spanish) in a broad range of learning contexts (Bahrain, Brazil, Canada, Egypt, Finland, Hungary, Ireland, Israel, Japan, Spain, and the US).

520 pp., ISBN 0-8248-2458-X $25.

A FOCUS ON LANGUAGE TEST DEVELOPMENT: EXPANDING THE LANGUAGE PROFICIENCY CONSTRUCT ACROSS A VARIETY OF TESTS

THOM HUDSON & JAMES DEAN BROWN (EDITORS), 2001

This volume presents eight research studies that introduce a variety of novel, non-traditional forms of second and foreign language assessment. To the extent possible, the studies also show the entire test development process, warts and all. These language testing projects not only demonstrate many of the types of problems that test developers run into in the real world but also afford the reader unique insights into the language test development process.

230 pp., ISBN 0-8248-2351-6 $20.

STUDIES ON KOREAN IN COMMUNITY SCHOOLS

DONG-JAE LEE, SOOKEUN CHO, MISEON LEE, MINSUN SONG, & WILLIAM O'GRADY (EDITORS), 2000

The papers in this volume focus on language teaching and learning in Korean community schools. Drawing on innovative experimental work and research in linguistics, education, and psychology, the contributors address issues of importance to teachers, administrators, and parents. Topics covered include childhood bilingualism, Korean grammar, language acquisition, children's literature, and language teaching methodology. *[in Korean]*

256 pp., ISBN 0-8248-2352-4 $20.

A COMMUNICATIVE FRAMEWORK FOR INTRODUCTORY JAPANESE LANGUAGE CURRICULA

WASHINGTON STATE JAPANESE LANGUAGE CURRICULUM GUIDELINES COMMITTEE, 2000

In recent years the number of schools offering Japanese nationwide has increased dramatically. Because of the tremendous popularity of the Japanese language and the shortage of teachers, quite a few untrained, non-native and native teachers are in the classrooms and are expected to teach several levels of Japanese. These guidelines are intended to assist individual teachers and professional associations throughout the United States in designing Japanese language curricula. They are meant to serve as a framework from which language teaching can be expanded and are intended to allow teachers to enhance and strengthen the quality of Japanese language instruction.

168 pp., ISBN 0-8248-2350-8 $20.

FOREIGN LANGUAGE TEACHING & MINORITY LANGUAGE EDUCATION

KATHRYN A. DAVIS (EDITOR), 1999

This volume seeks to examine the potential for building relationships among foreign language, bilingual, and ESL programs towards fostering bilingualism. Part I of the volume examines the sociopolitical contexts for language partnerships, including:

- obstacles to developing bilingualism
- implications of acculturation, identity, and language issues for linguistic minorities.
- the potential for developing partnerships across primary, secondary, and tertiary institutions

Part II of the volume provides research findings on the Foreign language partnership project designed to capitalize on the resources of immigrant students to enhance foreign language learning.

152 pp., ISBN 0-8248-2067-3 $20.

DESIGNING SECOND LANGUAGE PERFORMANCE ASSESSMENTS

JOHN M. NORRIS, JAMES DEAN BROWN, THOM HUDSON, & JIM YOSHIOKA, 1998, 2000

This technical report focuses on the decision-making potential provided by second language performance assessments. The authors first situate performance assessment within a broader discussion of alternatives in language assessment and in educational assessment in general. They then discuss issues in performance assessment design, implementation, reliability, and validity. Finally, they present a prototype framework for second language performance assessment based on the integration of theoretical underpinnings and research findings from the task-based language teaching literature, the language testing literature, and the educational measurement literature. The authors outline test and item specifications, and they present numerous examples of prototypical language tasks. They also propose a research agenda focusing on the operationalization of second language performance assessments.

248 pp., ISBN 0-8248-2109-2 $20.

SECOND LANGUAGE DEVELOPMENT IN WRITING: MEASURES OF FLUENCY, ACCURACY, & COMPLEXITY

KATE WOLFE-QUINTERO, SHUNJI INAGAKI, & HAE-YOUNG KIM, 1998, 2002

In this book, the authors analyze and compare the ways that fluency, accuracy, grammatical complexity, and lexical complexity have been measured in studies of language development in second language writing. More than 100 developmental measures are examined, with detailed comparisons of the results across the studies that have used each measure. The authors discuss the theoretical foundations for each type of developmental measure, and they consider the relationship between developmental measures and various types of proficiency measures. They also examine criteria for determining which developmental measures are the most successful and suggest which measures are the most promising for continuing work on language development.

208 pp., ISBN 0-8248-2069-X $20.

THE DEVELOPMENT OF A LEXICAL TONE PHONOLOGY IN AMERICAN ADULT LEARNERS OF STANDARD MANDARIN CHINESE

SYLVIA HENEL SUN, 1998

The study reported is based on an assessment of three decades of research on the SLA of Mandarin tone. It investigates whether differences in learners' tone perception and production are related to differences in the effects of certain linguistic, task, and learner factors. The learners of focus are American students of Mandarin in Beijing, China. Their performances on two perception and three production tasks are analyzed through a host of variables and methods of quantification.

328 pp., ISBN 0-8248-2068-1 $20.

NEW TRENDS & ISSUES IN TEACHING JAPANESE LANGUAGE & CULTURE

HARUKO M. COOK, KYOKO HIJIRIDA, & MILDRED TAHARA (EDITORS), 1997

In recent years, Japanese has become the fourth most commonly taught foreign language at the college level in the United States. As the number of students who study Japanese has increased, the teaching of Japanese as a foreign language has been established as an important academic field of study. This technical report includes nine contributions to the advancement of this field, encompassing the following five important issues:

- Literature and literature teaching
- Technology in the language classroom
- Orthography
- Testing
- Grammatical versus pragmatic approaches to language teaching

164 pp., ISBN 0-8248-2067-3 $20.

SIX MEASURES OF JSL PRAGMATICS
SAYOKO OKADA YAMASHITA, 1996

This book investigates differences among tests that can be used to measure the cross-cultural pragmatic ability of English-speaking learners of Japanese. Building on the work of Hudson, Detmer, and Brown (Technical Reports #2 and #7 in this series), the author modified six test types that she used to gather data from North American learners of Japanese. She found numerous problems with the multiple-choice discourse completion test but reported that the other five tests all proved highly reliable and reasonably valid. Practical issues involved in creating and using such language tests are discussed from a variety of perspectives.

213 pp., ISBN 0-8248-1914-4 $15.

LANGUAGE LEARNING STRATEGIES AROUND THE WORLD: CROSS-CULTURAL PERSPECTIVES
REBECCA L. OXFORD (EDITOR), 1996, 1997, 2002

Language learning strategies are the specific steps students take to improve their progress in learning a second or foreign language. Optimizing learning strategies improves language performance. This groundbreaking book presents new information about cultural influences on the use of language learning strategies. It also shows innovative ways to assess students' strategy use and remarkable techniques for helping students improve their choice of strategies, with the goal of peak language learning.

166 pp., ISBN 0-8248-1910-1 $20.

TELECOLLABORATION IN FOREIGN LANGUAGE LEARNING: PROCEEDINGS OF THE HAWAI'I SYMPOSIUM
MARK WARSCHAUER (EDITOR), 1996

The Symposium on Local & Global Electronic Networking in Foreign Language Learning & Research, part of the National Foreign Language Resource Center's 1995 Summer Institute on Technology & the Human Factor in Foreign Language Education, included presentations of papers and hands-on workshops conducted by Symposium participants to facilitate the sharing of resources, ideas, and information about all aspects of electronic networking for foreign language teaching and research, including electronic discussion and conferencing, international cultural exchanges, real-time communication and simulations, research and resource retrieval via the Internet, and research using networks. This collection presents a sampling of those presentations.

252 pp., ISBN 0-8248-1867-9 $20.

LANGUAGE LEARNING MOTIVATION: PATHWAYS TO THE NEW CENTURY
REBECCA L. OXFORD (EDITOR), 1996

This volume chronicles a revolution in our thinking about what makes students want to learn languages and what causes them to persist in that difficult and rewarding adventure. Topics in this book include the internal structures of and external connections with foreign language motivation; exploring adult language learning motivation, self-efficacy, and anxiety; comparing the motivations and learning strategies of students of Japanese and Spanish; and enhancing the theory of language learning motivation from many psychological and social perspectives.

218 pp., ISBN 0-8248-1849-0 $20.

LINGUISTICS & LANGUAGE TEACHING: PROCEEDINGS OF THE SIXTH JOINT LSH-HATESL CONFERENCE

Cynthia Reves, Caroline Steele, & Cathy S. P. Wong (Editors), 1996

Technical Report #10 contains 18 articles revolving around the following three topics:

- Linguistic issues—These six papers discuss various linguistic issues: ideophones, syllabic nasals, linguistic areas, computation, tonal melody classification, and wh-words.
- Sociolinguistics—Sociolinguistic phenomena in Swahili, signing, Hawaiian, and Japanese are discussed in four of the papers.
- Language teaching and learning—These eight papers cover prosodic modification, note taking, planning in oral production, oral testing, language policy, L2 essay organization, access to dative alternation rules, and child noun phrase structure development.

364 pp., ISBN 0-8248-1851-2 — $20.

ATTENTION & AWARENESS IN FOREIGN LANGUAGE LEARNING

Richard Schmidt (Editor), 1996

Issues related to the role of attention and awareness in learning lie at the heart of many theoretical and practical controversies in the foreign language field. This collection of papers presents research into the learning of Spanish, Japanese, Finnish, Hawaiian, and English as a second language (with additional comments and examples from French, German, and miniature artificial languages) that bear on these crucial questions for foreign language pedagogy.

394 pp., ISBN 0-8248-1794-X — $20.

VIRTUAL CONNECTIONS: ONLINE ACTIVITIES & PROJECTS FOR NETWORKING LANGUAGE LEARNERS

Mark Warschauer (Editor), 1995, 1996

Computer networking has created dramatic new possibilities for connecting language learners in a single classroom or across the globe. This collection of activities and projects makes use of e-mail, the internet, computer conferencing, and other forms of computer-mediated communication for the foreign and second language classroom at any level of instruction. Teachers from around the world submitted the activities compiled in this volume—activities that they have used successfully in their own classrooms.

417 pp., ISBN 0-8248-1793-1 — $30.

DEVELOPING PROTOTYPIC MEASURES OF CROSS-CULTURAL PRAGMATICS

Thom Hudson, Emily Detmer, & J. D. Brown, 1995

Although the study of cross-cultural pragmatics has gained importance in applied linguistics, there are no standard forms of assessment that might make research comparable across studies and languages. The present volume describes the process through which six forms of cross-cultural assessment were developed for second language learners of English. The models may be used for second language learners of other languages. The six forms of assessment involve two forms each of indirect discourse completion tests, oral language production, and self-assessment. The procedures involve the assessment of requests, apologies, and refusals.

198 pp., ISBN 0-8248-1763-X — $15.

THE ROLE OF PHONOLOGICAL CODING IN READING KANJI

SACHIKO MATSUNAGA, 1995

In this technical report, the author reports the results of a study that she conducted on phonological coding in reading kanji using an eye-movement monitor and draws some pedagogical implications. In addition, she reviews current literature on the different schools of thought regarding instruction in reading kanji and its role in the teaching of non-alphabetic written languages like Japanese.

64 pp., ISBN 0-8248-1734-6 $10.

PRAGMATICS OF CHINESE AS NATIVE & TARGET LANGUAGE

GABRIELE KASPER (EDITOR), 1995

This technical report includes six contributions to the study of the pragmatics of Mandarin Chinese:

- A report of an interview study conducted with nonnative speakers of Chinese; and
- Five data-based studies on the performance of different speech acts by native speakers of Mandarin—requesting, refusing, complaining, giving bad news, disagreeing, and complimenting.

312 pp., ISBN 0-8248-1733-8 $15.

A BIBLIOGRAPHY OF PEDAGOGY & RESEARCH IN INTERPRETATION & TRANSLATION

ETILVIA ARJONA, 1993

This technical report includes four types of bibliographic information on translation and interpretation studies:

- Research efforts across disciplinary boundaries—cognitive psychology, neurolinguistics, psycholinguistics, sociolinguistics, computational linguistics, measurement, aptitude testing, language policy, decision-making, theses, dissertations;
- Training information covering program design, curriculum studies, instruction, school administration;
- Instruction information detailing course syllabi, methodology, models, available textbooks; and
- Testing information about aptitude, selection, diagnostic tests.

115 pp., ISBN 0-8248-1572-6 $10.

PRAGMATICS OF JAPANESE AS NATIVE & TARGET LANGUAGE

GABRIELE KASPER (EDITOR), 1992, 1996

This technical report includes three contributions to the study of the pragmatics of Japanese:

- A bibliography on speech act performance, discourse management, and other pragmatic and sociolinguistic features of Japanese;
- A study on introspective methods in examining Japanese learners' performance of refusals; and
- A longitudinal investigation of the acquisition of the particle ne by nonnative speakers of Japanese.

125 pp., ISBN 0-8248-1462-2 $10.

A FRAMEWORK FOR TESTING CROSS-CULTURAL PRAGMATICS

THOM HUDSON, EMILY DETMER, & J. D. BROWN. 1992

This technical report presents a framework for developing methods that assess cross-cultural pragmatic ability. Although the framework has been designed for Japanese and American cross-cultural contrasts, it can serve as a generic approach that can be applied to other language contrasts. The focus is on the variables of social distance, relative power, and the degree of imposition within the speech acts of requests, refusals, and apologies. Evaluation of performance is based on recognition of the speech act, amount of speech, forms or formulæ used, directness, formality, and politeness.

51 pp., ISBN 0-8248-1463-0 $10.

RESEARCH METHODS IN INTERLANGUAGE PRAGMATICS

GABRIELE KASPER & MERETE DAHL, 1991

This technical report reviews the methods of data collection employed in 39 studies of interlanguage pragmatics, defined narrowly as the investigation of nonnative speakers' comprehension and production of speech acts, and the acquisition of L2-related speech act knowledge. Data collection instruments are distinguished according to the degree to which they constrain informants' responses, and whether they tap speech act perception/comprehension or production. A main focus of discussion is the validity of different types of data, in particular their adequacy to approximate authentic performance of linguistic action.

51 pp., ISBN 0-8248-1419-3 $10.

www.ingramcontent.com/pod-product-compliance
Lightning Source LLC
Chambersburg PA
CBHW080335170426
43194CB00014B/2578